Monetarist Perspectives

Monetarist Perspectives

David Laidler
University of Western Ontario

Philip Allan

First published 1982 by
PHILIP ALLAN PUBLISHERS LIMITED
MARKET PLACE
DEDDINGTON
OXFORD OX5 4SE

British Library Cataloguing in Publication Data

Laidler, David E. W.
  Monetarist perspectives.
  1. Quantity theory of money
  I. Title
  332.4   HG221

ISBN 0-86003-042-3

Set and printed in Linotron Times 10/12
in Great Britain at
The Camelot Press Ltd, Southampton

Contents

Introduction

Economists are not subject to any 'truth in packaging' legislation. Even so, when anyone labels a group of essays with an adjective as slippery as 'monetarist', a little small print is in order to explain just what he means by it. First of all, this book is 'monetarist' in the very simple sense that its author had that label pinned upon him over a decade ago, and has long since given up trying to unpin it. The label was affixed in Britain and not in North America, however; and that is important because, as is now well known, it by no means indicates the same ingredients on the two sides of the Atlantic. The first of the essays which follow is concerned with defining and assessing the particular brand of monetarism underlying this book, so there is no need to go into great detail about its characteristics at this point. A brief outline will suffice to indicate to the reader the common threads which link them.

Above all, the essays which follow are motivated by the belief that the behaviour of the quantity of money is very important (though not all-important) for the behaviour, not just of real income and employment, but also and in particular of the general price level. This belief in turn is related to another belief, which, I insist, is the *sine qua non* of monetarism: namely, that there exists a stable aggregate demand function for money. As the reader will see in due course, this latter proposition permeates the arguments presented in the following pages. However, stability of the demand for money function is not treated as a basic and unquestionable axiom in what follows, but rather as an hypothesis whose central role requires that it be subjected to the closest critical scrutiny. Thus these essays are monetarist in a scientific, not in an ideological, sense.

The case for regarding the stable demand for money function as a key ingredient of monetarism is one of the themes of the first essay. The connection between this relationship and Patinkin's (1956, 1967) real balance effect, and what that connection implies for the interpretation of the so-called 'short-run' demand for money function, provides the subject matter of the second. In the third essay, I examine the implications of this same evidence for the hypothesis that the world may usefully be modelled 'as if' made up of continually clearing competitive markets; while the role of the demand for money function in the 'transmission mechanism' of monetary policy is one of the matters discussed in the fourth essay. The last essay is directly concerned with monetary policy, particularly as an anti-inflation measure; and draws out what seem to me to be certain key policy implications of what has been argued earlier, not least about the demand for money.

There is, of course, more to monetarism than the demand for money function. As I assert in my first essay, a belief that the inflation–unemployment trade-off is transitory (but not necessarily trivial) has also been a key ingredient of monetarist economics over the last decade. This relationship therefore also figures prominently in the following essays. In them, I am concerned with the role of inflation expectations in the Phillips curve, and with the question of whether the existence of such a curve in the short run represents the observed outcome of the functioning of continuously clearing competitive markets, or whether it is instead a manifestation of disequilibria produced by a failure of markets to clear in the face of exogenous shocks. Nowadays, critics of monetarism too often argue that the first of these alternatives is at least as much, or even more, a *sine qua non* of monetarism as is a stable demand for money function (see e.g. Hahn 1980 and Godley 1981). In terms of the history of the monetarist debate, it is grossly misleading to argue along these lines. Some monetarists, and very important ones at that (e.g. Friedman 1975), have recently adopted this clearing markets hypothesis; but others, including myself, have never subscribed to it. As the reader will see, the third of the following essays is devoted to examining critically the hypothesis of clearing markets and to arguing that it probably should be rejected in the light of empirical evidence; while the fourth essay presents an account of the transmission mechanism of monetary policy explicitly cast in disequilibrium terms. Furthermore, the possibility of unemployment caused by market failure looms large in the case for monetary gradualism as it is presented in the final essay.

The reader may wonder at this stage whether some kind of semantic trick has been played on him. Surely the notion that market prices fail to change quickly enough to equate supply and demand, so that trading at false prices is an important real-world phenomenon, is a key postulate of Keynesian economics. This is not the place to get involved in a discussion of what we mean by 'Keynesian', which may well be the only adjective in economics more slippery than 'monetarist', but nevertheless I do not believe that any trick, semantic or otherwise, has been played here. The fact is that the monetarism which this book is devoted to elaborating is closer in its theoretical foundations to Keynesian economics than to what is often called 'new-classical' economics. In the following essays I prefer to use the adjective 'neo-Austrian' to describe the latter work. In their methodological individualism, their stress on the market mechanism as a device for disseminating information, and their insistence that the business-cycle is the central problem for macroeconomics, Robert E. Lucas Jr, Robert J. Barro, Thomas J. Sargent, and Neil Wallace, who are the most prominent contributors to this new body of doctrine, place themselves firmly in the intellectual tradition pioneered by Ludwig von Mises and Friedrich von Hayek. Certainly their work is much more closely related to traditional 'Austrian' economics than to the 'Classical' macroeconomics of Alfred Marshall and Arthur C. Pigou.

Be that as it may, the fact that there is a strong Keynesian element in the following essays does not mean that I have recanted any earlier beliefs. All it means is that neo-Austrian economics represents a new development in the subject, which is separate and distinct from monetarism as far as matters of economic theory are concerned. None the less, the theoretical similarities between monetarism and Keynesianism do not, as the terms are usually used, extend to policy recommendations. Such issues are dealt with briefly in the first and third essays and at greater length in the last one. It will be apparent to anyone who reads these pieces that the monetarist is characteristically pessimistic about what monetary policy can accomplish. This pessimism stems in large measure from the role which expectations play in his view of the transmission mechanism of monetary policy, a subject discussed in detail in the fourth essay.

The idea that inflation expectations constitute an important endogenous variable (it might be better to say set of variables) in the inflationary process has been at the centre of monetarist analysis since Friedman's 1967 Presidential address to the American Economic Association (Friedman 1968). Initially, in monetarist models this endogeneity was captured with distributed lags on the past behaviour of the inflation rate (see e.g. Cagan 1956 and Laidler 1975, Chs 7 and 9), but more recently the neo-Austrians, notably Robert E. Lucas Jr (e.g. 1976), have reminded us of the fact that economic agents are reasoning beings capable of adapting their learning behaviour to the environment in which they find themselves. Among other things, this means, as I follow Lucas in arguing in the fourth essay, that the transmission mechanism for monetary (or any other) policy is likely to vary with the manner in which policy is conducted. It is this interaction between policy and its transmission mechanism which makes its effects so hard to predict, and which nowadays underlies the monetarist's pessimism about the likely effectiveness of activist monetary policy.

As the foregoing remarks indicate, the essays which make up this book are interlinked by a number of themes, so that they do, I hope, amount to more than a random collection of articles. Nevertheless, this book is not a monograph. In preparing it, I have tried to ensure that each essay is sufficiently self-contained to be fully comprehensible when read by itself. Thus, I hope the book will be useful to the reader, particularly the student reader, who wants to find out what monetarist analysis has to say about particular topics, without first having to digest a two-hundred-odd page argument which deals with a lot of other things as well. The price of achieving piecemeal readability of this kind is a certain amount of overlap among the individual essays. In editing them for publication in their present form I have been on the look out for repetitive passages, but I have only eliminated such repetition where, in my judgement, to do so would not make it unnecessarily difficult to follow the arguments of the individual essay considered in isolation. The reader who works his way through the following pages in a systematic fashion will, therefore, from time to time, and particularly towards the end of the book, find the same material turning up in the context of different topics. I can only express the hope that he does not find this happening so often as to be irksome.

Of the five essays which follow, two are brand new (numbers two and three), one represents a reworking of an earlier effort sufficiently thorough as to make it to all intents and purposes a new piece (number five), while the remaining two are reprints, with relatively minor revisions, of recently published work (numbers one and four). The revisions which I have made in the case of the reprinted essays are of three kinds. Firstly, where what seems to me to be important new work has appeared on the topics with which they deal since the time of their first publication, suitable references have been added. Secondly, as I have learned from previous experience, very few people, even reviewers, read footnotes. Thus, to conform to the footnote-free style which I have adopted for the new work included here, I have either incorporated into the main body of the text material originally put in footnotes, or dropped it altogether. Finally, wherever I have changed my mind about an issue since writing a particular passage, or wherever I made what I now believe to be errors, I have revised the text to reflect my current views.

Although I hope that specialist monetary economists will find this book worthwhile, it is nevertheless aimed at a broader audience. Each essay contains a fair amount of survey material, while algebra has been kept to a bare minimum. Thus, all of it should be readily accessible to economists specialised in other areas, to first-year graduate students and to final-year undergraduates, while some of it, particularly the first and last essays, should be accessible to anyone with a serious interest in economic matters. This is not a textbook; the point of view it espouses is undoubtedly too narrow for that; but I hope it will prove a useful source of information about the monetarist viewpoint for people trying to achieve a balanced view of the current state of macroeconomics.

A number of institutions and individuals have made the completion of these essays possible. I have prepared them for publication in this form during a sabbatical leave from the University of Western Ontario. I am grateful to Western, and to the Social Science and Humanities Research Council of Canada, for financial and other support during the academic year 1980–81. I am also grateful to the

University of Konstanz, and particularly to Professor Nikolaus Laüfer, for having invited me to give a short series of lectures there in the early summer of 1980, in which I was able to try out and develop the outlines of much of what is included here. Many of my friends and colleagues have commented helpfully on one or more of these essays and my thanks are due to Russell Boyer, Karl Brunner, Victoria Chick, Eddie Clarke, Alan Coddington, Edgar Feige, Malcolm Fisher, John Flemming, John Foster, Joel Fried, Milton Friedman, Herschel Grossman, John Helliwell, Peter Howitt, Peter Jonson, Geoffrey Kingston, Axel Leijonhufvud, Clark Leith, Richard Lipsey, Thomas Mayer, James MacKinnon, Allan Meltzer, Ross Milbourne, Michael Parkin, Don Patinkin, Bill Poole, Douglas Purvis, Tom Rymes, Ronald Shearer, Richard Snape, Franco Spinelli, Jerome Stein, Michael Sumner, William White, Ronald Wirick and George Zis. None of them is to be held responsible for the finished product. Monica Malkus, Terry Caverhill and Yvonne Triesman have all coped admirably with the arduous and boring task of typing and retyping these essays, and their efforts are deeply appreciated.

Finally, various editors and publishers have graciously permitted me to include already published work in this volume. I am grateful to: the Editors of the *Economic Journal* and the Cambridge University Press for permission to reprint as the first essay of this book a revised version of my paper 'Monetarism: An Interpretation and an Assessment' from the *Economic Journal*, March 1981; and the Editors of the *Journal of Monetary Economics* and North Holland Publishers for permission to reprint as the fourth essay a revised version of my paper 'Money and Money Income – An Essay on the Transmission Mechanism' from the *Journal of Monetary Economics*, May 1981. My fifth essay builds upon and incorporates material taken from a paper entitled 'An Alternative to Wage and Price Controls' which appeared in *The Illusion of Wage and Price Control* edited by Michael Walker and published by the Fraser Institute of Vancouver, British Columbia, in 1976. I am grateful to Dr Walker and to the Fraser Institute for permission to use this material here.

1

On Monetarism

1. INTRODUCTION

Like beauty, 'monetarism' tends to lie in the eye of the beholder, and before it can be assessed it must be defined. Though there have been a number of valuable attempts over the years to specify monetarism's key characteristics (for example, James Boughton 1977, Karl Brunner 1970, Victoria Chick 1973 (Chs 3 and 7), David Cobham 1978, Timothy Congden 1978, Nicholas Kaldor 1971, Harry Johnson 1972, Franco Modigliani 1977, Thomas Mayer 1978, Douglas Purvis 1980) I shall not rely upon them in this essay. Each of them has been heavily conditioned by its time and place of writing, and monetarism has evolved over the years in response to changing circumstances, and in different ways in different places, as new hypotheses have either been developed or absorbed. Thus, I will begin this paper with my own, inevitably somewhat subjective, characterisation of monetarism. In my view, its key features are as follows:

I A 'quantity theory' approach to macroeconomic analysis in two distinct senses: (a) that used by Milton Friedman (1956) to describe a theory of the demand for money, and (b) the more traditional sense of a view that fluctuations in the quantity of money are the dominant cause of fluctuations in money income.

II The analysis of the division of money income fluctuations between the price level and real income in terms of an expectations augmented Phillips curve whose structure rules out an economically significant long-run inverse trade-off between the variables.

III A monetary approach to balance of payments and exchange rate theory.

IV (a) Antipathy to activist stabilisation policy, either monetary or fiscal, and to wage and price controls, and (b) support for long-run monetary policy 'rules' or at least pre-stated 'targets', cast in terms of the behaviour of some monetary aggregate rather than of the level of interest rates.

I categorises the theoretical core of monetarism as it developed in the 1950s and '60s; II and III represent theory developed or absorbed by monetarists since the mid-1960s; while IV summarises a view of macroeconomic policy issues which, even though it is neither logically implicit in their positive analysis nor their exclusive property, has remained rather constant among monetarists for the last quarter century.

Before discussing these characteristics of monetarism in detail, let me deal briefly with two propositions that some might feel should be included in the above list. First, on the one hand monetarists have frequently been accused of failing to give any account of the transmission mechanism linking monetary policy and aggregate demand, and have had attributed to them a belief in some mysterious 'direct' influence of money on expenditure; on the other hand they have themselves sometimes referred to a characteristically 'monetarist model' of that same transmission mechanism cast in terms of portfolio substitution among a wide variety of assets including reproducible capital, and even perhaps non-durable consumption goods. I believe that this is and always has been a non-issue. The claim that monetarists have failed to specify their transmission mechanism has never been true from the very outset (see e.g. Brunner 1961, Friedman and Meiselman 1963, Friedman and Schwartz 1963b), and although the mechanism propounded in those papers is a good deal more sophisticated and better grounded in relative price theory than that embodied in the textbook macro models of the 1950s, or in the econometric models of that vintage, there is, as Johnson (1962), Brunner (1970), and Douglas Purvis

(1980) among others, have argued, no essential difference between it and that analysed for example by James Tobin and his associates. (See also Essay 4 below.)

Second, monetarists are often said to prefer 'small' to 'big' econometric models, and their views about the importance of the quantity of money for the determination of the general price level have undoubtedly led them to take highly aggregated systems seriously. On the other hand, early large-scale econometric models were not constructed so as to highlight any strong effects of money on economic activity, and monetarists criticised them as much for being Keynesian as for being 'big'. Even so, subsequent developments have clearly shown that 'big' models can take on some very monetarist characteristics. Consider, for example, the London Business School model of the UK economy (see Ball and Burns 1976), the Canadian RDX2 model and the smaller RBA76 model of Australia (see Jonson, Moses and Wymer 1976 and for the revised RBA79 version of the model see Jonson and Trevor 1980). At the same time, the Ando and Modigliani (1965) and De Prano and Mayer (1965) papers demonstrate that single-equation reduced-form techniques can as well produce 'Keynesian' as 'monetarist' results.

Empirical analysis of all sorts has been used by both sides in the monetarist controversy, and if there is a method of empirical research more frequently found in monetarist work than Keynesian, it is not small-model or single-equation econometrics, but National Bureau techniques of business cycle analysis. Certainly Friedman and Schwartz (1963) and Cagan (1979) use these techniques extensively, although such monetarists as Brunner and Meltzer do not. They are mainly associated with the Chicago branch of monetarism. In short, though empirical techniques have, in specific instances, provided something to argue about, there seems to me to be no clear dividing line between the statistical methodology of monetarists and their opponents about which one can usefully generalise.

2. THE QUANTITY THEORY OF MONEY

It has often been said that Friedman's celebrated essay on the Quantity Theory could just as well have been called 'The Theory of

Liquidity Preference – a Restatement'. Harry Johnson (1962) argued that Friedman's work on the demand for money should be viewed as a development of a fundamentally Keynesian capital theoretic approach to monetary theory and Don Patinkin (1969) later documented that it was indeed just that. However, I would stress the word *development* here; for 'Keynesian' though Friedman's model is, it is no more *Keynes'* model than Keynes' 'Marshallian' theory of income determination is Marshall's theory; and it differed from other developments of Keynes' theory of liquidity preference that appeared at about the same time in a number of ways.

First, it abstracted from any specific characteristics that money might have because it is a financial asset; Friedman treated money instead 'as if' it was a service-yielding consumer durable to which the permanent income hypothesis of consumption could be applied, just as Margaret Reid (1962) applied it to housing, or the contributors to Arnold Harberger (1960) did to a variety of other durable goods. In this respect Friedman's approach stands in sharp contrast to the analyses of Baumol (1952) and Tobin (1956, 1958), as it does in its claim to be a theory of the total demand for money in the macroeconomy rather than of some component of that demand. Second, Friedman explicitly recognised inflation as an own rate of return on money and postulated a well determined functional relationship between the demand for money and the inflation rate, whose existence Keynes (1936) (and some of his disciples) explicitly denied. (See Harrod 1971.)

Finally, and so obviously that the matter is usually overlooked, Friedman asserted that the demand for money was, *as an empirical matter*, a stable function of a few measurable arguments. Keynes did not believe that – his empirically stable relationship was the consumption function – and nor did (or perhaps do) many of his British followers. Thus, the Radcliffe Report (1959) is largely based on the proposition that the demand for money function is essentially non-existent as a stable relationship, while Nicholas Kaldor (1971) and Joan Robinson (1970) later stated essentially the same point of view. On the other hand, pre-Keynesian monetary theorists did not believe in an empirically stable demand for money function either. Though they often enough assumed a constant velocity of circulation, that is by no means the same thing; and in any event they typically did so in order to make their analytic points with the maximum of clarity, and not with the intention of stating a belief about the nature of the real world. (Irving Fisher (1911) is, however, an exception here.)

It is only with the publication of Friedman's essay that statements to the effect that the demand for money is, *as a practical matter*, a stable function of a few arguments become central to debates about monetary economics. Its stress on this hypothesis makes monetarism a very different doctrine from Classical and Neo-classical economics, no matter what other similarities there may be here. However, it should be noted explicitly that the econometricians among American Keynesians have not found it necessary to adopt a monetarist label as a result of contemplating the possibility of the empirical stability of the relationship. For example, the Keynesian James Tobin was the author of a pioneering econometric study of the demand for money function (see Tobin 1947) and his review of Friedman and Schwartz (1963a) (Tobin 1965) presented further econometric estimates of the demand for money function.

Ten years ago I argued that this characteristic monetarist belief in a stable demand for money function was well supported by empirical evidence (Laidler 1971). However, the last decade has produced a good deal of evidence to suggest that the relationship has shifted in an unpredicted way in a number of countries. There is not space to go into details here, but I have defended the following assertions at some length (Laidler 1980).

First, the instability in question is often presented, particularly in the United States, as a matter of a cumulative deterioration in the ability of the function to track data. This cumulative deterioration is largely an illusion stemming from the use of dynamic simulations of relationships containing a lagged dependent variable. A *one-time shift* of such a function will, as a matter of arithmetic, lead to a *cumulative deterioration* of its dynamic simulation goodness-of-fit, which should not be read as implying a *continuous* tendency of the relationship to shift. On the other hand, I do not believe we can safely conclude that one-time shifts in the demand for money function have not occurred, despite the fact, again particularly in the United States, that some formulations of the relationship turn out to deteriorate significantly less than others during the 1970s. When important issues like the stability of the demand for money function begin to depend, for example, on just which interest rate or rates one uses to proxy the opportunity cost of holding money, I believe that the correct conclusion is not that the variable which provides the best fit this time around is the 'right' one, but that our knowledge of the details of the relationship is more fragile than we thought. (See also Essay 2.)

Finally, arguments to the effect that the demand for money function has not 'really' shifted, that we can restore its stability by taking note of institutional change and redefining 'money' so as to take account of its effects, need to be handled carefully. They are relevant to the interpretation of economic history, but the successful conduct of policy requires that specific actions be taken *vis à vis* precisely defined aggregates in order to achieve particular policy goals. To say, after the event, that our policy didn't work because new assets evolved whose existence affected the outcome of those policies in a way which we could have forecast had we only been able to foresee their invention, may be true; but it is not very helpful in enabling us to do better next time, unless the evolution in question was, as it sometimes can be, the predictable outcome of some policy action or other.

Shifts in the measured demand for money function are not in fact a new phenomenon. Evidence drawn from more than one country shows that the demand for money function shifted as the institutional framework evolved long before 1974. To cite but four examples: the income elasticities of demand for money seem to have fallen significantly in both the USA and Britain during the twentieth century (see Laidler 1971), the abolition of interest payments on demand deposits in the United States in 1933 was associated with a change in the nature of the demand function for narrow money (see Lieberman 1980), as was the growth of Savings and Loan Associations in the 1940s (see Cagan and Schwartz 1975), or in Britain, the introduction of 'Competition and Credit Control' in 1971 (see Artis and Lewis 1976). Shifts in the demand for money function are not new, then, but they are important. Though two of the above examples were the result of policy changes and might have been predicted *ex ante*, two were not. In any event, these effects of institutional change on the demand for money function have important implications for the proper conduct of monetary policy, as I shall argue in section 5 below.

In the traditional vocabulary of economics, the phrase 'quantity theory of money' referred to a theory of (or better, an approach to the analysis of) the relationship between the supply of money and the general price level. The characteristic monetarist belief that variations in the supply of money are the 'dominant impulse' (to borrow Brunner's phrase) causing fluctuations in money income is clearly related to this traditional version of the quantity theory. Modern monetarists are on the whole more clearcut in their attribution of a dominant causative role to the money supply than were quantity theorists of earlier vintages (again, note that Irving Fisher (1911) provides an exception to this judgement). The difference between modern monetarists' views on this issue and those of most earlier Quantity Theorists is surely attributable to monetarists' belief in a stable demand for money function. Earlier quantity theorists spent much of their time contemplating the empirical possibility of autonomous shifts in velocity. However, it takes more than a belief in a stable demand for money function to yield the monetarist conclusion that variations in the quantity of money are the main cause of money income fluctuations. Setting aside the important complications which arise in the open economy, there are two ways in which a conventional analytic model of the IS–LM variety can be made to produce such a 'monetarist' result.

First, in its under-employment form, if the demand for money is insensitive to interest rates relative to expenditure, then the quantity of money comes to dominate the determination of the level of real income. Now, obviously a monetarist must deny that the interest elasticity of demand for money is infinite, and this has been done often and explicitly; but it is mainly in Britain that such a denial has been thought to amount to a distinctively monetarist statement. A number of textbook writers (including myself), have gone to the other extreme and used the assumption of a zero interest elasticity of demand for money to generate monetarist propositions from an under-employment IS–LM model. However, Friedman's (1959) study of the United States function is a notable exception to the general tendency of demand for money studies – including those of such monetarists as Brunner and Meltzer (e.g. 1963) – to find a statistically significant interest elasticity of demand for money, and his inability to find such a relationship turned out to be due to a faulty statistical method (see Laidler 1966 and Friedman 1966).

In fact the existence or non-existence of a statistically significant interest elasticity of demand for money has not been a serious issue between monetarists and their opponents for at least fifteen years.

If it had been, it is hard to see how monetarists, not least Friedman, could have contributed to the analysis of the welfare costs of inflation, or how Friedman and Meiselman could have accepted their own evidence of the importance of autonomous expenditure as an influence on money income during the Depression years with such equanimity. This of course is not to say that Friedman has always paid as much attention to the interest elasticity of the demand for money as his critics might have wished. However, among the various reviewers of the *Monetary History of the United States*, the monetarist Allan Meltzer (1965) was as critical as any on this score, and this leads me to conclude that what we are dealing with here is a characteristic of some of the work of one, albeit the most important, monetarist, rather than of monetarism in general.

If we rule out the vertical LM curve, we can still get an IS–LM model to produce monetarist results if we assume full employment, and then postulate that the major source of disturbance is variations in the level – or rate of change of – the nominal money supply. With the determinants of velocity, except the expected rate of inflation, thus pinned down at full employment, and with fluctuations in money income thus reduced to fluctuations in the price level, the characteristics of the demand for money function – other than its stability and homogeneity in the general price level and its sensitivity to fluctuations in the expected inflation rate – become quite irrelevant to the relationship between the quantity of money and money income. A Keynesian of course would agree, as an analytic matter, with this proposition, but would probably deny what the monetarist would claim: namely that, if the IS–LM model is to be used as a framework for discussion at all – and there are some monetarists, notably Brunner and Meltzer who would not want to use it – then this full employment version of it is frequently the empirically relevant one.

To put matters this way is, in effect, to say that monetarists' belief in the quantity theory as a theory of money income boils down to the view that sustained inflation is caused by an expanding money supply. This is not too far from the mark, and much of the spread of monetarism in the last fifteen years stems from its ability to provide a readily comprehensible explanation of inflation along these lines. However, to cast the monetarist approach to the analysis of inflation in terms of a 'full employment' IS–LM model is difficult to justify except as a very first approximation. Though monetarists are among those who have written at considerable length about the interaction of the quantity of money and the price level in models where 'full employment' is the rule, the models in question have been long-run equilibrium growth models, not versions of short-run IS–LM analysis.

In any event, the 'money and growth' literature and, to a lesser extent, that dealing with 'money and welfare', even though it builds on Friedman's formulation of the relationship between the demand for real balances and the expected rate of inflation as a well-defined inverse function, is properly viewed, not as an offshoot of monetarism, but as an extension of Patinkin's (1956, 1965) theoretical analysis of the classical dichotomy and the neutrality of money; to deal with the *long-run* properties of a *growing* economy, in the presence of variations in the *rate of change* of the nominal money supply. Mayer (1978, pp. 5–6) correctly argues that this analysis is not monetarist in nature. This is not to deny the important influence that Patinkin's work had on subsequent monetarist analysis (see, for example, Jonson 1976a), but it is to stress that, in dealing with the interaction of the quantity of money, money income, and prices, the essential monetarist contribution has been to postulate the existence of stable relationships among these variables as an *empirical* matter, and to draw *practical* conclusions about the proper conduct of *short-run* stabilisation policy from studying their nature. The 'money, growth and welfare' literature has next to nothing to say about these matters.

When it comes to empirical propositions about the relationship between money and money income, what was once monetarist heresy is now close to being received orthodoxy. In this respect monetarism has made an important positive contribution to macroeconomics. In the United States it seems now to be rather widely accepted that the correlation between the quantity of money and money income which long runs of time series data display, is not just the result of coincidence, but does in fact constitute evidence for the existence of a causative relationship which has run primarily from money to money income rather than *vice versa*. The weight of the evidence produced by Friedman and his various collaborators, not to mention such predecessors as Irving Fisher (1911) and Clark Warburton (see Bordo and Schwartz 1979), and the persuasiveness of their arguments, has changed enough minds to warrant the conclusion that, in an important sense, 'we are all monetarists' now.

Elsewhere in the world, not least in Britain, there has been a similar movement of opinion. Certainly one no longer hears much about velocity being variable almost without limit. One does, though, hear more about 'reverse causation' in Britain, as an explanation of the correlation between money and money income, than one does in the United States. However, it is convenient to defer further discussion of this particular issue to section 4 below. (See also Essay 4.)

3. THE EXPECTATIONS AUGMENTED PHILLIPS CURVE

Monetarist doctrine asserts not just that variations in the quantity of money lead to systematic variations in money income, but also that those variations are primarily in prices rather than real income. Although, as I have already noted, much of monetarism's popular appeal stems from its claim to provide an easily comprehensible explanation of inflation, that explanation of inflation is by no means universally accepted. The view that the influence of money on money income falls on its real income component and not on prices has constituted a 'Keynesian' alternative to the monetarist position on these matters. In Britain in particular, the 1960s and 1970s saw a systematic shift in 'Keynesian' opinion from the Radcliffe view that money doesn't matter at all, to the view that money matters for real income but not for prices. This shift can be seen, for example, by comparing the evidence of Richard Kahn to the Radcliffe Committee with, for example, Kahn (1976). The 'expectations augmented Phillips curve' has provided a focus for debate about these issues, and that is why a particular set of beliefs about its nature is a vital ingredient of monetarist doctrine.

The notion of a trade-off between inflation and unemployment was widely prevalent in Keynesian literature even before Arthur Brown (1955), William Phillips (1958) and Richard Lipsey (1960) formalised it in terms of what seemed to be an empirically stable functional relationship. Monetarists have long doubted its existence, instead asserting a belief in the 'inherent stability' of the private sector in the absence of policy-induced monetary disturbances, by which they have usually meant nothing more complex than that the system tends in and of itself to operate at or near 'full employment' regardless of the inflation rate if policy makers do not upset matters. The papers of Edmund Phelps (1967) and Friedman (1968) provided a framework in terms of which differences of opinion about these matters could be stated sharply enough to be confronted with empirical evidence. Although some commentators (e.g. Frisch 1978) treat the Phillips curve as providing an alternative theory of inflation to the monetarist approach, that is surely a mistake. In its expectations augmented form, it emerged at the turn of the decade to provide what Friedman (1970) called 'the missing equation' in the monetarist model of inflation.

It is possible to derive this 'missing equation' from two very different theoretical bases, and disagreements here are of quite fundamental importance for macroeconomics; but the first round in the debate about the expectations augmented Phillips curve, and the one that was crucially relevant to monetarism, paid little attention to these matters. It was almost entirely empirical, because the relationship in question enabled alternative viewpoints about important and pressing policy issues to be formulated and investigated in an easily manageable way. With Δp the inflation rate, Δp^e the expected inflation rate, and y some measure, either direct or indirect, of the deviation of output from its 'full employment' level, and v a catch-all vector of other influences, systematic as well as random, the general linear form of the relationship may be written as follows:

$$\Delta p = gy + b\Delta p^e + v \qquad (1)$$

A whole spectrum of beliefs about inflation may be expressed in terms of this simple equation, depending upon the values assigned to its parameters. Thus, the extreme 'sociological' view of the determination of the price level, which was widely prevalent in Britain in the early 1970s, would predict that the parameters g and b were essentially equal to zero, implying that monetary policies, if they had any effect on money income, would influence real income. The behaviour of prices, in this view (of which Wiles 1973 provides a particularly vivid example) was determined by exogenous factors which would all go into the catch-all vector v. At the other extreme, the typical monetarist of the early 1970s would argue that g was positive, so that inflation would, relative to expectations, be low in a depressed economy and high in an over-expanded one. He would also argue that the coefficient b on expected inflation would be equal to unity, and would supplement equation (1) with some formula for the formation of expectations, typically based on the error learning hypothesis. This ensured that, eventually, any constant actual inflation rate would come to be fully anticipated. For him, therefore, any trade-off between inflation and deviations of output from full employment was a temporary one which vanished in the long run. The typical 'American Keynesian' of the same vintage, for example Solow (1969) or Tobin (1972), would agree with the monetarist about the parameter g and about the reasonableness of assuming that expectations would eventually catch up with experience, but would nevertheless assign a value of less than unity to the parameter b, thus ensuring that though the price in terms of inflation of increasing output was higher in the long run than in the short run, it did not, as the monetarist asserted, ever become infinitely high. He might also argue that equation (1) omitted to mention explicitly many factors that in particular times and places might have an important influence on the inflation rate, and which it will suffice here to think of as being captured in v.

There is not space here to survey the extensive empirical literature which these issues generated, but its upshot may be summarised easily enough. The evidence that, other things equal, inflation varies with the level of aggregate demand is overwhelming. To the extent that differences of opinion here ever set monetarism apart from other points of view – and I think they probably did in Britain, though not in North America – then surely we have here another case of 'we are all monetarists now'. (See Santomero and Seater 1979 for a recent and well-balanced survey of the evidence on these matters.) There has also been a swing towards the typically monetarist belief that in the long run there is no economically significant inflation–output trade-off. The more rapid inflation of the 1970s, and the more sophisticated methods of modelling expectations developed over the same period, have provided empirical evidence of a type which we did not have a decade ago to support this belief. There is still substantial disagreement, though, on the question of how fast the economy converges on the long-run solution. Finally, there is more of a consensus about the importance of the influence of 'other' variables on the inflation rate than there was. Monetarists are now willing to agree that factors such as the activities of OPEC and perhaps even the anchovies (see McCracken *et al.* 1977, p. 65), or sudden changes in the level of indirect taxes, can affect the behaviour of the price level 'temporarily' against the background of long-run trends determined by monetary factors; Keynesians, particularly American ones, in their turn are now willing to agree that the long-run trend of inflation may well be determined by monetary factors, while continuing to stress the importance of special factors for the short run.

There is much less of a consensus about the theoretical basis of the Phillips curve than there is about its empirical properties. As originally analysed by Lipsey, the Phillips curve dealt with the reaction of the money wage level to the existence of a general condition of excess demand for labour in the economy, and therefore of the general price level to the excess demand for goods. Excess demand was conceived of, not as a purely *ex ante* notion such as we meet in theoretical analyses of Walrasian tâtonnement, but as a realised quantity such as appears in models of economies made up of markets characterised by sticky prices. In their original critiques of the Phillips curve, Friedman (1968) and Phelps (1967) both concentrated on the point that disequilibrium in the labour market might be expected to bring pressure to bear on real wages rather than on money wages *per se*, and that what happens to the latter would therefore be critically influenced by what was thought to be happening to the general price level. Each of them, though Phelps more explicitly so than Friedman – who in some of his subsequent writings (e.g. 1975) on inflation–unemployment interaction adopts an aggregate supply curve interpretation such as I describe below of the Phillips curve – treated unemployment as a quantity signal that conveyed to economic agents the desirability of varying prices. Hence they seemed to be providing a crucial correction to what remained a fundamentally Keynesian approach to the analysis of wage and price stickiness.

On the other hand, most of the contributors to the well-known Phelps (1970) volume started from a very different theoretical basis to provide an explanation of the interaction of output and prices, though the similarity of their conclusions to those stated by Phelps and Friedman at first distracted attention from what in retrospect was the much more important theoretical matter of different premises. (See the papers by Armen Alchian, Robert E. Lucas and Leonard Rapping, Donald Gordon and Alan Hynes, and Dale Mortensen, all in the Phelps 1970 volume.) According to this alternative approach, which was anticipated by Irving Fisher (1911,

Ch. 4, 1926), the expectations augmented Phillips curve is in fact an aggregate supply curve. Equation (1) is derived from

$$y = \frac{1}{g}(p - p^e) \qquad (2)$$

combined with the following definition of the expected rate of inflation

$$\Delta p^e \equiv p^e - p_{-1} \qquad (3)$$

Among monetarists, Brunner and Meltzer were quick to adopt this interpretation of the expectations augmented Phillips curve. They had already developed a view of the transmission of monetary impulses in asset markets which stressed the role of relative prices as signalling devices, and found it easy enough to extend that line of reasoning to the markets for output and labour services as well (see Meltzer 1969). By now there can be no doubt that this Fisherian aggregate supply curve interpretation of inflation–unemployment interaction is the dominant one among monetarists; although it might be noted that in later work carried out by Brunner and Meltzer and their associates, a version appears of the aggregate supply curve in which the rate of change of output, rather than the level of output, affects the rate of inflation. This form of the relationship appears to stem from their tendency to treat the expected inflation rate as synonymous with the rate of change of the expected price level. (See Brunner and Meltzer (eds) 1978 and particularly the comments there by Bennett McCallum.) Even so, not all monetarists have accepted the aggregate supply curve interpretation of the Phillips curve (see e.g. Cagan 1979) and, as I shall now argue, it raises issues which go well beyond the traditional subject matter of the monetarist debate.

To say that the Phillips curve is an aggregate supply curve is to say that fluctuations in output and unemployment represent the voluntary choices of individuals operating in markets which are continually clearing but in which agents make expectational errors about prices. (See Essay 3 for a fuller analysis of this matter.) Since voluntary choices made on the basis of erroneous expectations about prices are by no means the same thing as choices that lead to the outcome which agents would have desired, this is not to deny that deviations of output and unemployment from the 'natural' levels they would attain were expectations fulfilled, represent a serious problem. Therefore, though I agree with much of what

Willem Buiter (1980) has to say about this theory of unemployment, I cannot accept his characterisation of it as 'The Macroeconomics of Dr Pangloss', except perhaps to the extent that it makes the natural unemployment rate a long-run equilibrium concept; whereas in the Lipsey–Phelps price reaction function interpretation of the relationship, it seems to be synonymous with the Keynesian concept of the minimum feasible unemployment rate. (For a perceptive discussion of some of the issues involved here see Thomas Wilson 1976.)

As I have already noted, the 'Fisherian' aggregate supply curve approach to the Phillips curve locates the cause of unemployment, not in the failure of markets to bring together all willing buyers and sellers in *ex ante* mutually satisfactory trades, but rather in a failure of markets (and other social institutions as well, perhaps) to convey sufficient information to enable the expectations upon which those trades are based to be formed accurately in an economy subjected to stochastic shocks. Thus the manner in which expectations are formed must play a vital role in the analysis of fluctuations in output and employment about their natural rates, and the Rational Expectations Hypothesis is therefore a natural supplement to the aggregate supply curve interpretation of the Phillips curve. If agents suffer losses in utility as a result of making expectational errors, they have an incentive to use all available information in forming their expectations up to the point at which the marginal benefit from improving their accuracy equals the marginal cost of doing so. The rational expectations hypothesis does *not* necessarily say that every agent's expectations are always as accurate as they would be if he were equipped with a 'true' econometric model of the economy in which he operated (though it is sometimes convenient to formulate it that way in analytic and empirical exercises), but it does say that his expectations will not *systematically* be wrong over time and to that extent will resemble those generated by such a 'true' model. An agent who forms expectations in a manner which leads to systematic error will find himself persistently making the wrong choices: hence in the very course of his market activities, he will be provided *gratis* with the information necessary to eliminate that systematic error.

If each individual makes only random errors in forming expectations, and if, in the presence of such errors, markets nevertheless clear, two questions naturally arise: how does it happen that at a particular moment the expectations of a predominant number of agents in the economy should be in error in one particular direction so that aggregate output and employment come to deviate from their 'natural rates'? And how does it happen that the fluctuations in output and employment which are observed in any actual economy come to display that pattern of serial correlation summarised in the term 'business cycle'? Answers to these questions have been provided by Lucas (1972, 1975 and 1977) and Sargent (1977) and I have taken up the issues which they raise in considerable detail in Essay 3 below. Here it will suffice to note that the questions are answered in a logically coherent way, and that implicit in those answers is an embryo theory of the business cycle of considerable elegance and power.

The theory in question is reminiscent of the Austrian business cycle theory of the 1920s and 1930s and that is no accident. It is the Austrians, and not, as Solow (1980) has suggested, Pigou, who are the predecessors of Lucas, Sargent and their associates. Like Ludwig von Mises and Friedrich von Hayek, they have set themselves the task of producing a theory of the business cycle which is firmly based on the notion that all market phenomena represent the outcome of the voluntary choices of maximising individuals, but these neo-Austrians have gone beyond their predecessors to produce a theory in which output and employment, as well as prices, fluctuate as a result of voluntary choice exercised in markets that always clear. Whatever we may think of the empirical relevance of that theory, and its proponents, notably Robert J. Barro (1978), McCallum (1975) and Patrick Minford (1980), show an admirable, and un-Austrian, willingness to submit their ideas to empirical tests, there is no doubt that its very construction represents an intellectual achievement of the highest order.

One can admire a theory without agreeing with it, and there are many, including myself, who would challenge the basic assumption upon which the Lucas–Sargent–Barro theory of the Business Cycle is based, namely that it is legitimate to model the economy 'as if' markets always clear. It is one thing to agree that commodity and asset markets dominated by specialist traders ought to, and indeed do, display the characteristics associated with continuous clearing and rational expectations; and quite another to attribute similar characteristics to the markets for many components of final output, and above all to the labour market. One may follow Hicks (1974) in distinguishing between 'flexprice' and 'fixprice' markets, assign the labour market to the latter category, and argue that the interaction of inflation and unemployment is best analysed on the premise that the Phillips curve represents the disequilibrium response of prices to a mismatching of supply and demand.

Such a line of analysis is as 'Keynesian' in spirit as the clearing markets approach is 'Austrian', and its existence permits one to subscribe to the expectations augmented Phillips curve without also being committed to a clearing-market–rational-expectations approach to the analysis of economic fluctuations. Moreover, such an approach does *not* differ from the clearing-market view in denying that individuals perceive, and then engage in, all available mutually beneficial trades. It simply denies that they do so infinitely rapidly. It is not true, as for example Barro (1979, p. 58) has recently suggested, that to postulate an infinite speed of price adjustment in the face of excess demand or supply is to conform to sound microeconomic principles, and to postulate anything significantly slower is to rely on a 'non-theory'. One postulate is as *ad hoc* as the other, for the simple reason that we do not have a microeconomic theory of the speed of price adjustment upon which to base our macroeconomics.

The non-clearing market approach to analysing inflation–unemployment interaction is not obviously incompatible with the notion of rational expectations, particularly if the latter concept is interpreted a little flexibly. (See Essay 4 below.) If output fluctuations convey information about appropriate behaviour concerning price setting, as this approach suggests, they can be regarded as constituting one of the ingredients of the expectations upon which such behaviour is based. In that case the term Δp^e in equation (1) can be thought of as summarising influences upon expectations *other than quantity signals*. To say this begs the question of what those 'other influences' on expectations might be, but leaves open the possibility that the same type of information to which the rational expectations hypothesis draws our attention could be incorporated without difficulty into models based on the non-clearing market approach. Observations on the past behaviour of the money supply, for example, might well provide agents with information about the appropriate way to set prices, and might be included among those 'other' influences, as might, in an open economy, variations in prices ruling elsewhere in the world economy, variations in exchange rates, and so on. (On this see e.g. Clements and Jonson 1979.)

The non-clearing market interpretation of the Phillips curve needs to be reconciled with the basic facts of the business cycle. Once given, why do output signals, generated as a response to a conventional transmission mechanism between money and aggregate demand, not result in an immediate adjustment of prices to a market clearing level? The answer here is straightforward – a quantity signal is more likely to lead to a response in price behaviour the more strongly do agents believe that the shock which gave rise to it will persist into the future, and the more free are agents to act on that belief. Inability to disentangle short-term from persistent shocks will, as I have argued elsewhere (Laidler 1975, Ch. 1), lead to a tendency to under-react to quantity signals, as will the existence of contracts that prevent wages and prices being varied, and hence to cause those quantity signals to be drawn out over time and perhaps amplified by multiplier–accelerator effects as well. (See also Essay 4.)

Similar arguments might also have a role to play in the clearing markets model. Brunner, Cuckierman and Meltzer (1980) provide an analysis of persistent shocks within an aggregate supply curve framework, while Peter Howitt (1979) argues that, once explicit attention is paid to the role of inventories in the price setting process, the contrast between clearing market and non-clearing market approaches to economic modelling becomes blurred, and to some extent semantic rather than substantive in nature. However, Howitt's analysis does not extend to the labour market, for obvious reasons, and this fact highlights the fundamental difference between the two approaches. Put simply, for the neo-Austrian *all* unemployment is *voluntary*, and for other macro-economists *some* of it is *involuntary*.

Although theoretical analysis of the interaction of output, employment and prices in terms of an expectations augmented Phillips curve can thus proceed along two very different lines, it is misleading to treat debate about these issues as the latest round in the monetarist controversy. Though monetarists and their opponents are in much closer agreement than they were about the empirical stability of the demand for money function, and about the empirical nature of output–inflation interaction, they still take the same diametrically opposed views on the proper conduct of macroeconomic policy that they did a quarter century ago. Divisions of opinion here *do not* depend upon differences of view about the theoretical basis of price–output interaction. The policy debate has been part of the monetarist controversy for the last two decades. Disputes about the theoretical basis of the Phillips curve, on the other hand, have been going on for ten years at most. That is why it is a mistake to treat the neo-Austrian view of price–output interaction as synonymous with monetarism, as for example Frank Hahn (1980) does. I shall discuss the policy aspects of the monetarist controversy in section 5 but, before I do so, it will be convenient to discuss the place of the monetary approach to balance of payments and exchange rate theory in monetarist doctrine.

4. THE MONETARY APPROACH TO BALANCE OF PAYMENTS AND EXCHANGE RATE ANALYSIS

The monetary approach to balance of payments and exchange rate analysis represents in some respects a revival of the English Classical approach to these problem areas. However, the monetary approach as utilised, for example, by the contributors to Frenkel and Johnson (1975), differs in important ways from classical analysis, as Dietrich Fausten (1979) has pointed out; and the very characteristics that thus distinguish it are borrowed from closed economy monetarism. Most important, advocates of the monetary approach postulate the existence of a stable demand for money function, not just as a working simplification, but as an empirical hypothesis; it is this hypothesis which transforms the approach from an accounting framework into a body of substantive theory. Furthermore, in early statements of the doctrine its proponents tied down the real income argument of that function by assuming full employment, but they soon learned how to replace this assumption with an expectations augmented Phillips curve approach to price–output interaction. (See, for example, Laidler 1975, Ch. 9 and Jonson 1976b.) In effect the monetary approach to balance of payments and exchange rate analysis provided the means whereby these characteristically monetarist hypotheses were made relevant to economies other than the United States which, under the Bretton Woods system, was about as close an approximation to a closed economy that was also a separate political entity as the world has ever seen. Monetarism thus only came to be important outside the United States, not least in Britain, in alliance with the monetary approach to balance of payments and exchange rate analysis.

Until 1971 the world was on a system of fixed exchange rates against the United States dollar. Under such a system, in any country other than the United States, the existence of a stable demand for money function, whose arguments are beyond the direct control of the domestic authorities, implies that the money supply must be an endogenous variable which must adjust to the demand for money. Given this insight, evidence which suggests, for example in the United Kingdom in the 1950s and 1960s, that causation seems to have run predominantly from money income to money, rather than *vice versa*, is no embarrassment to a monetarist provided that he is also willing to attribute most of the variation in money income experienced over that period to causative factors originating abroad. Moreover, although the expectations augmented Phillips curve tells us that in general we should expect to find no stable and persistent inverse trade-off between inflation and unemployment, post-war United Kingdom data do display just such a well-determined relationship down to 1967, and this fact needs explaining. The monetary approach to balance of payments analysis suggests two complementary reasons why this should be the case.

First it notes that, so long as a fixed exchange rate is to be maintained, the prices of tradeable goods sold domestically are going to be determined in the long run, not domestically, but on world markets; it follows from this that the domestic price level's long-run behaviour is going to be constrained by the behaviour of prices in the world at large. Economic agents do not have to be more than merely sensible to perceive this fact and to incorporate it into their expectations. If world prices are relatively stable, and they were until the late 1960s, then so are inflation expectations, and our expectations augmented Phillips curve, equation (1), no matter how we interpret its microeconomic origins, will predict that the data will generate a stable and persistent inflation–unemployment trade-off, because the expectations term will be essentially an exogenous constant or time trend.

This explanation of the existence of a persistent inflation–unemployment trade-off in post-war Britain is an important component of what may fairly be called monetarist hypotheses, about the nature of the stop–go cycle in the 1950s and 1960s and about the degeneration of that economy's performance in the 1970s, which contrast strongly with conventional 'Keynesian' accounts of the same phenomena. The latter begin from the proposition that Britain has a peculiarly high marginal propensity to import, so that, under the Bretton Woods system, attempts to run the economy at a high degree of capacity utilisation, though they produced only a small and on the whole acceptable amount of inflation, were frustrated by balance of payments pressure which forced a reversal of policy. The monetarist hypothesis about stop–go, on the other hand, has it that high levels of demand were associated with high rates of domestic credit expansion which, under fixed exchange rates, generated balance of payments problems in large measure as an *alternative* to domestic inflationary pressure.

The conventional view seemed to imply that Britain's economic performance could be improved by adopting exchange rate flexibility and allowing a depreciation of the currency to offset the balance of payments effects of a high propensity to import. With a flexible exchange rate, the economy could be run at a higher level of capacity and could grow more rapidly without interference from a balance of payments 'constraint'. According to this view a series of exogenous shocks and the autonomous activities of trade unions undermined a basically well-founded strategy when it was adopted in the 1970s. The monetarist view, on the other hand, argues that the adoption of exchange rate flexibility replaced a balance of payments problem with a domestic inflation problem when expansionary policies were pursued, and did nothing to influence the economy's ability to sustain either a higher level or rate of growth of real income. For the monetarist, therefore, the deterioration of British economic performance after 1972 was the predictable (and predicted) consequence of a policy of expanding aggregate demand against a background of exchange rate flexibility. (On this, see my 1972 Lister Lecture, Laidler 1975, Ch. 10 and Laidler 1976.)

Now the monetary approach to balance of payments analysis does far more than make monetarist analysis relevant to Britain. It also permits the explanation of the international spread of inflation in the late 1960s in terms of the repercussions in the world economy of United States monetary expansion, and it treats the breakdown of the Bretton Woods system as the culmination of this process. However, it is only fair to note that such analysis performs less well in the face of the behaviour displayed by the international monetary system since exchange rates began to float in the early 1970s. The prediction that the behaviour of exchange rates can fruitfully be analysed as if determined in efficient asset markets does seem to be supported by the data. However, a basic postulate of the monetary approach is that the equilibrium value of the exchange rate between any two currencies reflects purchasing power parity. Just as data generated under fixed rates show that the price levels of particular economies can display considerable autonomy for substantial periods of time, so under flexible exchange rates systematic and persistent deviations of exchange rates from purchasing power parity do seem to be possible. Though purchasing power parity considerations underlie the behaviour of long period averages of data, implying that, ultimately the terms of trade between countries are independent of monetary factors, there seems to be ample room for short-run deviations from the long-run pattern. Just why this should be the case, and what explains the patterns of such deviations as we observe, are important and open, though by no means neglected, questions. (See Frenkel 1980 for an accessible overview of the issues involved here.)

Be all that as it may, the present regime of flexible exchange rates came into being as the authorities in various countries learned that they could not control such politically important variables as domestic inflation and unemployment, while continuing to adhere to the Bretton Woods arrangements. The diversity of inflation rates among countries since 1971 supports the view that the adoption of flexible rates allows such variables to have their behaviour predominantly determined at home; and long before the 1970s monetarists, not least of course Friedman, argued that the adoption of exchange rate flexibility was a necessary prerequisite to the pursuit of what would now be called monetarist policies in individual countries. In the 1970s we have seen the emergence of conditions under which individual countries could implement independent monetary policies, and as I have suggested above, it is mainly on the matter of policy prescriptions that sharp differences between monetarists and their opponents persist. I shall therefore devote the penultimate section of this essay to a discussion of these matters.

5. POLICY ISSUES

As we have seen, when it comes to propositions about the demand for money function, the relationship between money and money income, and output–inflation interaction, there is a real sense in which 'we are all monetarists now'. The issues that continue sharply to distinguish the views of monetarists from those of their opponents concern the conduct of economic policy. As he did in the 1950s, the monetarist still wants fiscal policy to stick mainly to its traditional tasks of influencing resource allocation and the distribution of income and wealth, and monetary policy to adhere to some simple rule under which the monetary aggregates do not react to short-run fluctuations either in real output or prices; the Keynesian, on the other hand, is still a proponent of activist stabilisation policy.

These policy issues are not independent of the theoretical questions which we have discussed earlier, and indeed, much of the current popularity among monetarists of the neo-Austrian approach to the analysis of price–output interaction stems from the erroneous belief that it provides the only sound basis for scepticism about the effectiveness of activist stabilisation policies. Many Keynesians focus their attacks on that same piece of analysis in the belief, just as erroneous, that if they succeed in refuting it, they also succeed in restoring the case for activist stabilisation policy. Now, the approach in question does indeed imply that output and employment can be influenced by policy only to the extent that it causes prices to vary in a way that agents in the private sector do not anticipate, while the rational expectations hypothesis tells us that if such effects were systematic, the private sector would discover the fact, adapt to it, and thereby render policy ineffective. It follows at once that the only macroeconomic policy which can influence income and employment is a purely random one, and no supporter of 'fine tuning' could possibly recommend that.

The argument just sketched out is logically coherent. So is the counter-argument that, if inflation–output interaction reflects the role of quantity signals in the mechanism whereby various shocks, including those imparted by policy, have their effects transmitted to prices, the way is opened for monetary and fiscal policy to exert a systematic influence upon output and employment. However, there is much more than this to be said about the feasibility and desirability of activist policies. If there was not, how could it be that

Friedman (1960) was able systematically to state his views on policy more than a decade before Lucas (1976) and Sargent and Neil Wallace (1975a and b) developed the theoretical arguments which are now so widely regarded as the only logical underpinning of those views? The Lucas–Sargent–Wallace analysis certainly provides a *sufficient* basis for monetarist policy prescriptions, but is not a *necessary* basis for them: it is one thing to say that the world is so structured that policy can systematically influence output and employment in the short run, and another thing altogether to say that policy makers have enough knowledge to use that ability in a beneficial way.

If it is agreed that in the long run the Phillips curve is essentially vertical – or perhaps even positively sloped if allowance is made for super-non-neutralities – then that certainly does not rule out the possibility of the economy slipping below its natural rate of output in a short run that may be of considerable duration, or the possibility that there exists an appropriate menu of monetary and fiscal policies which might hasten its return to that natural rate without generating any serious costs during the transition. As a first step to exploiting this possibility though, those in charge of policy would need to know what the natural rates of output and employment actually are. As a second step, they would need accurate information upon where the economy actually is, and where it would move in the absence of a policy change, not to mention at what pace. Armed with this not inconsiderable amount of information, policy makers would know that they were in a position where it might be useful to deploy some policy measure or other. To design the policy would of course require them to know about the size and time path of the economy's response to the measures they might take, factors which even the loosest application of the rational expectations idea tells us are likely to be influenced by the policy measures themselves.

Now, I will readily agree that we have the mathematical and statistical tools available for tackling the design of stabilisation policy along the foregoing lines, and I also agree that our econometric models contain answers to all the quantitative questions which I have just raised. However, the conclusion which I draw from all this is that we are probably rather good at fine-tuning econometric models. One can base the monetarist case against activist policy on the proposition that markets always clear and that expectations are rational, but one can also base it on the much more down to earth proposition that we are too ignorant of the structure of the economies we live in, and of the manner in which that structure is changing, to be able safely to implement activist stabilisation policy in the present environment, or in the foreseeable future; although this is not to deny that the rational expectations notion does much to strengthen this latter argument. (See Essay 3, pp. 103–105.)

Among the penalties for making errors in fine tuning which concern monetarists are those which come in the form of the uncomfortably high, and perhaps accelerating, inflation which would result from setting over-optimistic targets for employment and output. Thus, if there is something in the policy environment which weakens the ability of the inflation rate to accelerate, the penalties for such errors are milder, and the case against fine tuning developed above can be softened a little. In the 1950s and 1960s, there can be little doubt that the British authorities did succeed in fine tuning income and employment variables within the rather narrow bounds laid down by what then appeared to be balance of payments constraints. The monetarist interpretation of that period implies that the background of monetary stability implicit in the commitment to a fixed exchange rate was the real constraint on how far fine-tuning policy could be pushed and also that it provided the necessary conditions for its limited success. However, the fact remains that the experience in question does show that a limited degree of fine tuning is feasible if only a background of long-run price stability is assured, and is seen to be assured.

In the kind of sociological theorising about inflation which was particularly popular in Britain in the early 1970s, incomes policy was to be assigned the task of stabilising prices and expectations; but a monetarist would, of course, look to monetary policy to provide such stability. Indeed the Radcliffe Committee (1959) also regarded the task of monetary policy to be the achievement of background stability for the economy. Their view differed from the monetarist approach to the same issue in putting interest rates (and a fixed exchange rate) at the centre of the policy-making process rather than any monetary aggregate. A fixed exchange rate against a stable currency is in and of itself one means of tying down the behaviour of a monetary aggregate, but the adoption of some sort of a money supply growth rule is an alternative. In either case, fine tuning would have to be by fiscal policy. Such a conclusion will be of little consolation to American Keynesians, who are forced by the inability of American political institutions reliably to deliver rapid changes in fiscal variables to assign to monetary variables a far more important role in stabilisation policy than their British counterparts ever did. However, it may do a little to cheer up the British, for whom a return to the days of 'never had it so good' might be a welcome relief from the consequences of 'going for growth'.

As should be apparent from the last few paragraphs, I regard the question of whether governments should or should not indulge in a limited amount of fiscal fine tuning as a secondary issue for monetarists; this is not a new position on my part, being one that I have taken since the early 1970s. Of course questions about the effectiveness of fiscal policy are important ones for macro-economists, and the Brown University Conference on Monetarism (see Stein 1975) dealt almost exclusively with such issues. I accept Purvis' (1980) judgement that the outcome of that conference was to show beyond a reasonable doubt that 'fiscal policy matters'. I also accept his judgement that in retrospect the debate about the effectiveness of fiscal policy has not been central to the monetarist debate, however important an issue it might be in its own right for macroeconomics. Related questions concerning public sector borrowing and the share of the public sector in National Income are even more peripheral to the monetarist debate. No matter what the public perception of these matters might be, I insist that monetarist doctrine tells one that there are severe limits to the extent to which public sector borrowing can be financed by money creation, and beyond that has nothing to say about whether a 'high' or 'low' level of such borrowing is in and of itself desirable. Similarly, monetarism offers no guidance as to how big the public sector of any economy ought to be. It is a macroeconomic doctrine and the issues at stake in debates about the size of the public sector, the welfare state, and so on are fundamentally microeconomic in nature. (These issues are discussed further in Essay 5 below.)

Monetarists have had a good deal to say about wage and price control policies, however. They have opposed them, not just for ideological reasons, though there has been a considerable ideological content to the monetarist debate, but for the much more down to earth reason that they have not expected them to work. This position has been mainly and justifiably defended on the basis of empirical evidence: in the post-Korean war period it is hard indeed to find any wage–price control scheme which has not produced disappointing results over any period longer than a few months. However, monetarists have also sometimes opposed controls on theoretical grounds, particularly in the context of open economies. They have noted that under fixed exchange rates the behaviour of world prices and hence the domestic prices of traded goods cannot be controlled by domestic regulations, any more than can the money supply. They have also pointed out that under flexible rates, though the money supply is under control, neither the exchange rate nor world prices can separately be regulated. In either case, in an open economy wage and price controls inevitably impinge only upon 'the domestic component' of the price level and hence are policies towards relative prices. For that reason, they cannot for long influence the behaviour of the general price level, unless they are accompanied by a battery of quantitative restrictions, not least on foreign trade, that very few of their advocates have been willing to contemplate.

In the 1960s wage and price controls came to be regarded as an alternative to monetary policy in the control of inflation, and in the early 1970s serious attempts were made in both Britain and the United States to use them as such. In both cases the attempts failed sufficiently dramatically that such proponents of controls as, for example, the McCracken Committee (see McCracken *et al.* 1978, Ch. 8) now regard them at best as supplementary devices to be deployed in harmony with more traditional demand-side policies, rather than as a serious alternative to such measures. Though such a viewpoint stops short of the blanket opposition to controls which, along with other monetarists, I would still be willing to defend, it does represent a substantial move in a monetarist direction from positions taken a decade ago. Here again, as in other instances, much of the heat has gone out of the monetarist controversy largely as a result of the accretion of empirical evidence. (Parkin, Sumner and Jones 1973 is still an admirable source of information about wage and price controls in the British economy, while Walker 1976 contains much useful information on other countries.)

There is more to practical monetarism than scepticism about fiscal fine tuning and opposition to wage and price controls. Its key positive tenet is that monetary weapons, and in particular the growth rate of some monetary aggregate, should be assigned to the attainment and maintenance of long-run price stability, and hence that those same monetary weapons not be used for fine tuning purposes. In this respect, as with the other components of the doctrine which we considered earlier, there has been a considerable growth in the acceptance of monetarism. It is now widely accepted that the influence of inflation expectations on nominal interest rates make them unreliable guides to the tightness or otherwise of policy, while propositions about the desirability of setting rules and targets for the growth of monetary aggregates are now commonplace in the statements of Central Banks. If monetarists complain – and they do – about the failure of Keynesian policies since the mid-1960s, then simple fairness requires them to say something about the lessons that they have learned about the viability of their own policy proposals from what many observers believe to have been widespread and sustained efforts to apply them during the 1970s.

The first thing to be said on this score is that the case for monetary growth rate rules, as initially stated by Friedman (and Edward Shaw), was put in terms of the capacity of such a policy to *maintain* stability in an already stable economy – it was a policy prescription for *staying out* of trouble. However, it has been only since our economies have found themselves deeply *in trouble* that monetarist policy proposals have attracted the attention of policy makers. There is much less unanimity among monetarists about how to tackle the problem of restoring stability than there is about how to maintain it. Though all monetarists would agree that a return to a modest growth rate of some monetary aggregate or other is the long-run goal, the neo-Austrians would favour a rapid return to such a rule, while those of us who take a more traditional view of the nature of the Phillips trade-off have advocated 'gradualism'.

Unless we take the cynical view that the rhetoric of central bankers bears no relationship to their intentions, we must conclude that in a number of places attempts have been made to implement gradualist policies. There are two questions to be asked about those attempts: first, is it the case that those attempts have resulted in a systematic and gradual reduction in the rate of growth of any monetary aggregate? and second, if such attempts have anywhere been successful, did that success lead to a reduction in the inflation rate? As is well known, policy has in the main failed on the first count because only in Canada, to the best of my knowledge, have the authorities on the whole succeeded in achieving pre-stated monetary growth targets over an extended period. It is equally well known that the single most important reason for this failure, at least in the United States and Britain, has been the unwillingness of those in charge of monetary policy to give up setting targets for interest rates, unreliable indicators of the stance of policy though they may be, when they adopted targets for money supply, combined with a proclivity to stick with the interest rate target when the two came into conflict, as they inevitably had to sooner or later. Germany and Switzerland have had difficulty sticking to money supply targets because of concern with the behaviour of the exchange rates rather than interest rates *per se*, as Sumner (1979) has noted, but of course exchange rates and interest rates are hardly independent of one another; and concern over the exchange rate and interest rates during the period 1979–81 posed a serious threat to the continuation of the Canadian experiment. (See Essay 5, pp. 188–9, for further comments on the Canadian experiment.)

It would be easy enough to argue in the light of all this that recent experience offers essentially no test of monetarist gradualism, but that seems to be going too far. Monetarists have usually treated questions of income distribution and resource allocation as separate and distinct from those of monetary policy. This dichotomy is a useful one when the problem for monetary policy is to *maintain* already existing stability, but can all too easily lead one to neglect the way in which monetary policy interacts with allocation and distribution when its implementation requires sharp (albeit temporary) increases in interest rates. A key factor here, at least in Britain, is the political importance of the housing market, and of the behaviour of mortgate interest rates. In retrospect, it is clear that monetarists did not do a very good job of educating policy makers – both elected and otherwise – about the problem that adopting monetarist policies would generate in this area. Some of us did raise these matters, but apparently not loudly enough. High interest rates have turned out to be at least as difficult for politicians to deal with as have high unemployment rates, and that was not foreseen. (See Laidler *et al.* 1976, particularly Chapters 7 and 9, for an earlier statement of my own views on the role of the housing market and its interaction with monetary policy and inflation. I readily acknowledge that the source is an obscure one.)

There are also technical problems with implementing monetarist policies. The manipulation of interest rates as the centrepiece of monetary policy long antedates the Keynesian revolution, and was quite appropriate in economies whose monetary rule was to maintain convertibility into gold or some other currency at a fixed price. However, the day-to-day operating procedures of central banks, the very organisation of their decision making processes, not to mention the structure of the private markets in which they operate, are all geared by force of tradition to making and implementing decisions about interest rates. Although monetarists have gone a great deal of work on the basic economics of the money supply process under different policy regimes, and though some of them, notably Brunner and Meltzer, have frequently scolded their colleagues for neglect of these issues, hindsight suggests that they did not place enough emphasis upon the extent to which the problem of implementing a different monetary policy might require a basic overhaul of institutions if it was to be solved; an overhaul that might involve a considerable break with traditional practices, and hence be hard to implement. Such work as has been done on these issues, for example by William Poole and Charles Lieberman (1972) for the United States, and Nigel Duck and David Sheppard (1978) for the United Kingdom, seems to have had no effect in convincing policy makers to undertake such an overhaul at the same time as they adopted monetarist rhetoric.

If central banks have not on the whole succeeded in smoothly slowing down monetary expansion rates in a sustained way, a number of them have nevertheless managed to create contractions in monetary growth rates which have been sharp and persistent enough to bite. Associated with these contractions have been the 'shifts' of the demand for money function that I discussed earlier in this paper. As the reader will recall, I argued that these shifts were, in all probability, real phenomena and not statistical artifacts, that such shifts were nothing new, and that they were probably to be explained, at least in part, by institutional changes which themselves might plausibly be interpreted as a response to monetary policy. It should be noted explicitly that it has perhaps been a tightening of policy *per se*, rather than the adoption of money supply targets, that has lain at the root of the problem, at least in the United States, and a tightening of policy in the context of legal restrictions on movements of bank interest rates at that. Nevertheless, these shifts of the demand for money function, relatively small though they have been, force us to reassess a fundamental tenet of practical monetarism, namely the injunction to fix *ex ante* a specific quantitatively expressed growth rate rule for the money supply, and then ensure adherence to it by taking away from the monetary authorities the discretion to do otherwise.

Objections to such a proposal have frequently been cast in terms of the question 'How are you going to define the money supply for purposes of implementing this policy?' The answer typically given has been that it doesn't much matter, because if the rate of growth of one monetary aggregate is pinned down, all the others will end up behaving consistently, at least on average over the kind of time periods for which stability in monetary policy is really important. That answer is surely valid if one is dealing with an economy in which there is no institutional change in the private sector, but that does not make it as adequate a response to the question as I once thought it did. Suppose we agreed to set a rule for the growth rate of M1 and that initially we could agree on what assets to include in that aggregate. What if, after the rule had been implemented, some new asset, for example a new kind of chequing account, evolved? Perhaps the demand function for M1 as initially defined would then shift, but if *ex post* we included the new asset in our definition of M1 we might still be able to show that the demand for narrow money hadn't 'really' shifted, after all.

Such problems would not arise if we were not too specific in laying down the precise definition of money which was to bind policy makers in the future. However, to do that would leave it open to the discretion of someone at some time in the future to decide just how to define the monetary aggregate whose rate of growth was tied down with a rule, and that amounts to giving them the discretion to ignore the rule in question. It is hard to resist the implication that it does not seem to be possible, let alone desirable, to eliminate all scope for discretionary policy in a world in which the monetary system is in a state of evolution. I hasten to add that this does not imply that attempts to implement short-run fine tuning of the economy by way of manipulating interest rates are all of a sudden all right, or that it is fruitless to require central banks to announce target ranges for the expansion of precisely defined monetary aggregates over, say, one or two year time horizons. However, it does imply that it is, as a practical matter, impossible to prevent policy makers doing the wrong things, if they so wish, by tying them down to a quasi-constitutional monetary growth rate rule. Unless we can accurately foresee the path which innovations in the financial sector are going to take, someone somewhere is going to have to be granted the discretion to deal with them when they arise. The monetarist injunction not to use monetary policy for fine tuning is not affected by these considerations, but the proposal that the once-and-for-all enactment of a simple quantitative rule, to be followed ever afterwards, can lead to that injunction being implemented is undermined. That seems to me to be a rather severe criticism of much received monetarist policy doctrine. (The above argument is elaborated in Essay 5.)

6. CONCLUDING COMMENTS

As the reader will by now have seen, it is my view that the core of monetarism has consisted of a series of empirical propositions and policy prescriptions, all of which are quite consistent with mainstream economic theory. One can approach the analysis of social questions in terms of the maximising behaviour of individual agents without believing in a stable demand for money function, or a vertical long-run Phillips curve, but evidence that such relationships exist need in no way disturb one's theoretical preconceptions. Although there have been episodes in the monetarist debate where the relevance of mainstream economics to the analysis of such social questions as inflation and unemployment has been vigorously questioned, particularly in Britain, that debate has mainly been about questions amenable to being settled with reference to empirical evidence, as Mayer (1978) has also argued.

Viewed in this light, I would suggest that, in all but one aspect, the monetarist debate is as close to being over as an economic controversy ever is. The demand for money function does seem to be more stable over time than the early critics of monetarism suggested, while shifts in it have been neither new phenomena, nor of sufficient magnitude seriously to undermine long-run relationships between money and money income. Puzzles about 'reverse causation' in the data for countries such as Britain cease to be puzzles when the openness of the economy and the nature of the exchange rate regime are taken into account. There is now much less disagreement about the empirical nature of the interaction of real income and inflation: there is a short-run trade-off between inflation and unemployment ànd it does seem to vanish in the long run, though there is still debate about how quickly that 'long run' is approached. We should not under-rate the importance of the consensus which has been achieved on the foregoing issues – or neglect to mention explicitly that the consensus in question is not universal – but this does not mean that there is now no controversy in macroeconomics. As we have seen, two areas remain contentious.

First, one aspect of the monetarist debate remains alive, and that concerns the proper conduct of monetary policy. I doubt that my own view, that the case for governing monetary policy by long-run rules is impossible to sustain in the face of careful consideration of the influence of institutional change on the behaviour over time of the demand for money function, will find a great deal of support among monetarists at present; while I would be surprised to find it regarded as sufficient of a concession to proposals to 'fine tune' money income, and it really is no such thing, to satisfy the Keynesians. Thus, I would expect debates about this matter to keep the monetarist controversy alive for a while yet.

The other, and in my view far more important, issue has to do with the market–theoretic foundations of macroeconomics. The issues raised by Lucas and his collaborators are not the issues which have traditionally concerned participants in the monetarist debate and it is misleading to approach them as if they were. The debate about the assumptions of clearing markets and rational expectations as a basis for macroeconomics is a new one and, as Brian Kantor (1979) has suggested, it is really about whether Keynes' *General Theory* carried economics forward or took it on a fruitless detour. Though it has very little to do with monetarism, it nevertheless concerns issues of fundamental theoretical importance for macroeconomics. Let us hope that this new controversy (which I discuss in detail in Essay 3) proves to be as fruitful as the monetarist controversy has been.

2

On the Demand for Money and the Real Balance Effect

1. THE LONG- AND SHORT-RUN DEMAND FOR MONEY

No proposition in macroeconomics has received more attention than that there exists, at the level of the aggregate economy, a stable demand for money function. When we say that the demand for money function is stable we mean at the very least that money holdings, as observed in the real world, can be explained, to conventionally acceptable levels of statistical significance, by functional relationships which include a relatively small number of arguments. We also mean, or should mean, that the same equation is capable of being fitted to samples of data drawn from different times and places, without it being necessary to change the arguments of the relationship in order to achieve satisfactory results, and also without the estimated quantitative values of the parameters changing too much.

Now of course a cavalier treatment of the requirements that the number of parameters be 'relatively small', and that parameter values not change 'too much' when the data are changed, could permit claims to be made on behalf of the stability of almost any relationship, but, in this case, there is no need to abuse the English language. In practice a 'small' number of arguments has meant three or four – typically including a scale variable such as income, permanent income or wealth, an opportunity cost variable such as a nominal interest rate or some measure of the expected inflation rate, and, if nominal balances have been the dependent variable, the general price level. The requirement that parameters not change 'too much' has meant not only that they have been expected to take their theoretically predicted sign, but also to stay within reasonable quantitative ranges as well, in the region of 0.5–1.0 or a little greater for the real income elasticity of demand for money, somewhere around −0.1––0.5 or less for the interest elasticity depending upon the interest rate, not to mention the definition of money, utilised, and since economic theory predicts that the demand for money is a demand for 'real' balances, a price level elasticity of demand for nominal balances of close to 1.0.

I have surveyed empirical work on the demand for money elsewhere (Laidler 1977, 1980), and there is no need to go into detail about these matters again here. It will suffice to note that, although not every test on every set of data has proved satisfactory, the demand for money has turned out to be 'stable' in the sense in which I have used the word above quite often enough to convince the majority of monetary economists, some of whom twenty years ago were quite sceptical (see e.g. Modigliani 1978), of the importance of the relationship for our understanding of macroeconomic phenomena. One characteristic of the results generated by empirical work on the demand for money which seems to be rather general is that, unless one is dealing with data which are highly aggregated over time – business cycle phase averages for example (see Friedman 1959) – or which cover such a long period of time – fifty years or more, say – that the variation in the data used is dominated by secular changes, it has proved necessary to distinguish between the 'long-run' and the 'short-run' demand for money in order to achieve satisfactory results.

The long-run aggregate demand for money function may be thought of as being generated by the outcome of the following thought experiment: consider an economy in which, given the values of the various arguments in the function, the aggregate of agents desire to hold a certain quantity of money and are able to do so; then ask how much money they would be observed to hold in various *alternative* circumstances in which the variables that determine money holding took different values. If the tastes of agents *vis à vis* money holding did not change over time, and if there were no barriers to their moving instantaneously from holding one amount of money to another, the outcome of this experiment would be the same as that generated by varying the values of the arguments of the demand for money function over time and then observing the changes in cash balances associated with those variations. However, if agents face any costs of adjusting their money holdings, so the argument goes, they will not move immediately to a new point on their long-run demand for money function when one of its arguments changes. They will begin to move towards that point, but the speed of the approach will be determined by their response to the adjustment costs involved in getting there.

It will help with the clarity of the argument to put all this into a familiar algebraic form at this point. It is convenient to work with a log linear (constant elasticity) form of the demand for money function, and to divide time up into discrete periods, Hicksian 'weeks' say. Thus, with X a vector of factors determining the demand for real balances, p the log of the general price level, m^* the log of the quantity of money demanded as determined by the long-run function, we write

$$m^* = f(X) + p \qquad (1)$$

which is the long-run aggregate demand for money function.

Following practices which I shall in due course criticise, we may also write, with the subscript -1 denoting a one-period time lag and with m the log of nominal money demanded,

$$m - m_{-1} = b(m^* - m_{-1}) \qquad 0 < b \leq 1 \qquad (2)$$

which tells us how much of the gap between actual and ultimately desired money holdings will be closed during one period. Together these equations yield the short-run demand for money function

$$m = b\{f(X) + p\} + (1-b)m_{-1} \qquad (3)$$

An equation such as (3), or something very like it, has been used in an enormous number of studies of the demand for money, and the lagged dependent variable has almost invariably proved an important addition as far as increasing the relationship's explanatory power is concerned. The addition in question has usually been regarded as quite innocuous, because the kind of adjustment cost argument which I have just sketched out has been widely applied, not just to the demand for money, but to the consumption function as well, not to mention the demand for various durable goods (see Harberger 1960). Indeed, one well-known, and still frequently cited, article on this particular aspect of the demand for money (Chow 1966) was explicitly an application to money of techniques which its author had used when working on the demand for automobiles, techniques which, in essence, give econometric content to the Marshallian distinction between the long-run and short-run response of quantity demanded of some good to a change in some argument of its demand function, a distinction which seems at first sight to be universally applicable.

The bulk of this essay will be devoted to elaborating upon the proposition that, notwithstanding the widespread practice of adding a lagged dependent variable to the demand for money function, the belief implicit in this practice that the demand for money *in the aggregate economy* can be modelled in the long and short runs 'as if' money was a consumer durable good, is fallacious. It will also examine some of the implications of this proposition for what we do and do not know about the aggregate demand for money. The phrase 'in the aggregate economy' is italicised, because the problem to be discussed arises at the level of what Patinkin (1956) called the market experiment, and not at the level of the individual experiment at all. It will nevertheless be helpful to begin the argument with an examination of the relevant individual experiment.

2. THE INDIVIDUAL EXPERIMENT AND THE REAL BALANCE EFFECT

Though it was a controversial matter at one time, it is by now as near to universally accepted as anything in economics ever is that once the relevant object of choice is recognised to be 'real balances' (money holdings measured in constant purchasing power terms), and once their durability is taken account of, the individual agent's demand for money can, and indeed should, be analysed along with his demand for everything else. The amount of real balances which he will hold will be the outcome of the interaction of his utility function with his budget constraint, just like the quantity of anything else he will demand. It was at one time widely questioned whether it made sense to argue that money yielded 'utility' to the individual in the same way as other goods, but it is by now well established that, from the point of view of the individual experiment, the 'story' which one tells about this matter makes no critical difference.

One may argue that, by holding real balances, the individual agent is able to avoid the embarrassment of being unable to pay up promptly when unexpectedly called upon to meet his obligations in cash (Patinkin 1965, Ch. 5); one may argue that he is enabled to cut down on the transactions costs involved in liquidating income earning assets when cash is required (Baumol 1952, Tobin 1956); one may argue that the agent can avoid the uncertainties about future command over resources inherent in holding variable capital value assets such as bonds (Keynes 1936, Ch. 15, Tobin 1958); and so on. What is postulated here turns out to make no difference to our ability to integrate the analysis of the demand for money with that of other aspects of the agent's choices, any more than the motives we attribute to the owners of automobiles make any difference to our ability to apply choice theory to analysing the demand for that durable good.

What is important, as Patinkin (1965, Chs 5–7) showed quite clearly, is that agents *do* desire to hold real balances, and not *why*. This is not to deny that if we formulate some precise hypothesis about the nature and source of the 'utility' which money holding yields the individual, we might thereby put ourselves in a position also to formulate more precise hypotheses about the quantitative nature of the agent's demand for money function than generalised choice theory would yield. After all, the Baumol–Tobin 'square root rule' is an example of just this possibility working out in practice. However, if the qualitative predictions yielded by the basic theory of choice are sufficient for any particular purpose, then there is no need to ask why cash balances yield utility before applying that theory to analysing the demand for money. This is *not* to say that, when we engage in economic analysis, we never need to pay attention to those special characteristics of money as a social institution which facilitate the processes of exchange; but it is to say that, when considering the money holding behaviour of an individual agent acting alone, it will suffice to treat real money balances 'as if' they are a service-yielding consumer durable.

Using the same symbols as before, but attaching to them, where appropriate, the subscript i to indicate that we are indeed dealing with an individual, we may write the individual agent's long-run demand for money function, where 'long run' is defined in a manner analogous to that already used above, as

$$m_i^* = f_i(X)_i + p \qquad (4)$$

Here, it is as well to note explicitly that m_i^* refers to the quantity of nominal balances the individual will plan to end up holding at the end of the current period, given the price level and the values of the variables included in X that rule during the period, if he faces no costs of adjusting his money holdings. If we are willing to entertain the possibility of our agent being off his long-run demand for money function over a time span longer than one period, and we should be, if only because Archibald and Lipsey (1958) established one set of mechanisms that make this a reasonable postulate, we might also argue that he moves back towards it slowly according to

$$(m_i - m_{i-1}) = b(m_i^* - m_{i-1}) \qquad (5)$$

Once again then, we can derive a short-run demand for money function of the conventional form

$$m_i = b\{f_i(X)_i + p\} + (1-b)m_{i-1} \qquad (6)$$

Here m_i is the amount of money the agent *actually* plans to hold at the end of the current period, and m_{i-1} is the amount of money with which he *begins* the current period; as we shall see in a moment, m_{i-1} may or may not be the amount of money he *chose* to hold in period -1. Be that as it may, the adjustment parameter b is easily enough motivated in the individual experiment. If, by the end of the period for which he is choosing his cash holdings, our agent is not on his long-run demand for money function, he obviously enjoys less utility, or incurs greater costs somewhere or other, than he otherwise would. Suppose, however, that in moving back towards that long-run relationship over the period in question he also incurs transactions costs of some sort. Call the first cost K_1 and the second K_2, and let them be determined in the following way:

$$K_1 = \alpha_1(m_i^* - m_i)^2 \qquad (7)$$

$$K_2 = \alpha_2(m_i - m_{i-1})^2 \qquad (8)$$

The agent seeking to minimise the sum of these costs will adjust his cash balances over time according to equation (5) where

$$b \equiv \alpha_1/(\alpha_1+\alpha_2) \tag{9}$$

The above cost functions are undoubtedly arbitrary; their quadratic form has much more to do with the fact that this enables us to derive a linear, and therefore easy to handle, adjustment process, than with any well thought through microeconomic analysis; also, the existence of an adjustment cost function such as (8) for the individual is not easily reconciled with the lump sum adjustment costs which are sometimes used in deriving the long-run demand for money function (when, for example, the Baumol–Tobin inventory approach is used), but such criticisms are not of any great importance for present purposes. Nothing fundamental in the arguments which follow depends upon the linearity of the adjustment process, but the simplicity of the argument is enhanced if we make the arbitrary assumptions which have to be made in order to keep the individual's short-run demand for money function in the form given by (6), not least because that is the form which is usually thought of as underlying the similar relationship used in empirical work on aggregate data.

Equation (6) tells us that the amount of nominal money we will observe our individual holding at the end of any time period will depend upon the general price level at which trade takes place during the period, whatever factors we might put in X – let us say, real income and a representative nominal interest rate over the period – and the quantity of nominal money he held at the beginning of that period. Such an equation makes perfectly good economic (and econometric) sense. The price level and nominal interest rates are quite beyond the individual's control, as is real income – unless we go into a model in which the labour–leisure choice is endogenous; and if we did that we ought to put the real wage, and some endowment of labour power, into the relationship instead. Beginning of period money is also exogenous from the point of view of current period behaviour, however it may be determined. The only endogenous variable in the equation is indeed the one which appears on its left-hand side.

Equation (6) is a meaningful, if rather trivial, expression, which can form the basis for a series of equally meaningful, and equally trivial, individual experiments. We can start our individual out on his long-run demand for money function, face him with changes in his real income, the interest rate, or the price level, and use equation (6) to generate the resulting time path of his nominal money holdings. In this case, note that m_{-1}, beginning of period money holdings, will be given by the value taken by the dependent variable of equation (6) in period -1. We can also present our individual with a windfall gain in nominal money holdings (perhaps as a result of the passage of a helicopter, cf. Friedman 1969), hold interest rates, prices and his income constant, and once again use equation (6) to tell us about his reaction. In this case, of course, beginning period money will not be equal to the individual's money holdings at the end of period -1.

We do not usually come across this latter experiment in the discussions of the demand for money, finding it instead in discussions of the 'real balance effect' where the influence of money on expenditure flows is at the centre of attention. However, it is a point too often taken for granted, and perhaps for that reason not fully enough appreciated, that, in the individual experiment, whenever there arises a discrepancy between desired long-run money holdings and actual money holdings, for no matter what reason, there must be accompanying effects on expenditure flows, either on current consumption goods and/or on the acquisition of other assets. The change in money holdings on the left-hand side of equation (5) must have its counterpart in the agent's expenditure if his budget constraint is to be satisfied. That is to say, when we talk of the adjustment over time of the agent's money holdings towards their long-run equilibrium, we are also talking about what is, to all intents and purposes, a real balance effect, or as Chick (1973, pp. 76–77 following Mishan 1958) called it, a 'cash balance effect'. This is true whether the experiment we are describing is set in motion by a variation in the arguments of the agent's long-run demand for money function, or by a change in his endowment of nominal money.

I am here using the phrase 'real balance effect' in a rather broader sense than did Patinkin (1956), because he reserved the term to characterise only wealth effects. He used the phrase 'substitution effect' to describe the consequences of those disturbances to the individual which required him to change only the composition of his assets. Here I am bringing both types of reaction under the one heading as Patinkin himself tended to do (1967). Moreover, this analysis of the dynamics whereby desired long-run money holdings are reached, presented above, is different from the account offered by Archibald and Lipsey (1958) to which I have already alluded, in their extension to the multi-period case of Patinkin's (1956) analysis of the operation of the real balance effect in the individual experiment. However, these differences reflect the fact that the foregoing analysis has started from the literature on the Demand for Money, rather than that which deals with the integration of Monetary Theory and General Equilibrium Theory. They do not imply that the conclusions which have been stated above about the relationship between monetary adjustments and expenditure flows are in any way misplaced. Thus, we may use the insights yielded by Patinkin's and Archibald and Lipsey's work to illuminate the connection between the individual and market experiments in the analysis of the role of adjustment costs in the demand for money function. This is a matter of considerable importance because, as Patinkin showed, the operation of the real balance effect in the market experiment is very different from its operation in the individual experiment. I now turn to a discussion of these issues.

3. THE MARKET EXPERIMENT WITH EXOGENOUS NOMINAL MONEY

The way in which a market experiment having to do with the demand for money, the real balance effect, and so on, works out must obviously depend on the nature of the market in which it is performed. It is convenient to begin here with the kind of economy analysed by Patinkin (1965, Chs 10 and 11): that is, one in which perfect competition reigns throughout, prices are perfectly flexible, tastes, technology and resource endowments are given and held constant over time, the money supply consists of tokens whose nominal quantity is exogenously given at the beginning of each period, and individual agents face no portfolio adjustment costs. In such a case, one conceivable source of disturbance would be a change in the nominal money supply: given perfect price flexibility (and setting aside distribution effects), the outcome of the operation of the real balance effect in the market experiment would be an *instantaneous* change in the price level. Its effect as far as the demand for money is concerned would be to keep the economy on its *long-run* function.

This does not imply that in empirical work it would be appropriate to substitute the logarithm of actual money supply for m^* on the left-hand side of equation (1), and estimate that relationship as a demand for money function, because, with the money supply exogenous and the price level endogenous, these two variables ought to change places. However, because the price level is endogenous in this economy, so are real balances and it would be appropriate to re-write the long-run demand for money function as

$$m^* - p = f(X) \qquad (10)$$

Then, provided there was some exogenous variation over time in the factors included in X, a long-run demand for real balances function could be estimated in this form if m_s was substituted for m^*.

All this is somewhat academic, since we have noted already that the kind of quarterly and annual data which we use in our empirical work on the demand for money will not permit us successfully to estimate such a long-run relationship. We have also noted that it is usual to deal with this problem by adding a lagged dependent variable to the demand function, and that this practice is often defended by referring to the existence of adjustment costs. Suppose that we attempted to introduce these costs into the kind of economy we have briefly described above. Could we account for the presence of a lagged dependent variable in our aggregate demand for money function in these terms? We could not, as I shall now argue. To begin with, recall that equation (3) pictures nominal balances adjusting slowly over time in response to a change in some argument or another of the demand for money function, and note that in the economy I have just described it is the nominal money supply which changes to disturb agents' money holdings, and exogenously at that. In such an economy, where prices are perfectly flexible, individual adjustment costs would have no observable consequences for aggregate behaviour in the face of an exogenous change in the nominal money supply.

The latter assertion seems to fly in the face of certain conclusions which have a well established place in the existing literature of monetary economics. As long ago as 1966 Donald Tucker embedded an aggregate demand for money function, essentially the same as equation (3), in an IS–LM model, and showed that the presence of such an equation in a model of that type implies that at least one of the arguments of the demand for money function overshoots its long-run equilibrium value as an instantaneous response to a change in the money supply. This result is *mathematically* coherent, but it is *logically* incompatible with the existence of the individual adjustment costs on which the presence of a lagged dependent variable in the demand for money function is usually supposed to be based.

To see why, consider how Tucker's result would apply to an economy in which all the arguments of the demand for real balances (X) are held constant (at their 'full employment' levels, perhaps) and in which, therefore, only the price level can adjust to absorb a change in the quantity of money. In such an economy, let the nominal money supply be increased by a certain amount. If there is no lagged dependent variable in the demand for money function, that change in the quantity of money will lead to an equi-proportional change in the price level as a result of the pressure of demand exerted on goods markets as all agents try to restore their cash balances. The algebra here is trivial: from (1), if we postulate that the demand and supply of money are to be in equilibrium, we have

$$m_s = m^* = f(X) + p \qquad (11)$$

and

$$p = m_s - f(X) \qquad (12)$$

so that

$$\partial p / \partial m_s = 1 \qquad (13)$$

Now suppose that we maintain the 'supply and demand for money are in equilibrium' assumption, but add a lagged dependent variable to the demand for money function. When the nominal money supply changes, a *greater than proportional* change in the price level *seems* to be required. From (3) we have

$$p = \frac{1}{b} m_s - f(X) - \frac{1-b}{b} m_{-1} \qquad (14)$$

from which it *seems* to follow that

$$\frac{\partial p}{\partial m_s} = \frac{1}{b} > 1 \qquad (15)$$

This is a very strange result indeed. Faced with portfolio

adjustment costs, the individual experiment tells us that the typical agent in the economy is prepared to take time about getting back to equilibrium, and that he therefore changes his demand for goods by less than he would in the absence of such costs when he receives an addition to his holdings of money. Yet we are asked to believe that the aggregate effect of this *smaller* increase in demand, this *weaker* real balance effect, is to cause the price level to change by a *greater* amount than it otherwise would. The conclusion is obvious nonsense.

The problem here has arisen because we have given the wrong interpretation to the variable m_{-1} in the aggregate demand for money function. The individual experiment which must underlie the market experiment we are discussing here is one in which the typical agent receives a windfall gain in money holdings and sets in motion expenditure which enables him to adjust his money holdings towards their long-run equilibrium level. As we have seen, in this individual experiment it is crucial to distinguish the cash balances the individual agent chose to end up holding at the end of period -1 on the one hand, and those with which he begins the current period on the other, because these two amounts are not the same when the individual's holdings of nominal money are exogenously disturbed. If he faces portfolio adjustment costs, the individual attempts to move his holdings of nominal money part of the way from where they are at the *beginning* of the period to the value given by his long-run demand for money. That is the meaning of equation (6). The individual can always do this, but when the nominal money supply is exogenous, the whole economy can not. In the aggregate, the money which is available to be held must be held.

But does not equation (15) tell us by how much the price level must change in order for the increased stock of nominal money to be held willingly? It does not, and the reason why it does not may be seen by considering equation (6), the individual short-run demand for money function. The aggregate demand for money is, of course, obtained by adding up the latter expression over all individuals in the economy. However, in the experiment we are considering we must substitute the individual's beginning of period money holding for the variable m_{i-1} on the right-hand side of (6). Therefore, the *current period's money supply* rather than the *previous period's aggregate demand for nominal money* ought to be substituted for the variable labelled m_{-1} on the right-hand side of equation (3). If we do this, equation (14) becomes

$$p = \frac{1}{b} \, m_s - f(X) - \frac{1-b}{b} m_s \qquad (16)$$

which of course reduces to the long-run equation

$$p = m_s - f(X) \qquad (12)$$

so that we have

$$\partial p / \partial m_s = 1 \qquad (13)$$

Thus, the 'overshoot' effect is non-existent, and the economy is always on its long-run demand for money function even in the presence of portfolio adjustment costs.

A similar argument can be mounted against Tucker's (1966) analysis, where output and interest rates, rather than prices, respond to the change in the money supply, and indeed William White (1978, 1981) essentially does just that. I shall return to this point below, but for the moment let it be clear that what is at stake here is not whether Tucker's results follow from the model which he writes down, because they do, but whether the experiments he carried out with his model are compatible with the underlying adjustment lag assumptions used to justify the presence of a lagged dependent variable in the aggregate demand for money function. An alternative motivation for lags in the demand for money function, for example one based upon sluggishness on the part of expectations to respond to experience, in a world in which the demand for money depends upon the expected rather than actual values of the arguments in the function, would be quite consistent with Tucker's market experiment. His results retain their interest even if we quarrel with one set of premises from which they might be derived. The results are in fact very similar (though not identical) to those discussed in Laidler (1968) where the existence of lags in the demand for money function, and elsewhere, is justified, following Friedman (1959), along expectational lines.

The above qualification is of some importance, because a good deal of work on the demand for money function has been devoted to investigating whether or not expectation lags are, in fact, a better explanation of the need to distinguish between a short-run and a long-run demand for money function in our empirical work than are adjustment lags. Specifically, it is well known that, if we substitute the logarithm of real permanent income y^*, and the logarithm of some interest rate r, for X in equation (1), and generate permanent income according to the log–linear error learning formula

$$y^*-y^*_{-1}=q(y-y^*_{-1}) \qquad (17)$$

then, with the δs being the parameter of the long-run demand for money function, the short-run demand for money function is given by

$$m = q\delta_0+q\delta_1y+q\delta_2r+qp+ \\ (1-q)m_{-1}-(1-q)\delta_2r_{-1}-(1-q)p_{-1} \qquad (18)$$

If this were the true short-run demand for money relationship, we would need to posit no adjustment lags in the individual experiment; agents could always be thought of as holding just the quantity of money they desired, and the long-run–short-run distinction, upon which successful empirical work seems to depend, would hinge upon discrepancies between current and permanent income.

However, it does not seem possible to defend the proposition that (18) is the true form of the demand for money function in the face of available empirical evidence, even though Feige's (1967) seminal paper on this subject seemed to show that it was. To begin with, Feige used annual data and did not rule out the possibility that quarterly data might reveal a role for adjustment lags. Subsequent work with quarterly data does seem to show that they have a role to play even in the presence of expectation lags, or at least Laidler and Parkin (1970) claimed that this was the case for the United Kingdom. Stephen Goldfeld (1973) went further and concluded that a lag structure of the type captured in equation (3) left nothing for expectations lags to explain in the context of recent United States quarterly data. Furthermore, with similar data, also for the United States, Laidler (1980) found that equation (18) systematically performed worse than an adjustment lag formulation of the function (though not of quite the same form as Goldfeld's, as we shall see in a moment). He found that this result held up with annual data too. Moreover, none of this is to mention that recent work on the notion of Rational Expectations must imply that equation (17) is a very dubious formulation of the relationship between permanent income and current income.

In short, appealing though the expectations lag hypothesis is as a solution to the problem of linking individual and market experiments

while maintaining the distinction between the short- and long-run
demand for money functions, the empirical evidence in favour of
this solution is weak. Equations like (3) do fit the data rather well,
but if that was because they were really good approximations to
equation (18), then the latter would fit even better; and it does not
do so on any systematic basis. However, this does not alter the fact
that, in an exogenous money supply world, portfolio adjustment
costs cannot be used to motivate the long-run–short-run demand
for money distinction.

There is yet a third explanation of the presence of the lagged
dependent variable in the aggregate demand for money relationship
to be found in the literature on the demand for money. The
explanation involves the 'real' (as opposed to 'nominal') adjustment model of the short-run demand for money. The model is
usually written in the following way:

$$m-p = bf(X)+(1-b)(m_{-1}-p_{-1}) \tag{19}$$

It is then estimated on the assumption that $m_s = m$. By way of
comparison, consider equation (3) once more and substract from
both sides of it the logarithm of the current value of the general
price level. This yields an expression which differs from equation
(19) only in the timing of the value of the price level observation by
which lagged nominal balances are deflated.

$$m-p = bf(X)+(1-b)(m_{-1}-p) \tag{20}$$

With this equation too, for empirical purposes the money supply is
substituted for the quantity of money demanded. Clearly, if one of
these expressions fits a particular data set well, so will the other,
unless the price level series is extremely erratic; but in practice the
series is highly autocorrelated. It was this real adjustment form of
the function which Laidler (1980) found to fit better than that
derived from an expectations lag, and in this study it also turned out
that the real adjustment form performed better than its nominal
counterpart, in the sense of providing an estimate of $(1-b)$ that was
less than unity. Benjamin Friedman (1977) also obtained this result.

At the level of the individual experiment, the 'real' adjustment
notion is, to say the least, decidedly odd. To apply it to the
individual experiment is to argue that, if the general price level
varies, the typical agent will instantaneously adjust his nominal
balances in order to keep his real money holdings constant, but that

a change in any other argument of the long-run function will meet with a lagged response. The price level is quite as exogenous as any other variable in the individual experiment, and any adjustment of real balances must involve the agent acquiring or running down nominal balances. It is therefore hard to see why this should be the case. However, when it comes to the market experiment, equation (19) perhaps makes more sense, because it tells us that real balances, rather than exogenous nominal balances, adjust slowly to any disturbance. As we have already noted, real balances are endogenous at the level of the market experiment even when nominal balances are not, and Alan Walters suggested as long ago as 1965 that an equation like (19) might be interpreted as a price level adjustment equation in an economy where nominal balances are exogenous.

In fact equation (19) is not quite accurately specified as a price level adjustment equation, as I shall now show. If we have, as our aggregate demand for money function,

$$m^* = f(X) + p \tag{1}$$

then with an exogenously given money supply, the equilibrium value for the price level p^* is given by

$$p^* = m_s - f(X) \tag{21}$$

Suppose that, for some reason, the structure of the economy was such that the price level moves slowly over time towards equilibrium according to

$$p - p_{-1} = b(p^* - p_{-1}) \tag{22}$$

Then, substitution of (22) into (21), and the addition of m_s to both sides of the equation, yields, with a little rearrangement,

$$m_s - p = bf(X) + (1-b)(m_s - p_{-1}) \tag{23}$$

This expression is very like both (19) and (20), and if it was in fact the true relationship describing the way in which the money supply and the arguments of the demand for money function interact over time, one would expect that the other two relationships would display considerable explanatory power as well. Indeed, econometrically speaking, if the 'true' relationship was

$$m_s - p = bf(X) + (1-b)(m_s - p_{-1}) + \varepsilon \tag{24}$$

then this would imply, for the 'real' adjustment model when m_s is substituted for m,

$$m_s - p = bf(X) + (1-b)(m_{s_{-1}} - p_{-1}) + u \qquad (25)$$

where

$$u = \varepsilon + (1-b)\Delta m_s \qquad (26)$$

and for the 'nominal' adjustment model

$$m_s - p = bf(X) + (1-b)(m_{s_{-1}} - p) + \eta \qquad (27)$$

where

$$\eta = \varepsilon + (1-b)\Delta(m_s - p) \qquad (28)$$

The importance of the presence of lagged dependent variables in empirical work on the aggregate demand for money function can then be explained in terms of price level stickiness, and this seems to me to be the best available explanation. The portfolio adjustment cost explanation is logically invalid, as we have seen, and the expectations lag explanation does not consistently stand up to empirical testing. However, if this conclusion is accepted, other problems immediately arise, problems which imply that attempts to bring empirical evidence to bear on this issue simply by attempting to fit equations (24), (25) and (27) to data would be unsatisfactory.

If the price level is sticky, then macroeconomics tells us that such variables as interest rates and real income will tend to change as the money market attempts to clear itself, but these are exactly the variables that one might expect to find in the vector (X). This in turn means that the use of single equation econometric techniques to estimate relationships such as (19), (20) or (23) in an economy where the nominal money supply is believed to be exogenous, is at the very least open to criticism for ignoring simultaneity problems. Jonson (1967a) has much to say about this matter in arguing that the demand for money function is best estimated as part of a complete macro system, rather than in isolation, and Cooley and Leroy (1981) have recently raised related issues in discussing the identifiability of the demand for money function.

Econometric questions are undoubtedly important, and it is not my intention to belittle them in any way when I say that, nevertheless, they are not central to the issues which I am attempting to tackle in this paper. The latter are economic in nature. I have shown in the last few pages that adjustment costs at the level of the individual demand for money experiment will produce no observable consequences at the level of the market experiment in an economy in which the nominal money supply is exogenous to the arguments of the demand for money function. It follows from this conclusion that there is something badly wrong with our habit of motivating the long-run–short-run demand for money distinction in terms of the existence of such adjustment costs. Nevertheless, we seem to need this distinction if we are to deal with a wide variety of real-world data on the determinants of money holding in a more or less satisfactory way.

I have argued that the best way out of this impasse is to interpret the typical short-run demand for money function as a slightly mis-specified price level adjustment equation. If this suggestion is accepted, it follows that the equation which we call a 'short-run demand for money function' is not a structural relationship at all, but a mixture of structural relationship (the long-run demand for money function whose parameters may or may not be being properly estimated if we use single equation techniques) and some reduced form of the whole economy. In particular, the adjustment parameter b must be interpreted as encapsulating the workings of those mechanisms whereby the price level moves slowly towards equilibrium after a monetary disturbance.

The fact that the adjustment speeds which are typically discovered in studies of the aggregate demand for money are very slow – it is not uncommon for money holdings to appear to move less than half way towards their long-run value within a year – has often puzzled monetary economists; but in the light of the above arguments, this fact would appear to tell us that sluggish price adjustment is an important fact of real-world economic life. This in turn means that the real balance effect is not just a factor which causes prices to change in some 'meta-time' when markets are clearing along Walrasian lines, but is an important empirical phenomenon underlying the generation of real-world data.

This conclusion might at first sight seem implausible, because it implies that the supply and demand for money can remain out of equilibrium for rather long periods of time, while the notion that the money market clears quickly is a commonplace of elementary macroeconomics. It is one thing to argue, however, that it is easy for the individual agent to rid himself of (or to acquire) cash, and quite another thing to argue that the economy as a whole can do so. In the latter case, as I have already pointed out, if the nominal money supply is exogenous, then any adjustment to the stock of real balances requires a price level change.

More to the point, even though, in the presence of price level stickiness, it is *possible* that the rate of interest can move to equate the supply and demand for money, it does not follow that this will in fact happen. In the standard classroom exposition of what Chick (1973, Ch. 3) has so aptly called the 'pseudodynamics of IS–LM', it is true that a change in the quantity of money is portrayed as causing a change in the rate of interest sufficiently large to keep the supply and demand for money in equilibrium, with changes in income and prices coming later. Nevertheless, there is no empirical basis for the proposition that in the real world the interest rate change in question is sufficient to establish money market equilibrium. All that is required to get the so-called 'transmission mechanism' to start working is that a change in the quantity of money move the interest rate away from a value which equates saving and investment at the current level of income, and not that the interest rate should attain a value which will equate the supply and demand for money. In any event, as White (1978, 1981) argues, interest rate changes are every bit as exogenous to money holders as price level changes. If the real world did indeed work as the above-mentioned 'pseudodynamics' suggest, we would never observe anything but a 'long-run' demand for money function. Hence this particular piece of analysis seems to be incompatible with the facts. However, this conclusion holds only for an economy in which the nominal money supply is determined independently of the demand for nominal money. As we shall now see, matters are more complex if the money supply is endogenous.

4. A DIGRESSION CONCERNING ENDOGENOUS NOMINAL MONEY

The arguments developed in the last few pages apply to an economy in which the nominal money supply is exogenous to the variables which determine the demand for it. It is sometimes suggested that, in many economies, not least in the United States and the United Kingdom, the actual conduct of policy in recent years has been such as to make it appropriate to think of the nominal money supply as responding passively to demand side factors in a manner which is reasonably captured by a nominal adjustment version of the short-run demand for money function similar to equation (3) or (20). That view is defended in the following way. Whatever changes there may or may not have been in the targets and indicators of monetary policy in the post-war period, its instruments have consistently been interest rates. The monetary authority has attempted to achieve whatever may have been its ends by standing ready to buy and sell securities at a price which, although not necessarily constant over time, is exogenously given at any moment. If over any reasonably short period – say a quarter – real income and prices may be regarded as predetermined, and if the monetary authority, and hence the banking system, stands ready to buy and sell securities at a given price, then there is no obstacle in the way of the economy as a whole adjusting its nominal money holdings towards a desired level at a pace of its own choosing. Given this view of the money supply process, equation (3) is sometimes defended as an appropriate and correctly specified tool for investigating the demand for money.

The argument just presented seems to me to be fallacious, or at least too simple. It rests upon a version of what Brunner and Meltzer (e.g. 1976) have termed the 'money market hypothesis' of the generation of the money supply, adapted to a situation in which the interest rate is the policy instrument; and they have argued that this hypothesis, though widely accepted, is crucially deficient. What Brunner and Meltzer term the 'credit market' hypothesis differs from it in correctly insisting that the non-bank public's supply of securities to the banking system is not simply the mirror image of its demand for the liabilities of that system. This is because the non-bank public also holds income-earning assets of a type distinct from those which it supplies to the banks when it borrows from them. It is convenient (but not logically necessary) to think of this third asset as reproducible physical capital. To see the significance of this characteristic of the credit market hypothesis for the issues under discussion here, it is helpful to begin with a situation of full portfolio equilibrium on the part of the banking system and the non-bank public, and then ask what happens, according to the two hypotheses, when the monetary authorities raise the price at which they are willing to buy securities.

The 'money market' hypothesis implies that the public will want to hold more cash balances, and will attempt to acquire them by offering securities to the banking system. It also tells us that any influence on output and prices will come later as a consequence of the effect of the lower interest rate on the level of aggregate demand for goods and services; and that, as output and price level changes materialise, more money will be forthcoming from the banking system as the public demands it. In short, the nominal stock of money will passively adjust to changes in the arguments of the demand function. If the money market hypothesis is true, nominal money will be just as much an endogenous variable in the market experiment as in the individual experiment, and equation (3) might indeed be an appropriate formulation.

The 'credit market' hypothesis leads one to tell a different story. Certainly a rise in security prices will lead the public to attempt to increase money holdings, but it will also, according to this hypothesis, lead agents to attempt to substitute physical capital for securities. In the market experiment, the whole of the non-bank public will try to make such a substitution, and the trick can only be accomplished by selling securities to the banks and taking the proceeds to buy physical capital – but of course the proceeds of such a sale of securities take the form of money, newly created, not because the non-bank public as a whole wants to hold it, but because each individual member of that public wants to use money to offer in exchange for capital. Once created, that money must be held, but its creation will coincide with, or even precede, the setting in motion of streams of expenditure which in turn will have consequences for the other arguments of the demand for money function, namely output and prices.

Eventually, the economy will end up with new long-run levels of income, prices, money holdings and so on, which may differ little from those which would be predicted by a model which ignored the distinction between securities and physical capital. However, we are here concerned with short-run adjustment, with the *process* whereby this equilibrium is approached, and that is critically different. It involves excess money operating upon expenditure flows which tend to force the arguments of the demand for money function to move towards new values; that is to say, it involves real balance effects. This is not to deny that money will also be created and extinguished in such a world in response to changes in the arguments of the demand for money function and in that sense be endogenous, but it is to argue that cause and effect will not run in the simple one-way manner from other variables to money which would be implied by the money market hypothesis, and which would justify equation (3) as a basis for empirical work.

The foregoing arguments fail to touch on yet another reason for not treating the nominal money supply as merely passively responding to the behaviour of the arguments of the demand for money function, even when the monetary authorities treat the interest rate as their principal policy instrument, namely that it is not only the extension of credit to the private sector, but also to the fiscal authorities, which leads to the creation of money. Even if, at a particular rate of interest, the values of income, prices, the rate of return on capital and so on are such as to render the supply of money and bank credit compatible with portfolio equilibrium on the part of the banking system and the non-bank public, that in no way guarantees either that the fiscal authorities' budget is in balance, or that, if it is not, the private sector will be willing to absorb just the right number of new government bonds to finance whatever deficit is being incurred. A fiscal deficit can therefore become an independent source of monetary expansion when the monetary authorities are treating the interest rate as their policy instrument. Once again, cause and effect will run from money creation to variations in the arguments of the demand for money function as well as *vice versa*, and real balance effects will be at work in influencing the outcome of any market experiment.

Closely related to the matters which I have just discussed are considerations having to do with the linkages between the balance of payments and the nominal money supply in an open economy operating a fixed exchange rate. It is true that the balance of payments can provide a channel whereby the nominal money supply will passively adjust to exogenous changes in the arguments in the demand for money function, and that, in a sample of data in which the only, or to put it more practically the major, source of money market disturbance lies in exogenous changes in those arguments, an equation such as (3) might be found to fit the data. In such a case, the parameter b would not be capturing the effects of adjustment costs which face individual agents attempting to re-arrange their portfolios; rather it would be summarising, in one statistic, the structure of the economy's balance of payments mechanism, and in particular the influence of real balance effects on that mechanism. This, however, is only part of the point. In a fixed exchange rate open economy, domestic monetary policy can obviously be an independent source of short-run disturbance to the domestic money market, while any shocks originating in the world economy which have balance of payments side effects can also lead to changes in the money supply which are exogenous to the arguments of the demand function. To say that, in such an economy, the nominal money supply is endogenous, is to say that variation in the nominal money supply is one equilibrating factor at work in the system. To this extent, the monetary behaviour of a fixed exchange rate open economy is different from that of the textbook closed-economy-with-an-exogenous-money-supply model, which we considered in the previous section of this essay; but the fact of long-run endogeneity of the nominal money supply stops far short of establishing the general validity of modelling the short-run demand for money along the conventional partial stock adjustment lines embodied in equation (3).

As to the flexible exchange rate case, here we are back to a system which is similar to the closed economy model, at least as far as the relationship between the factors governing the supply of money and the arguments of the demand for money function are concerned. Though the transmission mechanism for the effects of monetary changes to the price level may differ in this case from that to be found in a closed economy (see Essay 4, pp. 148–9, below), it is nevertheless that transmission mechanism, and not simply the portfolio adjustment costs facing individual agents, which must underlie any short run deviation of actual money holdings and those predicted by the long-run demand for money function.

5. CONCLUSIONS

The arguments presented in this essay have been rather taxonomic, but it is nevertheless possible to draw certain general conclusions from them, conclusions which in their turn yield important implications about our empirical knowledge of the properties of the demand for money function in particular and of the macroeconomy in general. The basic purpose of this essay has been to argue that the simple portfolio adjustment cost model, on which the distinction between the short-run and long-run demand for money hinges in the individual experiment, will not do to motivate that same distinction at the level of the economy as a whole. In an economy in which the nominal money supply is exogenous, it is possible for the individual agent to change his holdings of real balances by adjusting his holdings of nominal money; but the whole economy can only accomplish this by changing the general price level. If such an economy is kept 'off' its long-run demand for money function by adjustment costs, and the data seem to tell us that this is a pervasive phenomenon, then I have argued that the relevant costs are those of changing prices, not those involved in portfolio adjustment.

I have nevertheless argued that, for an economy in which it is believed that the nominal money supply is exogenous to the variables determining the demand for money, various widely used forms of the 'short-run' demand for money function *might* deal adequately with the data. They will do so if the complex transmission mechanism, which lies between money and prices, happens to be such that its dynamics can be captured in that single parameter b; if the simultaneity problems, which must arise here in principle, turn out to be unimportant in practice; and if the money supply and the price level are sufficiently highly autocorrelated that the mis-specifications involved in using the 'wrong' lagged dependent variable (cf. equations (19), (20) and (23)) are also unimportant.

In the case of economies in which the nominal money supply might reasonably be thought of as sometimes adjusting to the arguments of the demand for money function, rather than *vice versa*, either because of the way in which monetary policy is conducted, or because of the exchange rate regime, the above argument cannot be made as a general proposition. In such economies, whether nominal money does in fact predominantly adjust to demand side factors, or *vice versa*, depends upon the nature of the shocks to which the economy is being subjected. Even here though, where the shocks in question are such that the nominal money supply is a passively adjusting variable, any slowness on the part of the economy to get back 'on' its long-run demand for money function, after being driven 'off' it, will not simply be a matter of the adjustment costs facing individual money holders. Instead, it will involve the operations of the financial system, and perhaps of the balance of payments mechanism as well.

All this implies that the adjustment parameter b, which in empirical work on the aggregate demand for money plays such an important role in enabling us to get 'satisfactory' econometric results, must in general be thought of as summarising the dynamics of a good part of the economic system, and not merely the structural dynamics of the demand for money function itself. In the market experiment, a demand for money function which contains a lagged dependent variable can only be interpreted as being a structural relationship in and of itself if the presence of that variable is justified in terms of expectations lags; and as I have argued, such a justification is hard to sustain as the whole story – though it may be an important component of the story – in the face of available empirical evidence.

The question must arise as to what we are to make of all the empirical evidence which we have on the demand for money function in the light of the foregoing arguments. First, it must not be forgotten that there have been studies of the aggregate demand for money, using long time period samples, and/or data with a high degree of time aggregation, which have not invoked the 'short-run–long-run' distinction, and which have generated more or less satisfactory results (e.g. Friedman 1959, Meltzer 1963, Laidler 1966). Second, and this is important, the vast majority of studies of the 'short-run' demand for money *have* produced implicit estimates of the parameters of the 'long-run' relationship which are reasonably consistent with those derived from the studies just cited. On this basis, I am inclined to argue that, although the interpretation of short-run dynamics which has usually accompanied studies of the short-run demand for money is inappropriate and misleading, nevertheless, for most of the data which have been used, the practice of adding a lagged dependent variable to the function, crude and arbitrary though it is, has turned out to be an adequate way of allowing for the fact that the economy is not always in long-run equilibrium when we observe it.

The above argument presents a conjecture, not a well established truth, and it should not lead anyone to conclude that all is well with our empirical knowledge of the demand for money function. In order to find out whether the argument is true, we would have to construct explicit macroeconomic models, which permit the economy in general and the money market in particular, to deviate from long-run equilibrium; and then explicitly investigate the relationship between the structure of those models and the functional forms which typically have been fitted in studies of the short-run demand for money. The parameter b, it has been argued above, is a 'black box' parameter which summarises what we may loosely refer to as the dynamics of the real balance effect, and we do not currently know just what is buried in it.

A number of writers, notably Jonson (1967a) and Mervyn Lewis (1978) have noted that those samples of data that seem to give us the most trouble, as far as finding a stable demand for money function is concerned, are drawn from times and places where the monetary system has been subjected to particularly large shocks, for example the United Kingdom or the United States in the 1970s. They have speculated that the difficulties involved here have stemmed from inadequacy in our modelling of the dynamics of the monetary system. That too is a conjecture, but it is one which follows naturally from the arguments advanced in this paper, and it too could be investigated by carrying out the type of experiment suggested above. The work of Jonson and his associates, which builds upon that of Bergstrom and Wymer (1974), has involved the construction of complete econometric models in which expenditure flows of various sorts are explicitly modelled as responding to real balance effects (see e.g. Jonson 1976b, Jonson, Moses and Wymer 1976, Jonson and Trevor 1980) and could provide a framework in terms of which such an investigation could be carried out.

Be that as it may, the arguments which I have advanced imply a severe criticism of much econometric modelling of the conventional post-Keynesian sort. For example, in the FMP model of the United States economy as described by Modigliani and Ando (1976), a demand for money function complete with lagged dependent variable is estimated independently of the rest of the system, and is treated as a structural relationship to be included in the model, which is then put through all manner of simulation exercises. If the coefficient of the lagged dependent variable of that demand for money function is in fact capturing, in some approximate and unspecified fashion, aspects of the dynamic behaviour of the economy as a whole, then to treat the relevant function as if it were a structural relationship, and to use it in complete model simulation exercises, is inappropriate. When this is done, the economy's structure is being utilised twice, once in 'black box' form in the coefficient of the lagged dependent variable in the demand for money function, and once explicitly in terms of the rest of the model. This criticism, which of course applies to far more pieces of work than the FMP model, is in fact a variation on the argument advanced above when we commented on the incompatibility of Tucker's (1966) model with the adjustment lag hypothesis so often used to motivate its structure. There is no need, therefore, to repeat it here in any detail; enough has already been said to make the seriousness of its implications for much of our econometric work quite obvious.

The basic conclusion to be drawn from the arguments of this essay is very simple. In treating money as if it were just another durable good in our empirical work on the aggregate demand for money, we have overlooked the critical distinction between the individual and market experiments which Patinkin made so clearly in his theoretical work on the real balance effect. In doing so, we have used reasoning which should only be applied to the individual experiment when dealing with the market experiment. As a result, much of our empirical work on the demand for money, particularly on the 'short-run' relationship, has no proper theoretical basis in terms of which it can be interpreted, and our knowledge of that relationship is therefore much less robust than we might have thought. We do, already, have the basic tools with which we can set about remedying this state of affairs in the shape of those pioneering macro models which explicitly try to get to grips with the dynamics of real balance effects, but the work of developing those models and applying them to the issues raised here has only just begun.

3

On Say's Law, Money,
and the Business Cycle

---

1. MONEY AND THE ECONOMIC PROBLEM

As we all know, economics is about scarcity, about the fact that human wants exceed the means available to satisfy them. Economics is, therefore, concerned with choices, not only with how they are made by the individual agent, but also, and when we come to monetary economics, in particular, with how they are co-ordinated at the social level so that a 'solution' to the Economic Problem is generated. By the word solution, we mean, not a state of affairs in which scarcity ceases to exist, but rather a situation in which goods and services are produced, distributed and consumed in such a way that the relevant activities of each individual are compatible with those of every other, a situation in which the suppliers of various goods and services offer neither more nor less of any item than demanders will voluntarily take. Neo-classical economics is particularly concerned with the role played by prices and market mechanisms in coping with scarcity, and the General Equilibrium model which lies at the core of that body of doctrine can form the basis of strong claims about the effectiveness of such mechanisms. This model purports to show that, in a competitive market economy, knowledge only of his own tastes (technology too, if he is running a firm) and the prices of goods and services, is sufficient to enable, indeed to ensure, that the typical agent will act in such a way as to contribute to a coherent overall solution to the Economic Problem.

If it is accepted that the information requirements specified by the General Equilibrium model are sufficiently modest that they can in fact be met, then it is but a short step to defending market mechanisms as a practical means of solving the Economic Problem in the real world, as well as in the imaginary world of the economic theorist. It is uncontroversial that, in the absence of a monetary system, market mechanisms would founder upon problems of acquiring and processing information. To begin with, if there were no commonly used unit of account, individual agents would find the communication and processing of information about relative prices, if not entirely impossible, then at least extraordinarily cumbersome, for any but a very small number of items. If some arbitrarily chosen good was used as a *numeraire*, so that individuals could comprehend relative prices well enough to make coherent choices, the problem of carrying out the trades implicit in those choices would nevertheless be insurmountable in the absence of a generally acceptable means of exchange. Each individual would need to find out who had what to exchange for his own offerings before any trade could take place, and market mechanisms do not spontaneously generate and transmit such information to agents. (Brunner and Meltzer 1972, Ostroy and Starr 1974, Robert Jones 1976 and Jurg Niehans 1978, Chs 6 and 7), have all analysed aspects of these problems.)

The existence of money in its role as a generally utilised means of exchange enables acts of sale and purchase to be carried out at separate times and places. Hence, for all practical purposes it is the existence of money which makes multilateral trade possible, not least by making it feasible for some agents to act as specialist traders in particular commodities, or groups thereof. Moreover it is surely natural that the prices of those items which get traded should be quoted in terms of whatever it is they are to be exchanged against. Hence money, the means of exchange, also becomes the unit of account, the *numeraire* whose existence makes the processing of relative price information by individual agents feasible.

To say all this amounts to saying that a monetary system is a social institution every bit as necessary to the operation of markets as is, for example, a system of property law and the mechanisms for enforcing it. However, we do not usually pay any explicit attention to the legal system when we analyse the way in which markets allocate resources and distribute income, and in a wide variety of cases this does not seem to do too much harm to the empirical content of our analysis. Thus to say that General Equilibrium analysis frequently pays no attention to the role of money in making the operations of markets feasible, though it may be true, is not necessarily to advance a damning criticism of that body of theory and the insights it yields. It may be that the existence of money enables the informational problems, to which we have alluded above, to be solved without in any other important way rendering the outcome of market processes different from what they would have been, had those informational problems not existed in the first place.

A world with money cannot be literally identical to a world without it. When neo-classical theory treats a money economy as essentially the same in its structure as a barter economy (or at least a barter economy in which the information costs we have just alluded to are, for some unspecified reason, negligible), it asserts that the presence of money in the economy makes no more difference to the way in which it allocates resources and distributes income than does the presence of any other extra good in the array among which agents choose. From the point of view of the analysis of the choice making behaviour of the typical agent acting in isolation, what Patinkin (1956) called the individual experiment, it is difficult to argue with the claim that to bring money into the picture makes no essential difference; or at least I would not wish to do so. Once the relevant object of choice is recognised to be 'real balances', money measured in constant purchasing power units, and once the durability of real balances is taken account of, the individual agent's demand for money can be analysed along with his demand for everything else, and the amount that he chooses to hold emerges from the interaction of his utility function with a budget constraint, just like the quantity of anything else.

The characteristics of money which might set it apart from other objects of individual choice only become important in market experiments. To begin with, the equilibrium quantity of real balances in the economy as a whole is always demand determined (although, of course, the demand for real balances may itself depend upon the composition of the government debt and therefore indirectly upon the money supply – see Patinkin 1965, Ch. 12). In the typical case of token money – be it pure fiat or credit based is irrelevant – whose nominal quantity is exogenously fixed, this means that the quantity of real balances is changed by altering the price of goods in terms of nominal money. A change in the relative price of nominal money is not accomplished in the same way as a change in the relative price of anything else. A change in the relative price of a particular good can be brought about by a change of its nominal price in terms of the unit of account. Where *nominal* money itself is the unit of account, an alteration of its *relative price*, and hence a change in the *quantity* of *real* balances, will be accomplished by engineering equi-proportional changes in the accounting prices of everything else.

I have deliberately put the arguments of the last paragraph in tentative terms. Though I shall argue in this essay that these two characteristics of money make a money using economy crucially different from a frictionless barter economy, where there exists an object of choice that happens to be called 'money', there are those who would deny this proposition. In particular, a group of economists, prominent among whom are Robert E. Lucas Jr, Robert J. Barro, Thomas Sargent and Neil Wallace, to whom I shall refer in this essay as 'neo-Austrians' because of the similarity of aspects of their views to those propounded in the 1920s and 1930s by Ludwig von Mises and Friedrich von Hayek, argues that the behaviour of real-world economies may be interpreted 'as if' they were continually in a state of general competitive equilibrium in all markets. As I have already hinted, this latter proposition seems to me to be inconsistent with certain apparently well established facts. In order to make this case, I shall first of all give an account of the arguments which seem to support the neo-Austrians' position, and then show why the facts in question appear to refute those arguments.

2. SAY'S LAW AND UNEMPLOYMENT

The General Equilibrium model is highly abstract, a fiction, but nevertheless a fiction which might capture enough of reality to be relevant to the world we inhabit. It pictures an economy made up of self-interested individuals, each endowed with a particular bundle of goods, which in the general case includes the ability to perform labour services, as well as assets including money. It then addresses questions about whether and how the decisions of those individuals to produce, consume and trade can be so co-ordinated as to be in complete harmony with one another. The answer given to the first question is that decisions can be co-ordinated because there usually exists at least one set of prices at which all markets will clear, at which there will be zero excess demand for everything, at which, in other words, the plans of all agents are mutually compatible. If that set of prices rules, then the activities of self-interested individuals will, as they respond to those prices, result in a solution to the Economic Problem.

The key point here is that those individuals must respond, not just to any old array of prices, but to their 'market clearing' values. If trade takes place when prices are not at market clearing levels, then there will emerge excess supplies and demands for particular goods and services; the plans of individuals will not mesh with one another; there will be actual shortages of some goods, while others will go begging for buyers. In the case of labour services, a state of excess supply will involve those services being wasted, and in the perfectly reasonable sense that a scarce resource is not being devoted to the satisfaction of some human want or other, an excess supply of labour is a clear-cut sign that the market mechanism has failed to solve the Economic Problem.

The Classical Economists, who were not equipped with a formal analytic apparatus that in any way resembled our contemporary General Equilibrium model, were nevertheless well aware of these issues. The majority of them, although of course there were dissenters (see Corry 1959), drew a sharp distinction between the existence of temporary gluts and shortages of *particular* types of labour and commodities, which they regarded as quite possible, and that of a *general* over (or under) supply of goods and services, which they found inconceivable even as a temporary phenomenon. For them, since every offer to sell a quantity of a particular good or service was also an offer to buy something else in exchange for it, 'supply created its own demand', and the problem that markets sometimes failed to solve was that of bringing willing buyers and sellers together, not that of ensuring that there was sufficient demand in the aggregate to ensure that there existed a willing buyer for everything that was supplied.

The proposition just discussed is usually known as 'Say's Law'. The peculiar characteristics of money as an object of choice which I noted above, namely that the quantity of real balances can be adjusted by a change in the price of nominal money, and that this in turn requires a change in the money price of every other item being traded, mean that the truth of Say's Law in the context of a money using economy cannot be defended on purely logical grounds. What if the structure of prices is such that, in aggregate, agents want to hold more real balances than currently exist? In that case, as John Stuart Mill stated clearly as long ago as 1844, there will indeed be a general over-supply of commodities and services, including labour services, and scarce resources will be wasted for so long as this excess supply persists. To claim that such a state of affairs cannot, as a *matter of logic*, occur is to deny that one can conceive of the existence of an excess demand for money, and hence to deny that money is an object of choice for the individual agent. It is thus, as Lange (1942) and Patinkin (1956) argued, to deny the possibility of having a monetary theory at all within the neo-classical framework.

To entertain the logical possibility of some effect is not the same thing as asserting that it will be of importance in practice. On the contrary, it is the essence of a scientific proposition that it denies the empirical relevance of some event or events which are logically possible. The more which is ruled out the better, for then the stronger the predictive power of such a proposition and the more easily it is tested. Say's Law may be formulated to say, not that general excess supply in the economy is *logically* impossible, but that *as a matter of fact* it never occurs, or at least never persists long enough to matter. This version of Say's Law forms the foundation of what I have called neo-Austrian economics.

If there never exists a general excess supply or demand for real balances, that must be because, among other things, the price of nominal money is always at an appropriate level. Except in the uninteresting, empirically irrelevant (and very un-Austrian) case of an equilibrium price structure which never has changed nor ever will need to change, this in turn means that the money prices of individual goods and services are free to vary 'sufficiently rapidly' to maintain this state of affairs. In formal presentations of General Equilibrium theory, prices are pictured as being set by an entity, the auctioneer, who is not part of the economy under analysis and consumes none of its resources. Moreover the process of adjusting prices takes place in a 'meta time' in which the activities of production, consumption and trading are suspended until a structure of market clearing prices is achieved by way of a tâtonnement process.

The key characteristics of the tâtonnement process are that, on being faced with a set of prices, every agent submits his quantity plans to the auctioneer, who in turn fixes a new array of prices, the process continuing until a set of prices at which all quantity plans are compatible is achieved. 'Unrealistic' though the analysis is, it is not without interest, because it turns out that the simple instruction to the auctioneer to raise the prices of goods in excess demand and lower those of goods in excess supply will ensure that he does indeed eventually arrive at a set of market clearing prices in all but a few exceptional cases which it is customary to treat as unimportant. If the auctioneer treats nominal money as the *numeraire*, then the emergence of an excess demand for real balances during the tâtonnement leads him to lower the money prices of all goods and services until that excess demand has been eliminated. This lowering of goods prices raises the quantity of real balances, and hence serves to eliminate the excess demand for money. The auctioneer, in effect, presides over the operation of a 'real balance effect', which does not manifest itself as part of the trading process. In the General Equilibrium model, production, consumption and trading only take place subject to a set of prices at which Say's Law is satisfied.

No one takes the foregoing story literally. However, it can be argued that, in the real world, those who cannot sell all they want to sell do in fact tend to lower price, and that those who want to reduce their sales do in fact raise the price they ask. It has been shown by Howitt (1974) that an economy in which prices are set by specialised traders who respond *only* to the excess supply and demand for their own particular commodity, will converge upon an equilibrium similar to that generated by an auctioneer. How close to a 'complete' description of reality – whatever that may be – an economic model must come before one ceases to feel uncomfortable about its 'lack of realism' is a matter of taste, but this result surely enables the proponents of General Equilibrium theory to defend it against many attacks along these lines. To postulate the auctioneer may be a convenient way to show how a market solution to the Economic Problem can be generated, but he is not necessary to the generation of that solution. Thus his manifest absence from the real world is not, in the light of Howitt's analysis, conclusive evidence of the practical irrelevance of the General Equilibrium model.

Needless to say, Howitt's analysis does not guarantee the relevance of the General Equilibrium model either. One must refer to empirical evidence and not just to *a priori* argument to deal with such a question. Over the last couple of hundred years, economies which rely heavily on market mechanisms have operated at a sufficiently high employment level for a sufficiently high proportion of the time to enable neo-classical economists to argue that real-world markets, even the labour market, do tend to clear in a fashion akin to that described by the General Equilibrium model. However, unemployment, sometimes on a massive scale, has turned up regularly in all market economies as a temporary phenomenon, where temporary is an adjective which covers years and even decades, rather than weeks and months. This fact is frequently cited as *prima facie* evidence that, although the General Equilibrium model may be of some long-run relevance, it is far from complete as an account of how market mechanisms work to solve the economic problem in the real world.

The argument here is usually put as follows: if markets, including the labour market, always clear, then there cannot be such a thing as involuntary unemployment; therefore the very existence of such a phenomenon refutes the hypothesis that markets do indeed always clear. Not the least of the contributions made by the neo-Austrian economists to the development of economics has been to point out to us that the adjective 'involuntary' refers to the outcome of an agent's activities relative to his intentions, and to remind us that the fact that a man is unemployed tells us nothing whatsoever about his intentions. Moreover, they have gone on to show that they can explain observed unemployment in terms of a model in which it is the intended outcome of freely made choices. In doing this, they have not merely suggested that the conventional interpretation of unemployment might be faulty, but have quite explicitly asserted that it is. They have, as I have said earlier, propounded the *empirical* version of Say's Law as a fundamental basis for economic theory and have argued that it is compatible with available evidence.

3. NEO-AUSTRIAN BUSINESS CYCLE THEORY

It should go without saying that the fact of unemployment cannot be reconciled with the *conventional* version of the General Equilibrium model. Some modifications have to be made to it, and those which the neo-Austrians make have to do with the assumptions about the nature of the information available to agents. The usual version of the model is based on two propositions: that market clearing prices always rule; and, crucially, that *all* agents have knowledge of the values of *all* prices *before* they execute *any* decisions about quantities. In constructing an explanation of unemployment, the neo-Austrians maintain the first assumption, and hence Say's Law, but drop the second. The details of the analysis differ from exposition to exposition, as one would expect with a body of doctrine still under development, but the following account of what is involved is not, I hope, misleading in any way. It is based largely on my reading of Lucas (1972, 1975, 1977, 1980) and Sargent (1976).

To begin with, the world which the neo-Austrians analyse is not stationary any more than that of their Austrian predecessors was. Tastes are not given for ever, nor is technology; people leave the labour force, newcomers enter it; and so on. One result is that the market-clearing structure of relative prices is in a constant state of flux, so that agents are continually having to renew their stock of information about such prices. Crucial to neo-Austrian arguments is the proposition that agents must devote resources to generating such information. In particular, agents' stock of information about the structure of wages is thought of as depreciating if resources are not devoted to maintaining it; and for some agents at least, the generation of information about wages is posited to be a specialised activity so that to engage in it precludes working. Agents engaged full-time in generating for themselves information about wages are said to be engaged in 'job search' (misleadingly, since they are really seeking information about wages) and they are, beyond doubt, voluntarily unemployed. The relevance of this line of reasoning to the rationalisation of what is often called 'frictional' unemployment should be clear enough, and the argument proceeds to advance the hypothesis that, given the structure of any particular economy, given the way in which tastes, technology, and so forth are changing over time, there will exist a certain level of 'wage search' unemployment which is 'natural', which is, to borrow Milton Friedman's (1968) phrase, 'ground out by the Walrasian system of general equilibrium equations'.

Not only is the neo-Austrians' world in a state of perpetual long-term change, but it is also subject to a series of short-term random shocks as well, some of which affect the structure of market clearing relative prices, and some of which affect the market clearing value of the general price level. It is at this point that the crucial role of money as the *numeraire* of the system comes into the analysis, along with another specific and quite critical assumption about the nature of the information available to agents, namely that they learn about changes in the money prices of what it is that they sell (in the case of households, that means their labour) before they learn about the money prices of what it is that they buy (in the case of households again, of goods and services). The decision as to how much labour to supply in a particular occupation, however, and that includes the decision whether or not to search for a better alternative, or whether or not to carry on searching if one is already engaged in that activity, depends not upon the money wage, but upon the real wage. The availability of precise information about money wages where one is currently employed, or where one has recently 'searched', in the absence of equally precise information about money prices and alternative money wages, makes it possible for suppliers of labour to make errors about their current real wage and about the one that they might command elsewhere, and therefore to make errors in their employment decisions.

According to the neo-Austrians, it is changes in the nominal quantity of money which typically initiate output and employment fluctuations, and in order to appreciate fully the role of informational problems in their analysis, it is helpful to consider the effects, on an economy such as they postulate, of a fall in the nominal supply of money which requires an equi-proportional fall in all money wages and prices to absorb it without any real effects. In the wake of such a change, households will find themselves faced with lower money wage offers. Should they to any extent misread these offers as signifying a cut in real wages, they will reduce the quantity of labour which they offer at any *actual* value of the real wage. If we presume that firms know both output prices and the money wage rate, and to do so keeps the analysis manageable, they will respond to this shift in the supply curve of labour by cutting back output and employment. If all markets are to clear, output prices will fall by more than money wages fall, so that real wages will rise. At the same time employment will decrease and search unemployment will increase.

In due course, households will discover that they have made an error. They will find out that real wages have risen rather than, as they initially thought, fallen, and they will regret the labour supply and wage-search decisions they have taken upon the basis of this mistaken information. However, such *ex post* regret does not in any way alter the fact that the decisions in question were *ex ante* entirely voluntary. At the time when prices were formed and markets cleared in the foregoing experiment, no one who wanted to engage in wage search was prevented from doing so; no one who chose to work, at what he then (albeit mistakenly) perceived to be the real wage was unable to do so; no firm employed anything but just that amount of labour which enabled it to equate that factor's marginal product to the real wage; and no firm found any difficulty in selling just that level of output which it planned to sell at the going price. Thus, the unemployment rate increased in response to a cut in the quantity of money at the same time as money wages and prices and their rates of change as well (relative to expectations) fell, thus generating a typical observation on a 'short-run Phillips curve'. All this happened without Say's Law being violated.

Now, what we have described so far is the way in which, in the neo-Austrian version of the General Equilibrium model, a monetary contraction, if its effects on money prices are misread as relative price changes, can cause an increase in unemployment; but we have said nothing about a key characteristic of unemployment and output fluctuations in the real world, namely the serial correlation which these variables display. As a matter of simple fact, when output and employment fall, that fall persists for a while, and when they rise, that rise is also persistent. It is not random fluctuations in output and employment which need to be explained, but the business cycle. Broadly speaking, there are two approaches which can be taken to coming to grips with the persistence of output and employment fluctuations, while maintaining the empirical truth of Say's Law; but, although they are by no means mutually exclusive, the neo-Austrians have, for good reasons given the nature of their model, rejected the first of them.

The essential nature of this first approach is simply stated: unemployment departs from its 'natural' level because agents, who are forced to act upon incomplete knowledge about the money prices of goods, make errors in the expectations which they form about those prices. From this starting point, it is easy to go on to argue that if unemployment persists over time, that might be because the expectations upon which people act are systematically in error over time as well. However, to go in this direction does serious violence to the spirit of the neo-Austrian approach, which is to attempt to explain the facts of the business cycle in terms of a model firmly grounded in microeconomic principles. There is no assumption more important to microeconomics than that agents are self-interested maximisers.

No matter how an agent forms his price expectations, if those expectations are in error, and if as a result of that error the agent is led to take decisions which he later regrets, it is quite incompatible with the maximising assumption to postulate that he will continue to use the same method of forming expectations. By doing so he would continue systematically to make damaging errors, and that would be irrational. After all, information to the effect that his errors are systematic is presented to the agent without his having to devote any resources to its collection. It arises as a by-product of his market activity. To process such information so as to modify whatever rule was being used to generate expectations in the first place, though not quite costless, is, according to the neo-Austrian, a relatively trivial exercise. Thus, the neo-Austrian argues that, if making errors causes disutility, then a rational agent, even if he starts out making systematic mistakes, will learn about this and will stop doing so. Persistent expectational error cannot then, according to the neo-Austrian, be a permanent feature of a world populated by self-interested maximisers, and ought not therefore to be used as an hypothesis to explain the persistence of unemployment.

The 'rational expectations hypothesis' as originated by John Muth (1961) is thus an integral part of neo-Austrian theory. At first sight, that hypothesis, which here should be understood as the postulate that agents do not make systematic (i.e. serially correlated) expectational errors, seems to be difficult to reconcile with the existence of even random deviations of the economy as a whole from full employment. If each agent makes only random errors, why do they not cancel out as we aggregate to the level of the economy as a whole? Lucas (1972) provided the answer here. He argued that, because fluctuations in the quantity of money simultaneously impinge upon each agent and therefore upon the economy as a whole, to the extent that such fluctuations induce each agent to make an error in forming expectations about prices, and hence in making his quantity decisions, the error in question will be common to the actions of each agent. Thus, it will have similar consequences for the behaviour of each agent, and these consequences will still be observable when we aggregate to the level of the economy as a whole. In short, random events which simultaneously shock the whole economy have effects which are systematic across agents.

The foregoing argument does not explain why the effects of such random shocks persist over time to create the business cycle, but there is a whole array of arguments which can be pursued here, none of which is incompatible with the others, and which, taken together provide what most would regard as more than ample material for the construction of a theory of the business cycle. First of all, a genuinely random series will contain runs of values for whatever variable it is generating, and a series which is itself the sum of random series will display cyclical behaviour. The proposition that the business cycle is a reflection of purely random events is a time honoured one in economics going back at least to Eugen Slutsky (1937) (whose paper first appeared in Russian in 1927). The fact that we shy away from it has got more to do with our distaste for its implication that such an important fact of economic life is inherently unpredictable than it has with any gross logical or empirical weakness in the proposition in question.

Through neo-Austrians, again like their namesakes, are relatively pessimistic about the predictability of economic events, they nevertheless do not embrace the purely random events theory of the cycle. In their work on these matters, they concentrate on the other sets of arguments. The first is essentially a refinement of their basic theory of how the economy can be moved away from its 'natural' unemployment rate equilibrium while markets continue to clear. It is argued that the manner in which information about prices reaches agents is itself serially correlated (see Lucas 1975). Instead of learning about money wages instantaneously, and all other money prices with a single delay, agents are thought of as learning about different groups of prices with delays of different lengths. Whether one regards this type of argument as plausible or not is to some extent a matter of taste. It is a rather special one, to be sure, but households do shop for food, say, more often than for durable goods, so it is not totally without foundation in reality. Its effect is of course to introduce a systematic-over-time element into agent's expectational errors, but an element which is detectable only *ex-post*, and cannot be used to improve any future forecasts. The reader might note, though, that Edi Karni (1980) has shown that the existence of an economy-wide asset market would short-circuit the delays in the acquisition of information postulated here by ensuring that all relevant information was immediately incorporated in asset prices.

Whatever one might think of it, the above argument attempts to explain the business cycle in terms of systematic-over-time deviations of the unemployment rate from its natural level. Another element in neo-Austrian business cycle theory involves the proposition that the natural unemployment rate itself will vary. When the labour force misjudges the real wage, the supply curve of labour to firms, as perceived by them, shifts, and the pattern of households' demand for output also changes. This, in turn, means that the structure of output differs from what it would be in the absence of any error. To the extent that output decisions are costly to change once made, such effects will, in and of themselves, persist over time. Furthermore, to the extent that mistakes are made about the production of durable goods, and notably about producers' durable goods, the quantity of factors with which labour must co-operate in production in the future will be affected, and this in turn will influence the marginal physical productivity of labour in terms of consumption and producer goods and therefore the structure of real wages. With perfect knowledge of prices, and frictionless markets, all this will only change relative prices. However, when these very Austrian considerations are combined with the assumption that knowledge about prices must be produced by devoting resources to its production, it becomes possible that the division of household time among employment, job search and leisure, and therefore the natural unemployment rate, will also be affected. Because durable goods take time to wear out, such effects on the natural unemployment rate, once induced by an initial shock to the economy, will persist for a while.

Now the last few pages have not given a full account of neo-Austrian business cycle theory. However, their arguments do, I trust, say sufficient to indicate that there is no great logical difficulty in extending General Equilibrium analysis to cope with economy-wide fluctuations in real income and employment which persist over time, while continuing to maintain the basic assumption of that approach, namely that at every moment, all activities are the outcome of the voluntary choices of maximising agents freely exercised in clearing competitive markets. Once the basic proposition that expectational errors can lead to such decisions generating movements of output and employment away from the 'natural' levels which they would take in the absence of such errors is accepted, everything else can be made to follow without too much difficulty. The key factor here is expectational error, and I have already touched upon the rational expectations notion in the above discussion. I shall now take up this hypothesis in a little more detail.

4. RATIONAL EXPECTATIONS

As I have argued, the typical shock with which the neo-Austrian market experiment begins is a change in the nominal money supply. If such a shock immediately generated an equi-proportional fall in all money wages and prices, all markets would remain cleared at their 'natural' equilibria. It is a failure on the part of agents to see that such price changes must take place, and to act accordingly, which causes a cut in the quantity of money to have real effects. For the neo-Austrian, then, the way in which agents form their expectations about the behaviour of those prices of which they do not have immediate knowledge is crucial to an explanation of the short-run non-neutrality of money.

Consider, for the sake of argument, an economy in which each agent understands the operation of the General Equilibrium system of which he forms a part; suppose that each agent knows that a market clearing set of prices will always rule; suppose also that he knows that there has been a cut in the nominal money supply, and by what amount. In such an economy, populated by such agents, no one would misread the money wage signals that come in the wake of the money supply cut. Labour markets would, in effect, clear 'as if' all those involved in wage bargaining took account of the interaction of wages and prices in the aggregate economy, while settling matters in their own segment of the labour market. This example might seem to be far fetched, and to be based on a much more elaborate hypothesis about the nature of the typical agent's knowledge and expectations than that which I discussed a few pages ago. However, the two hypotheses about expectations are in fact intimately interlinked as we shall now see, so that the foregoing 'far fetched' story ought not to be dismissed too quickly.

The notion of 'rational expectations' was said earlier to amount to the proposition that agents learn how to eliminate systematic errors when forming the expectations upon which they base their activities. Now, I am talking about an economy in which each agent is equipped with knowledge of a model of the system which is sufficiently complete to enable him correctly to forecast the effects of a change in the supply of money on the money price of whatever it is he sells, so that he does not make false inferences about the behaviour of relative prices from that of those money prices. In this particular example, each agent reacts to a change in the supply of money so as to ensure that its effects are on money wages and prices alone, and not on real variables. The key question is whether agents who do no more than avoid systematic errors in forming expectations about the general price level will ever, in fact, act 'as if' they had foreseen the consequences of a change in the nominal money supply. The answer is clear: they will do so when the change in the nominal money supply is itself part of a systematic pattern of behaviour on the part of that variable, a pattern whose consequences have already been absorbed consciously or otherwise into whatever formula agents in fact use to form price expectations.

The assumption that agents do not make systematic errors – the formula they use to form their expectations is, subject to this assumption, quite irrelevant – is sufficient to permit the economist analysing their behaviour to postulate that they act 'as if' they understood the operation of the economy of which they form a part. So long as money supply fluctuations have a systematic component as well as a random component, it is only the latter which will have real effects. The systematic component of money supply fluctuations, 'anticipated money' to use Barro's (1978) phrase, will affect only prices. This might be because agents understand that the quantity of money determines the price level at full employment and therefore find it worthwhile to use the systematic behaviour of the money supply as a basis for expectations, but that does not have to be the case. They might just as well, for example, use information contained in the past history of the price level, which will itself reflect the consequences of systematic money supply behaviour and might well be cheaper to monitor, as Feige and Pearce (1976) argue.

This does not mean that the two versions of 'rational expectations' always yield the same implications. A crucial difference would arise if the nature of the systematic component of the money supply's behaviour were to change and if that change was announced. If agents really did understand the economy's operations, they would adapt at once to an announcement of such a change (here I beg the question of the credibility of the announcement), and the change in question would have no real effects. However, if agents did not understand the economy's operations, they would have to learn about the changed regime by making systematic errors, recognising them as such, and eliminating them by some unspecified trial and error method. While they were learning, the new policy regime would, albeit temporarily, have real effects.

The 'agent will eliminate systematic errors' version of rational expectations, which is after all the *a priori* plausible form of the hypothesis, does not say anything concerning how quickly agents will learn about a change in the policy regime and then act upon that new knowledge. It should not therefore (as I argue in more detail in Essay 5) be advanced as the basis for the argument that a quick attack on inflation by monetary policy, if only it is pre-announced, will be effective and have no real side effects. The latter prediction follows from the more narrowly formulated 'agents understand the working of the economy' version of the hypothesis and that version is much less plausible. It is also inconsistent with the evidence cited by Grossman (1981), which shows that contemporaneously observed changes in the money supply do in fact have systematic effects on the subsequent behaviour of real income and employment. Moreover, the prediction in question also requires that the announcement of a change in policy regime be believed by agents, and the rationality hypothesis tells us nothing either for or against the likelihood that this will be the case.

These matters are something of a side issue here. The key point as far as this essay is concerned is that fluctuations in the supply of money, whose effects on prices are not anticipated, will have real and persistent consequences for an economy made up of competitive markets which always clear. The neo-Austrians are quite right about that; and in claiming that this result is relevant to the real world, they offer an account of the business cycle very different from that which is familiar to those brought up on the macroeconomics of the 1950s and 1960s. Neo-Austrian theory *is* coherent and *does* deserve to be taken seriously; but that does not mean that it is correct, as I shall now begin to argue.

5. WAGE AND PRICE STICKINESS

The neo-Austrian approach to the analysis of the business cycle is, as I remarked at the end of the preceding section of this essay, very different from that implicit in orthodox macroeconomics; and the difference in question lies, not in the notion of rational expectations, important and fruitful though that notion is, but in the maintained hypothesis that prices always move so as to keep supply and demand equal to one another in all markets. It is by now widely agreed that much of the novelty of Keynes's economics, as set out in the *General Theory*, lay in postulating first, that prices, and particularly money wages, do not move sufficiently rapidly to keep markets cleared, and that, in the presence of price stickiness, quantities adjust instead to equilibrate markets. Thus, output fluctuations take place, not *because* of wage and price fluctuations, but *instead* of them.

Patinkin (1956), Clower (1965), Leijonhufvud (1969), Barro and Grossman (1975), and Malinvaud (1978) have all contributed to showing that, *given* the assumption of price stickiness, such phenomena as underemployment 'equilibrium', and the multiplier process, are quite compatible with the behaviour of maximising agents. They have thus provided a link between the microeconomics of General Equilibrium and orthodox macroeconomics. It is to miss the point of their work to criticise it as does Kantor (1980) for having failed to produce *new* empirical predictions, because what that work does is show that the abundant supply of predictions, tests, and what have you, which already exists in the published literature of macroeconomics, is compatible with the microeconomic postulates of utility and profit maximisation on the part of individual agents. However, the hypothesis of price stickiness is required to establish this compatibility, and the work in question is undoubtedly vulnerable to the criticism that it has not produced a foundation in the theory of maximising behaviour for this hypothesis.

Some commentators on Keynesian economics, for example Leijonhufvud (1969, 1981) stress interest rate stickiness rather than wage and price stickiness as a source of output fluctuations, but the difference between what they argue and the points which I am making here is one of emphasis rather than of kind. In this essay I am considering the ways in which the economy does and does not respond to a cut in the nominal money supply. Leijonhufvud is concerned with the ability of the interest rate mechanism to maintain the equality of savings and investment at full employment in the face of a fluctuating marginal efficiency of capital. An interest elastic demand for money, which does of course have a firm foundation in microeconomics, means that interest rate movements alone cannot accomplish this if the nominal money supply is held constant. The price level also has to vary in order to provide the quantity of real balances which the economy will want to hold at the new full employment equilibrium value of the rate of interest implied by the changed marginal efficiency of capital. If wages and prices were perfectly flexible, this would be accomplished instantaneously, and fluctuations in the marginal efficiency of capital would lead only to interest rate changes and not to fluctuations in real income and employment. Here too, then, the theoretically arbitrary assumption of price stickiness plays a vital role in the analysis.

Of course, neo-Austrian economics does not provide a foundation in maximising behaviour for its assumption of complete price flexibility either, and to this extent its handling of this matter is just as arbitrary as any other. However, price flexibility is the common assumption made in applications of the General Equilibrium model, and in this sense the neo-Austrian approach to macroeconomic issues is closer to micro theory *per se*. Moreover, empirical applications of conventional macro theory typically have money wages and prices fluctuating as a function of 'excess demand', the latter being proxied by some output or employment measure, with the values of the parameters governing the fluctuations in question left free to be determined by the data. To the extent that the neo-Austrian model can deal with the same data while maintaining *a priori* that the parameter in question is infinite in value, it is a simpler, and in that sense a 'better', model.

Some neo-Austrians, notably Barro (1979), have gone further than this and argued that the hypothesis that markets do not clear is incompatible with the basic assumption of economics that the world is populated by self-interested agents who will always engage in mutually advantageous trades. If Howitt's (1974) analysis of price formation in markets dominated by inventory holding specialist traders was universally relevant, and if it could be shown that such agents did not engage in trading at non-market clearing prices (a claim which Howitt did not make), it would be hard to disagree with this argument. Indeed Howitt (1979) has argued that in such a world the distinction between clearing and non-clearing markets reduces mainly to a matter of semantics. However, in the real world, not every market is so dominated, and in particular the labour market is not. The latter is, to use Hick's phrase, a 'fixprice' market, as opposed to a 'flexprice' market. In a flexprice market, so the argument goes, knowledge which enables a particular trader to foresee the time path of the market clearing price more accurately than his competitors enables him to make extraordinary profits. Hence, it is worth his and every other trader's while to invest a considerable amount of resources in generating that information. Therefore, if the market is competitive, the rate of return on resources devoted to generating and processing information is driven to a 'normal' level, the quality and quantity of available information is 'high', and actual prices are continuously 'close' to their market clearing levels.

Labour markets are not usually dominated by specialist traders. Typically, the level and structure of wage rates are fixed on a piecemeal basis by the decentralised activities of individual workers, or their representatives, and individual employers, or their representatives. For those involved in agreeing on a particular wage rate in a particular sector of the economy, the cost–benefit ratio for generating information about the market clearing structure of wages is likely to be relatively high, since there is no way of exploiting small increments to information by speculating on margin in the labour market. Furthermore, even when the market clearing wage rate changes and is perceived to have changed, it is not necessarily in the interests of everyone concerned in the wage fixing process to work towards an actual change in wages. For example, if the market clearing wage falls, those currently employed have no immediate interest in seeing their own actual wage rate cut. The logic of Barro's argument would seem to imply that, to move from a situation of excess supply of labour to one of full employment is in everyone's interest, so that those who are in employment have as much at stake in seeing the wage go to its market clearing value as anyone else. It is certainly true that in moving from a situation of unemployment to one of full employment, it is *possible* to make everyone better off, but it does not follow that the actual move will, in fact, have this result.

To put the case explicitly in the language of elementary General Equilibrium theory, for any point within the production frontier, there exists at least one Pareto superior point on that frontier; but not every point on the frontier is Pareto superior to any point inside it. Thus, members of the labour force who remain employed when there is an overall excess supply of labour may be perfectly correct in suspecting that to accept a wage cut will involve them in facing a lower real income even when full employment is restored. Hence, if they are self interested and rational, they will resist the tendency of wages to fall. To be sure, it is in the interests of those who are not employed, and of their potential employers, to attempt to bid wages down in these circumstances. However, one does not have to follow Hicks (1974) (who abandons the assumption of self interest and invokes the hypothesis that the spirit of 'fair play' leads employers and the unemployed to be half hearted in their attempts to bid down wages) to argue plausibly that, in the absence of an auctioneer, or of a group of specialist labour brokers, the resistance of what will usually be the majority of the labour force might lead to those efforts bearing fruit only rather 'slowly'.

I have used the word 'wages' in the last few paragraphs without attaching to it the adjectives 'real' or 'nominal', but it should be clear that, where money is the unit of account, all wage bargaining has to be about the money wage, even though its ultimate aim is to achieve a particular real wage. Moreover, where the labour market is not centralised, and money prices and their expected future behaviour appear as exogenous variables to those involved in the wage bargaining process, any attempt to lower money wages – or their rate of change – must appear to them as an attempt to influence real wages. Thus, even when an economy is subjected to a purely monetary shock, so that the market clearing value of the real wage is not changed, the considerations we have been discussing are relevant. Of course if wages were, literally, set by an auctioneer who would permit no trade to take place until a market clearing set of wages and prices had been achieved, this problem would not arise. However, the question we are addressing here is not *how* the world would function *if* an auctioneer was at work, but whether it would function in the same fashion in his absence, and in the absence of what Howitt's analysis seems to imply would be a substitute for his activities, namely a market in labour services dominated by specialist traders.

It might be argued that, in the wake of a cut in the nominal money supply, if each agent understood that no real wage changes were going to result from the acceptance of money wage changes because every other agent was expected to cut money wages and prices at the same time, the market would quickly clear. It would indeed do so, and clear at the natural unemployment rate as well, because the assumptions about information which I have just made describe a state of affairs in which the monetary shock in question has been 'fully anticipated'. However, the neo-Austrian model requires that markets in general, and the labour market in particular, also clear when monetary changes are not fully anticipated. It requires that, in the presence of systematic misapprehension about how the structure of wages and prices is actually changing, each wage bargain that gets struck be nevertheless consistent with an overall structure of prices and wages that will equate supply and demand in all markets. That model would therefore seem to require each agent to understand the nature of the misinformation ruling everywhere else in the economy, and to allow fully for its effects in his own wage bargaining.

The requirement that everyone have full information about everyone else's misinformation is odd, and not one which could literally be fulfilled in practice, not least because it is internally inconsistent except when there is no misinformation. However, the above reasoning should not be claimed to show that the neo-Austrian model is empirically false, but only that its *a priori* plausibility should not be defended by appeal to the propensity of rational agents to engage in all trades that are perceived to be mutually beneficial. It is not the basic propensity of economic agents to act in this way which is questioned by the critics of the neo-Austrian approach, or at least by this critic, but their ability quickly to *perceive* just what menu of trades is in fact open in a monetary economy where *multilateral* and not isolated *bilateral* trading is of the essence. What is at question is not the maximising propensity of self-interested agents, but the capacity of real-world markets to provide sufficient information and incentive always to harmonise their behaviour, or to put it another way, the empirical validity of Say's Law.

Now some might argue that the foregoing discussion is, in large measure, beside the point, because even casual observations of the real world show us that wages and prices do indeed change rather sluggishly in response to market forces. This argument, however, will no more do than will the closely related argument, already discussed, which refers to the observed fact of unemployment. We must not confuse the facts which we observe with a particular theoretical interpretation of those facts; and in this instance, we must recognise that it is now a commonplace of the literature which has grown from the original contributions of Donald Gordon (1974), Martin Neil Baily (1974) and Costas Azariadis (1975) that money wages may be modelled as being set by rather long-term contracts, which are themselves the outcome of a completely rational bargaining process. It cannot be inferred, from the fact that under the terms of such contracts money wages do not change with any great frequency, that labour markets do not operate 'as if' they cleared continuously. Barro (1977b) in particular has argued that if rational agents do engage in contracts, then the contracts themselves will contain clauses which enable appropriate quantity responses to be made to whatever shocks, systematic or random, might reasonably have been expected to occur during the lifetime of the contract at the time it was struck.

The wage stickiness associated with long-term contracts, under which the wage rate cannot plausibly be thought of as reflecting, at any particular moment, the marginal productivity of labour, and the apparently closely related phenomenon of fluctuations in employment brought about by lay-offs, is not necessarily incompatible with competitive maximising behaviour on the part of both parties to such contracts (see Robert Hall 1980). If employees are more risk-averse than their employers, then there will be an element of insurance in the wage bargain they strike; wages will be more stable over time than the marginal product of labour; and, when that marginal product falls below a certain threshold level, employment will be reduced not by the typical employee quitting in response to a wage cut, but by that employee instead being laid off. Thus the appropriate market clearing quantity is achieved without an intervening price signal being observed.

I find it awkward to reconcile such analysis with the underlying neo-Austrian hypothesis about the nature of the business cycle. The analysis is plausible enough at the partial equilibrium level, but the explanation of the business cycle requires that its results go through in General Equilibrium as well. The fundamental thrust of the neo-Austrian approach is to argue that the quantity fluctuations which we observe over the course of the cycle are generated by markets which clear, while the fundamental thrust of the contract literature is to argue that the quantity decisions which get taken, in labour markets at least (the analysis is surely applicable to certain output markets too), involve quantity solutions being achieved *without* the intervention of price signals. If one is to extend a proposition such as this from a single market to the whole economy, or a large segment of it, it must be explained how the information upon which quantity decisions get made is disseminated, if it is not by prices. This is not to argue that, if prices do not fluctuate in accordance with current conditions of supply and demand, then quantity decisions do not get made, or that those decisions will not, from the point of view of the immediate parties to them, be maximising decisions. However, it is to argue that it is not immediately obvious that such decisions will be mutually compatible across the economy as a whole, when prices no longer act as a means of co-ordinating them. If they are not mutually compatible, then of course the empirical version of Say's Law will be violated.

But once again, this argument is an *a priori* one; things might not work out as the neo-Austrians say they will, but then again they might. We are in effect arguing here about assumptions, and though that can often clarify just what the issues are in any debate, it cannot in and of itself settle anything. The phrase 'as if' is always available as a defence.

6. SAY'S LAW AND THE DEMAND FOR MONEY

The reference to the phrase 'as if' with which the previous section concluded was not intended as sarcasm. Our models, those in which we believe as much as those about which we have doubts, are after all models; they are not descriptions of reality. They always do leave things out and hence always do rest upon the often unspoken premise that the world operates 'as if' the factors which have been omitted are irrelevant to the outcome of whatever situations the model makes predictions about. However, it is the model itself, and not the economist who manipulates it, which determines what predictions are relevant to testing it. If a set of assumptions yields a conclusion which is false, even if that conclusion concerns some factor which was of no interest to those who put together that set of assumptions in the first place, then there is no alternative but to conclude that the set of assumptions in question is unsatisfactory and needs improving. This is not to say that a model which is in some way refuted must be discarded altogether, because a faulty model is not necessarily useless and may in any case be the best available to us at any time; but, to repeat, it is to say that the model cannot be regarded as satisfactory.

When it comes to macroeconomics and the business cycle, we are faced with (at least) two competing approaches. As things now stand, there is a strong case to be made for one of them, the neo-Austrian approach, on the grounds that it is simpler than its 'Keynesian' alternative, in the sense that it leaves one parameter fewer, that linking the rate of price change to excess demand, to be determined by the data; and also, and crucially, on the grounds that it has at least as much explanatory power as does the alternative framework. This is the main thrust of Lucas' (1980) argument. The previous section of this essay discussed certain aspects of labour market behaviour and concluded that there may be difficulties with the explanatory power of the neo-Austrian approach after all, but 'may be' stops well short of 'are', and our knowledge of facts and theory alike in this area seems to leave matters open. Whether or not labour markets work 'as if' they clear continuously in accordance with the predictions of competitive theory is a central question in the debate between the neo-Austrians and their critics. However, it does not follow that we are compelled to rely on the labour market to provide us with evidence about these matters.

The reason for this is inherent in the very nature of General Equilibrium theory, where any one market interacts with all the other markets in the system. If something is going wrong in the labour market, it will manifest itself not only there, but in some other market or markets as well, and perhaps in a way which will make it easier to see that something is indeed wrong. In this case, I shall now argue that it is possible to make inferences about whether the labour market clears from what happens elsewhere in the economy, and in particular in the market for real money balances, about which we have a good deal of theoretical and empirical knowledge. Specifically, I shall argue that this knowledge, if indeed it is valid, suggests that the neo-Austrian theory of the business cycle, in its insistence on the empirical validity of Say's Law, is probably unsatisfactory in the sense that it makes predictions which are contradicted by the evidence.

The behaviour of the demand for money is of particular relevance to judging the validity of neo-Austrian business cycle theory for a number of reasons. First of all, the typical shock which sets the cycle in motion in that theory is an unanticipated change in the nominal money supply. Second, as I pointed out explicitly above (p. 72), elementary monetary theory tells us that, when the nominal money supply is exogenous, the general price level must move so as to equate the supply of real balances to the demand for them, while the price level in its turn can only be changed if the money prices of all goods in the economy vary. These simple facts immediately make it difficult to reconcile neo-Austrian theory with the existence of any wage–price rigidity induced by long-term contracts. It cannot be valid to say that, in the presence of such contracts, and in the face of an unanticipated change in the money supply, the quantity decisions taken by firms and households in the absence of price changes are the same as those which would have been prompted by an auctioneer manipulating prices so as to keep markets cleared, because, in the absence of the appropriate price changes, the supply and demand for money cannot be brought into equilibrium.

The above argument is suggestive, surely, but it is not in and of itself convincing, because after all, in the real world, wages and prices do vary to some extent, and who is to say that the variations that we actually observe are not 'appropriate' to clear the money market? In order to answer this question we need to look more closely at the literature on the demand for money function. There we find that, in order to deal in a satisfactory way with the data that the world generates for us, it is necessary to distinguish between the 'long-run' and the 'short-run' demand for money. This is true, at least, unless those data are highly aggregated over time, to cycle phases for example, but we obviously need a lower level of time aggregation than that in our data if they are going to be able to tell us anything about the business cycle.

There is no need here to go into detail about the long-run–short-run distinction here, for I have already discussed the issues involved elsewhere (see Laidler 1977, 1980, and Essay 2). Suffice it to say that, in order to find 'stability' in the demand for money function, using annual or quarterly data generated over relatively short (thirty years or less, say) periods of time, a lagged dependent variable seems to be needed. Suffice it also to say that, in a world where the nominal money supply is exogenous, and that is after all the neo-Austrian world, it is logical nonsense to justify the presence of such a variable on the grounds that the nominal money supply adjusts with a distributed lag to variations in the arguments in the demand for money function. Nominal money is either exogenous or endogenous, and it cannot be both. That leaves two ways of accounting for the presence of the lagged dependent variable in the function.

The first of these involves postulating the existence of 'expectations lags' usually based on an application of the error learning hypothesis to the modelling of permanent income (on this, once more see Laidler 1977, Chs. 6 and 7, 1980, and Essay 2), but this will not do in the current context. First, the hypothesis in question does not seem to be entirely adequate in the face of the data; but second, the neo-Austrian who is devoted to the notion of rational expectations can hardly invoke the error learning hypothesis, which on all but the most special assumptions implies that agents make expectational errors which are systematic over time, in order to explain any empirical evidence. The only explanation for the presence of a lagged dependent variable in the aggregate demand for money function that is left, then, is that first suggested by Walters as long ago as 1965, namely that it reflects the slow adjustment of real balances, and therefore of the general price level, towards their long-run equilibrium value, rather than a slow adjustment of nominal balances.

To accept this last explanation of the presence of a lagged dependent variable in the demand for money function is, as I have argued in Essay 2 above, to conclude that the 'short-run' demand for money function is not, in fact, a structural relationship at all, but a hybrid which is part long-run structural demand for money function and part price level adjustment equation; and that the coefficient which measures the speed of adjustment is picking up, not the consequences of the costs that face individual agents trading in asset markets, but of the real balance effect operating on prices. If this interpretation is accepted, it ceases to be a puzzle that money market adjustment, so-called, is extremely slow, for it would imply, not that agents rearrange their portfolios slowly, but that in the real world the real balance effect works only slowly on prices. If the literature on the labour market provides us with all sorts of reasons to believe that money wages, and therefore perhaps prices, might display considerable sluggishness in moving towards market clearing levels in the face of a monetary shock, then empirical work on the demand for money function seems to provide us with a great deal of evidence that is consistent with that postulate.

The implications of the foregoing interpretation of the empirical evidence on the demand for money for neo-Austrian economics are profound, for they tell us that, far from being so flexible that they can keep markets continuously cleared in the face of fluctuations in the nominal money supply, prices take years to adjust to such fluctuations. If they do, if the working out of the real balance effect on prices is a significant fact of actual economic life, rather than a phenomenon which takes essentially no time at all, then we have ample time for the quantity variations, upon which the alternative non clearing market approach to the business cycle concentrates, to come into effect. I am here claiming that it is *almost* impossible to reconcile the neo-Austrian approach to the analysis of the business cycle with the evidence I am citing. The qualifying adverb is necessary because, with sufficient ingenuity it might be possible to construct a form for the long-run demand for money function which accomplishes such a reconciliation, but as we shall see the form in question is probably sufficiently far-fetched not to merit serious consideration. Before we get to this matter, however, there are a number of more direct objections to the position I am advancing which need to be faced and dealt with.

Perhaps the most obvious of these objections would start from the reasonable premise that, in the individual experiment on the demand for money, the agent who for one reason or another has too much cash on hand does not attempt to move all the way back to his long-run equilibrium if he faces transactions costs. It might seem to follow that, in the market experiment, we should not expect to find a quicker response. If each individual taken singly wants to restore his cash balances to equilibrium only slowly, then why should not all of them, acting collectively, achieve that end through markets which nevertheless remain continuously cleared? The answer here lies in the fact that the transactions costs which face the individual are irrelevant in the neo-Austrian market experiment, for there real balances are adjusted by changing the price level and not by any act of trading.

Now of course, if individual prices, not to mention money wages, are sticky, then real balances will in any event adjust only slowly; but it is the very essence of the neo-Austrian approach to argue that prices and wages are *not* sticky. Thus in the market experiment, prices change because there is an excess supply of money, and each agent finds his money holdings moving towards equilibrium as a result of a force which to him appears exogenous. He does not incur any transactions costs as a result of this adjustment, and will still find it worthwhile to attempt to incur such costs in order to move that bit closer to long-run equilibrium. When every agent does this, the price level must continue to rise, and the supply of and demand for money will not be in equilibrium until any discrepancy between actual and long-run desired cash balances has been removed.

The result here is essentially similar to that which we get from applying the Archibald–Lipsey (1958), Patinkin (1965) analysis of the dynamics of the real balance effect to the market experiment; there too a process which, at the level of the individual agent would be spread out over a number of periods, strictly speaking an infinite number since approach to equilibrium for the individual is asymptotic, when all agents are acting together, is accomplished instantaneously by the auctioneer adjusting prices to keep the market cleared. The matter can be put succinctly in terms of the behaviour of prices in a market presided over by an auctioneer. So long as there is any positive (negative) discrepancy between actual and long-run desired real balances, the plans of each agent involve him in being a net seller (or buyer) of real balances, and hence a net buyer (or seller) of goods and services, even if only for a fraction of the discrepancy that underlies the plans. Thus, the auctioneer will be forced to adjust prices until the discrepancy in question is removed and the economy is placed in its long-run demand for money function. Only then will trade be permitted to begin. (The above argument is developed more formally in Essay 2 above, especially pp. 49–51.)

In short, if we neglect the distribution effects discussed below, if Say's Law holds as an empirical proposition, and if the nominal money supply is an exogenous variable, it is impossible to observe the real balance effect working out over time because the economy is always *on* its *long-run* demand for money function. This, of course, does not preclude the possibility of prices moving systematically over time in response to a change in the money supply. If output responds to an unanticipated increase in the money supply by rising, as neo-Austrian theory predicts, and if that rise persists for a while, then, if current income is an argument in the long-run demand for money function, prices will not move instantaneously to a new higher long-run equilibrium level and stay there. However, the influence of these real income variations should already be captured by the presence of that variable on the right-hand side of the long-run demand for money function, and if its influence on real money holding is properly specified in the form of the long-run relationship, there should be no room for a lagged dependent variable to pick up any inertia in the behaviour of prices. A similar argument holds with reference to the possibility that interest rates may change in the short run so as to equilibrate the supply of and demand for money. Only such inertia as is independent of the current behaviour of the arguments of the long-run function should be captured in the coefficient of that lagged dependent variable; and according to the logic of the neo-Austrian approach there should not be any such inertia. Indeed, we can go further than this, because, as I shall now show, neo-Austrian theory predicts not merely that the price level should display no sluggishness in moving towards its long-run equilibrium value after the nominal money supply changes, but that it should *overshoot* that value unless the change in the money supply is fully anticipated.

It is uncontroversial that a fully anticipated change in the money supply will lead to a simultaneous and equi-proportional change in the general price level, leaving the quantity of real balances unchanged. To see why an unanticipated change in the nominal money supply should, according to neo-Austrian theory, lead to an overshoot of the general price level, it is necessary to consider once again the manner in which prices and quantities are thought of as reacting to unanticipated changes in the money supply by proponents of that theory. Prices, it will be recalled, must find a level at which all markets, including therefore the money market, are cleared. However, because agents know only about the prices of the items they actually sell at the time at which prices are set, they must make their quantity plans, including those about holdings of nominal money, upon the basis of expectations about the value of the general price level. We have seen that neo-Austrian theory explains the tendency of prices and output to move together in response to unanticipated monetary changes in terms of a general tendency on the part of agents to misinterpret changes in the money prices of what they sell as reflecting relative price changes, rather than changes in the general price level. They do this even if they form their expectations rationally.

However, as has already been stressed above, the money market has to clear at the same time as goods and labour markets, and that is a time at which agents underestimate the general price level. Thus, unless each individual agent regards only the price of what it is he has to sell as relevant to his money holding decision, the demand for nominal balances which must be satisfied to clear the money market will be conditional not upon the *actual* price level, but upon the *expected and underestimated* price level. Even when expectations are formed rationally, the expected price level rises with, but falls short of, the actual price level when there is an unanticipated change in the nominal money supply (see Lucas 1972). Therefore, when agents have to form expectations about the price level, the actual price level must move by more than it would need to move in a situation in which agents knew its true value. The result of this must be that *actual* observed holdings of real balances will lie below the quantity predicted by the demand for money function when there has been an unanticipated increase in the quantity of nominal money, and above the predicted quantity when there has been an unanticipated fall in the money supply.

We have some direct evidence on this very matter. Jack Carr and Michael Darby (1981), using quarterly data from a number of countries, and Laidler (1980) using annual US data, have both shown that there is a significant positive correlation between unanticipated nominal money and the quantity of real balances which the economy holds. Moreover, Laidler's results were derived with the very series on 'unanticipated money' which Barro (1978) constructed and used to explain price and output fluctuations in the United States. Now, the results I am citing here are vulnerable to the criticism that, in having the quantity of money on both sides of the equation, they might simply be the result of correlating the measurement error in that variable with itself. However, if there is more to them than that, and recent work by James MacKinnon and Ross Milbourne (1981) suggests that there may not be, they are not very difficult to explain if one does not insist that the money market be always cleared. When money is newly created, and if prices and other determinants of money holding have not adjusted to absorb it, it is bound simply to show up as extra real balance holdings. Indeed, the latter argument is tautological, but its premise that it takes time for prices to adjust in response to a change in the money supply is not a tautology. Indeed, that very premise denies the basic proposition of neo-Austrian theory, which is therefore inconsistent with the evidence to which I am referring here (or very probably so).

The qualifying phrase at the end of the previous paragraph is necessary because it is always possible that the empirical results just noted are the result of distribution effects, or have been derived from an erroneous specification of the long-run aggregate demand for money function. The Archibald–Lipsey–Patinkin result that, even in the presence of slow adjustment in the individual experiment, an exogenous change in the nominal money supply will lead to instantaneous long-run equilibrium, only goes through if the increase in question is distributed in proportion to initial money holdings, as Archibald and Lipsey (1958) explicitly demonstrated. If by some chance the distribution of new money when it is first introduced is weighted towards agents who have a relatively high propensity to hold money, then the price level will indeed adjust slowly over time towards a final equilibrium value, not because the market at any moment fails to clear, but because it takes time for market mechanisms to redistribute the money until it is once again held in proportion to initial endowments. Macro-economists are usually cautious about putting too much weight upon distribution effects at the best of times, and here I can think of no general reason why increases in the nominal money supply should always initially find their way into the portfolios of those agents with a particularly strong preference for holding increments to their assets in the form of money. Nevertheless, the logical possibility of rescuing neo-Austrian economics along these lines does exist.

If we set distribution effects to one side, we must nevertheless also note that, *ex post*, it is possible to construct a demand for money function which would reconcile the neo-Austrian model with the relevant evidence. Unanticipated monetary changes are associated with transitory changes in real income in that theory, and in this respect it is well supported by the data. If the demand for real money balances depended strongly on transitory income, and if this term was omitted from the demand for money function used to interpret data generated by an unanticipated rise in the money supply, then there might indeed appear to be more real balances being held than the demand for money function explained; and it might indeed be the case that the inclusion of transitory income in the function, with a sufficiently large coefficient, can explain this anomaly while maintaining the rest of the neo-Austrian model intact. Barro (1978) advances just such a suggestion in order to resolve certain puzzles arising from his empirical work on fitting a neo-Austrian model to the post-war United States. Since I know of no theoretical foundation for this property of the demand for money function, I find this line of argument quite unconvincing. However, further theoretical and empirical work on the function would surely be valuable in the light of the foregoing arguments.

7. CONCLUDING COMMENTS

This essay has covered a good deal of ground, and it would be as well to gather together the threads of argument which run through it. First and foremost, I have argued that it is very difficult to reconcile Say's Law, considered as an empirical proposition, with the empirical evidence on the demand for money. Anyone who wishes to maintain as a basic principle of analysis the proposition that market mechanisms in the real world operate to keep markets continually cleared 'as if' they were presided over by an auctioneer, will always be able to find a formulation of the demand for money function which will reconcile this proposition with any conceivable body of evidence. However, those who regard the proposition in question as being open to empirical test, will be likely to find it wanting in explanatory power in the light of the arguments I have presented. If this conclusion is accepted, then neo-Austrian economics must be regarded as probably constituting a fundamentally unsatisfactory account of the world we live in. If prices do not change quickly enough to keep markets cleared over the type of time interval that most of us regard as relevant – quarter by quarter, or year by year, say – then a number of things seem to follow.

If prices do not move quickly enough to clear markets, we must ask if any other factors will come into play as a result. Fortunately we do not have to grope for an answer to this question the way the economists of fifty years ago did. We do have Keynesian economics, as developed by Patinkin, Clower, Leijonhufvud, Barro and Grossman, and Malinvaud, which tells us that, in the absence of sufficient price flexibility, we may expect quantities to move to clear markets instead. It also tells us that such quantity fluctuations might tend to amplify the effects of disturbances rather than damp them, and therefore provides us with the basis of an alternative approach to the theory of the business cycle to that advanced by the neo-Austrians. In short, perhaps Keynes did not, after all, as some advocates of the neo-Austrian approach (see e.g. Kantor 1980) have suggested, lead economics up a blind alley.

However, this conclusion is not one about which anyone should be complacent. Though the facts seem to suggest that money wages and prices do not move quickly enough to clear markets, so that we may use the hypothesis of price stickiness as a starting point for macroeconomic analysis, we do not have anything approaching a satisfactory theory of why prices are sticky and, until we do, the predictive power of our macro models will be seriously impaired. A body of theory which cannot predict the pace at which prices will respond to excess demand can be reconciled *ex post* with an uncomfortably broad range of data by letting those data themselves determine the speed of price adjustment. This neo-Austrian criticism of orthodox macroeconomics remains valid, even if the neo-Austrian solution to the problem, namely constraining the speed of adjustment to infinity *a priori*, turns out to be as inconsistent with the empirical evidence as the extreme Keynesian alternative of constraining it to zero earlier proved to be. To have forced us to confront this critical gap in our theoretical understanding is an important contribution on the part of neo-Austrian economics. In this essay I am arguing that the basic premise of neo-Austrian economics is empirically refuted, but I am not also claiming that its proponents have led economics up a blind alley. They have asked too many pertinent questions and given too many interesting answers to those questions as well, for such a claim to be defensible.

Of course, we are not totally ignorant about the economics of price rigidity. Thus, at the level of the individual experiment, Barro (1972) has shown how the pace of price change might vary with the pressure of demand for a particular monopolist if he faces a stochastic demand curve, and is forced to incur lump-sum costs when he changes his price, while Mussa (1976) has extended this analysis to encompass labour market behaviour as well. Moreover, the notion that, from the point of view of the individual agent, money is a 'buffer stock' which reduces the costs incurred by making erroneous decisions as a result of acting on incomplete information, has been stressed by Brunner and Meltzer (1971), Laidler (1975, Ch. 1) and Jonson (1976a) among others. This notion surely helps us to understand why, in a money using economy, wrong prices might persist, because holding money reduces the costs faced by agents who fail to change them when they should.

Closely related, at the level of the market experiment, is the idea propounded among others by Georg Simmel (1907), Keynes (1936, pp. 269–271) and Sydney Frankel (1979) that a monetary system is not viable unless there is a certain rigidity and hence predictability to the purchasing power of money. This suggests that price stickiness, considered as a social phenomenon, is not altogether undesirable. It might be noted that this idea, which is also to be found in Austrian writing, at least on inflation, is strangely absent from the work of the neo-Austrians. The literature to which I am referring here does not yet amount to a coherent body of theory which would enable us to make quantitative predictions about the factors determining the pace at which money wages and prices might change with, say, the unemployment rate, but it does have enough to say about the social and economic aspects of price stickiness to give us grounds for believing that there is nothing inherently insoluble about the problem of constructing a model which will enable us to make such predictions. It would be easier if we did not have to face this problem, but the empirical evidence I have discussed here suggests that it has to be solved, rather than bypassed as the neo-Austrians would have us do.

To argue that Say's Law does not hold as an empirical proposition is to argue that there is a very real sense in which market mechanisms fail to solve the Economic Problem, and that the notion of a general over-supply of labour is not a figment of the Keynesian economist's imagination but a recurring fact of life in real-world market economies. If this is really the case, any generalised *a priori* arguments against government intervention in the economy based on the proposition that the operation of markets leaves no room for improvement cannot be sustained. The logical possibility of an activist stabilisation policy being able to bring the economic system closer to a solution of the Economic Problem than it would get of its own accord has to be entertained. However, to entertain that possibility is not to say that it can be realised, given the current state of knowledge.

Say's Law gets violated because individual agents do not know enough to be able to get wages and prices quickly to their market clearing levels. It would seem to follow, and Howitt (1981) argues that it is in fact the case, that a government could improve matters if it had better information, or could make better use of existing information, than the private sector. Here neo-Austrian economics, flawed though it may be, yields us an insight of basic importance. The idea of Rational Expectations, which is logically independent of the hypothesis that markets always clear, implies that once a government has information and begins to act upon it, that information becomes the property of at least some agents in the private sector as well, whose behaviour will then respond to it. If this is true, then the possibility of government intervention leading to a sustained improvement in the performance of the economy rests, not upon any once-and-for-all superiority in knowledge on the government's part, but upon the government getting and then *staying* one step ahead of the private sector. It is not just that, in the current state of knowledge, it is difficult to design an effective demand management policy, but that at some time in the future new knowledge will enable us to do so. Rather it is that the difficulty of designing such a policy arises from the state of the authorities' knowledge *relative* to that of agents in the private sector, and there is no reason to believe that future advances in economic knowledge will systematically tip the balance of advantage in the authorities' favour.

This conclusion (which plays a key role in Essay 5 below) is, in some respects, a pessimistic one. Markets do not really solve the Economic Problem for us in the real world as well as they do in the Economics textbook, and in a free society, where everyone has equal access to information, it seems that government intervention cannot be counted on systematically to help matters either now or in the future. It is important, then, to remind ourselves that this conclusion does not say that the state of the world has changed for the worse. Rather it says that the state of the world has always been what it now is in this respect, but that our understanding of this fact has improved.

It is a more than merely defensible proposition that the economic instability of the last couple of decades has stemmed in some measure from the attempts of well-motivated governments to improve the performance of markets and that those attempts have failed, indeed have made matters worse, because the governments in question were ill-informed and over-optimistic about just what they were in a position to accomplish. Undoubtedly that is not the whole story, for it is hard to blame the Cold War, the Vietnam War, the Arab–Israeli conflict, to name just a few obvious political sources of economic instability, on Keynesian economics; but it is a part of the story. If that is understood, developments in economics which make us more sceptical about what *either markets or governments* can accomplish in the way of solving the Economic Problem, might themselves turn out to be forces making for a closer approach to a satisfactory solution to it.

4

On the 'Transmission Mechanism'

1. INTRODUCTION

It is now widely agreed that variations in the quantity of money are an important cause, some would argue a dominant one, of variations in money income, and particularly, as Meltzer (1977) has stressed, of those variations which are long sustained over time. There can be no ignoring the simple fact that during the last fifteen years it has been those countries which have paid the most attention to the behaviour of their money supplies which have suffered the least from instability in money income, and those which have paid the least attention to monetary policy which have experienced the most instability in money income. Nevertheless, the subject matter of this essay, the nature of the causative links between money and money income – the 'transmission mechanism' – is still controversial.

Until recently, debates about the transmission mechanism were in the main carried on in terms of a common theoretical structure. That structure was usually one variation or another on the IS–LM model, which proved extremely flexible in its ability to accommodate opposing points of view as to how the macroeconomy operated. Disagreements thus seemed susceptible to resolution in terms of empirical tests designed to throw light upon one or another of the parameters of what may be termed a 'consensus' model which provided an agenda for empirical research in macroeconomics whose results were expected to lead to, among other things, agreement on the role of money in the macroeconomy and hence on the appropriate design of monetary policy. To give but one well-known example, much of the debate between Friedman and his critics, notably Tobin and Brunner and Meltzer (see Gordon 1974), was conducted in terms of such a model and the main issues at stake were agreed to be quantitative.

Quantitative knowledge has certainly grown rapidly in recent years. However, it is the contention of this essay that recent research has not so much filled gaps in our knowledge about an agreed theoretical framework, as it has cast doubt upon the comprehensiveness of that framework as a research agenda. In particular, research on price–output interaction, on the consequences of fiscal policy for the behaviour of the money supply, and on questions prompted by the openness of most economies, has emphasised the influence of expectations about price level behaviour on the activities of economic agents. This research will be discussed in some detail below, and it will be argued that it should lead us not just to reassess the answers to questions about the transmission mechanism cast in IS–LM terms, but to rethink the questions themselves. Even so, a good deal of recent work has been cast in the IS–LM tradition and it would give a misleading impression of the current state of knowledge to ignore it. I shall begin with an account of this work but, because there already exist several recent surveys of various subsets of it, this account will be reasonably brief. (See, for example, Gordon, Fisher and Sheppard 1974, Fisher and Sparks 1975, Goodhart 1975, Ch. 9, and Brainard and Cooper 1975.)

2. THE TRANSMISSION MECHANISM IN AN IS–LM CONTEXT

The basic IS–LM model is well known. Where E is real private expenditure, A is autonomous real private expenditure, Y is real income, G is real government expenditure, t the tax rate, M the quantity of nominal money demanded, M_s the quantity supplied and P the general price level, its static form can be written (in linear terms for simplicity):

$$Y-G=E=A+k(1-t)Y-ar \tag{1}$$

$$M_s = M_d = (l_1Y-l_2r)P \tag{2}$$

This model, whose expenditure function is sometimes augmented by a wealth effect, and which, for empirical purposes, is inevitably dynamised by introducing distributed lags into the structural equations which make it up, is concerned with the determination of aggregate demand. If we adopt the standard textbook 'reverse L' shaped aggregate supply curve, and consider the horizontal section of it along which the price level is constant, we may derive the following reduced-form equation for real income:

$$Y= \frac{1}{1-\{(1-t)k-(a/l_2)l_1\}}(A+G)+\frac{1}{(l_2/a)[1-\{(1-t)k-(a/l_2)l_1\}]}\frac{M_s}{P} \tag{3}$$

Clearly, in terms of this model, questions about the relationship between money and income concern the second term on the right-hand side of this reduced form, and these questions may be divided into two groups. First, the appropriateness of treating the behaviour of the quantity of money as determining that of income has often been disputed: this is the 'reverse causation' question. Second, there are questions about the stability and size of the money multiplier considered in isolation, and compared with the autonomous expenditure multiplier. The reverse causation question has usually been treated as being, by its very nature, a question about the conduct of monetary policy during particular historical episodes. It need not detain us at this stage, though we will have a good deal to say about it below.

Questions about the money multiplier seem, *from the point of view of the IS–LM model*, to be of a fundamentally different nature. They concern behaviour relationships in the private sector of the economy whose characteristics are to be regarded as independent of the conduct of policy. Thus, in the context of this model, quantitative knowledge about the money multiplier is thought of as conferring not only the power to answer questions about the channels whereby a given monetary policy *did* influence economic activity during a particular episode, but also to answer questions about how alternative monetary policies *would have* influenced activity had they been implemented instead. Moreover, such knowledge is also viewed as enabling predictions about the consequences of future policies to be made, so that their design may be improved. As we shall see below, much recent work questions the proposition that the structure of the economy is independent of the nature of the policy being carried out, but that proposition is a fundamental premise of the research on the transmission mechanism of monetary policy which is now to be discussed.

It is obvious from equation (3) that if the value of the money multiplier is to remain stable over time, then so must the parameters of both the demand for money function and the aggregate expenditure function (unless, of course, by some freak, fluctuations in one set of parameters just offset those in the other: see Driscoll and Ford 1980). It is equally obvious, not to say well known, that its value, both absolute and relative to the autonomous expenditure multiplier, is particularly sensitive to the values of the parameters a and l_2 which measure the interest sensitivity of expenditure and demand for money. Although the model as set out above is cast in linear terms, the relevant argument also goes through if we discuss the *elasticities* of expenditure and the demand for money with respect to the interest rate (see Laidler 1975, Ch. 3, p. 81). In the light of this property of the IS–LM model, it is hardly surprising that the role of interest rates in influencing agents' behaviour has been at the centre of empirical research concerned with the transmission mechanisms of monetary policy. Laidler (1977, 1980) extensively surveys both theoretical and empirical work on the demand for money function. Suffice it here to say that the existence of a stable aggregate demand for money function is reasonably well supported by empirical work (although see Essays 1, pp.7–8 and 2, pp. 63–64 above) and in particular, that a clearly defined negative relationship between the demand for money and an interest rate variable is a salient characteristic of that function. There is no question of the extreme 'quantity theory' special case of the IS–LM model being supported by empirical evidence; this fact implies that, if we take that model seriously, the nature of the relationship underlying the parameter a, both qualitative and quantitative, is of central importance to the linkage between money and economic activity.

The aggregate private sector expenditure function embodied in equation (1) is a convenient analytic simplification. Expenditure on currently produced goods and services by the private sector involves the behaviour of both firms and households. Firms' expenditure may be on producer durable goods as well as on inventories of raw materials and finished output. Households, on the other hand, buy both non-durable and durable goods. Even so, the qualitative nature of the linkage between money and expenditure which the IS–LM model attempts to summarise has not been a subject of much substantive controversy, although some, notably Brunner and Meltzer (e.g. 1976), have questioned the adequacy of the summary that this particular model in fact gives of this linkage.

Money is commonly regarded as one of a spectrum of assets held by firms and households, whose (not always very clearly specified) services yield diminishing marginal utility (or product) to their consumer. An increase in the quantity of money in an economy initially in asset equilibrium thus induces a disequilibrium in the structure of asset holding, because the implicit yield on money is thereby driven down. A generalised substitution from money into other assets takes place, driving down their rates of return, though not necessarily so far that the demand and supply of money are brought into equilibrium. Some of these rates of return are observable interest rates on securities, set by specialist dealers in response to supply and demand conditions in organised markets; some are observable borrowing and lending rates, set by financial intermediaries of one sort or another; and others are implicit, non-observable rates of return on assets such as consumer durables.

A general fall in rates of return involves an increase in the present value of the income streams yielded by existing assets, and hence a rise in their market values relative to the supply price of newly produced assets. The output of durables, both consumer and producer, therefore increases in response to this disequilibrium. At the same time, the price of current consumption in terms of future consumption foregone has fallen so that, in principle, an increase in expenditure on non-durables might also be expected to occur. This account of the first stage of the transmission mechanism is widely accepted. It appears, essentially as presented here, in the work of Tobin (see 1969), Friedman (see, e.g., Friedman and Meiselman 1963 for a rudimentary version) and Brunner and Meltzer (e.g. 1976) and in these authors' contributions to Gordon (1974). Furthermore, whatever the category of expenditure upon which impact effects fall in an IS–LM model, they are amplified by a multiplier process which is only partially offset by the subsequent behaviour of interest rates.

The argument of the previous two paragraphs says nothing about the quantitative significance of the various effects discussed, and it is here that substantive disagreements have arisen. Nowadays the extreme view that only the interest sensitivity of investment is relevant to the transmission mechanism is not found in North American literature, although some British economists still seem to regard this as the critical link in that mechanism. However, this position was quite widely held on both sides of the Atlantic in the 1950s and 1960s and the reader who is concerned about the issues, as regards both theory and policy, which this view raises should consult Brunner (1971). Even so, the qualitative issues raised above do have important implications for the interpretation of empirical evidence on the transmission mechanism, particularly that evidence which comes from certain large-scale econometric models, as Fisher and Sheppard (1974) have argued.

In principle, such models are capable of opening up to inspection the interior of the 'black box' which connects monetary policy to the behaviour of money income. In practice, these models, with certain notable exceptions (e.g. the Canadian RDX2 model – see Helliwell *et al.* 1971, and the US FMP model – see Modigliani 1975), have frequently omitted monetary variables from all but a subset of expenditure functions – typically involving firms' investment decisions – and in thus narrowing down the channels of causation which they investigate, virtually ensure that only relatively weak links between money and economic activity will be discovered. The 1972 version of the London Business School United Kingdom model (see Ball *et al.* 1975) and the CANDIDE 1.2 model of Canada (see Economic Council of Canada 1975) are open to this criticism, and although the results which these models produce are not necessarily wrong, what should be empirical questions have all too often been settled *a priori* in constructing them.

Because it is possible to construct a theoretically coherent case that all aspects of expenditure might respond to monetary variables, some would argue that it is necessary to investigate empirically all aspects of expenditure before one can conclude that monetary factors are, or are not, important. Others take the argument further. If reverse causation can be ruled out, and if a significant correlation between money and money income exists, then this, in and of itself, is *prima facie* evidence that a transmission mechanism between the variables also exists. Such reasoning underlies the preference sometimes displayed by some monetarists, for example Friedman and Meiselman (1963), for testing for the importance of monetary factors in the economy by way of highly aggregated models, not to mention reduced-form equations. If one accepts it, detailed work on the various aspects of the transmission mechanism should be interpreted, not as investigating the *existence* of such a mechanism, but as seeking information about its *nature*. It should be noted, however, that this is not the whole of the case for relying on reduced forms. It may also be argued that the structure of the transmission mechanism varies with the state of information in the economy and hence is, from an econometric point of view, unstable. I shall take up this matter below in considerable detail.

In practice, a variety of approaches have been taken to investigating the questions about linkages between monetary variables and economic activity which the IS–LM framework prompts. Reduced-form equations, of the type fitted to US data by Friedman and Meiselman (1963) and Andersen and Jordan (1968), certainly show that there is a positive and statistically significant relationship between the time paths of the quantity of money and money income, both over long runs of data and in the post 'Accord' period as well. The relationship between money and income also dominates that between autonomous expenditure and income. As far as more recent data are concerned, the statistical analysis of Christopher Sims (1972) suggests that causation runs predominantly from money to money income, rather than *vice versa*. However, Sims' test, building on the work of Clive Granger (1969), relies upon the timing of variations in the data and is controversial. Fisher and Sparks have argued (1975) that it is only possible to use data on timing to establish directions of causation in the context of a specific theoretical framework, while Feige and Pearce (1979) argue that Sims' results are extremely sensitive to variations in the pre-filtering procedures he used to remove systematic variations from his data. Be that as it may, for earlier periods, Friedman and Schwartz (1963, 1970), using the approach of the historian rather than of the econometrician, also conclude that causation has run in both directions, with that running from money to income predominating.

Reduced-form studies have been carried out for Britain by Barrett and Walters (1966) using data from the period 1878–1963, and by Artis and Nobay (1969), as well as the Bank of England

(1970) for post-Second World War data. Here too there can be no doubt that correlations between money and money income exist, but it is a fair generalisation that these are not nearly so strong and well determined as their counterparts for the United States. It is also notable that when Williams, Goodhart and Gowland (1976) applied Sims' techniques to British data for the period 1958–71, no clear-cut results on the direction of causation between money and money income emerged. Indeed, if anything, this study, taken at face value, supports the 'reverse causation' hypothesis. As to earlier periods, Susan Howson's (1975) work on inter-war Britain, like that of Friedman and Schwartz, is based on historical rather than econometric methods. Although she attributed an important causative role to monetary variables at certain times, notably during the upswing that followed the abandonment of the Gold Standard in 1931, she found it hard to attribute much influence to money in other episodes, for example in determining the economy's cyclical behaviour in the middle and late 1920s.

Problems like those encountered with British evidence occur in the Canadian case as well, as Fisher and Sparks (1975) have stressed. George Macesitch's (1966, 1969) attempts at replication of the Friedman and Meiselman study for that economy led to a debate which left the significance of the money–income relationship, and the direction of causation for that economy, open questions. Furthermore, Barth and Bennett's (1974) attempted replication of Sims' test for Canada for the years 1957–72 showed, at best (and then only provided that money was narrowly defined), that the interaction between money and money income involved causation running in both directions, and hence did nothing to solve the problems left open by the earlier work.

In short, it is easier to find a clear-cut correlation between money and money income for the United States than for Britain or Canada, but the details of an IS–LM type of transmission mechanism are just as hard to pin down for that country as for others. For the United States, the whole question of the importance of monetary factors in influencing business investment in fixed plant and equipment is an open one. Dale Jorgenson's theoretical work (e.g. 1967) on the neo-classical theory of investment clarified the role played by the rate of interest in determining the opportunity cost of the services of capital equipment, and the empirical studies which he and his associates (e.g. Jorgenson and Stevenson 1967, Jorgenson, Hunter and Nadiri 1970) carried out seems to show that investment responds with a distributed time lag to interest variations. However, those studies have been criticised on a number of grounds, notably by Frank Brechling (1974, 1975).

The time lags in Jorgenson's empirical work were introduced and specified arbitrarily. Brechling shows that Jorgenson's own neo-classical theory of investment, supplemented at least by a certain type of adjustment cost hypothesis, itself has definite implications for the time pattern of investment's response to interest rates, which can be incorporated specifically into the empirical formulation of time lags. He also shows that the neo-classical theory of investment, either as specified by Jorgenson or with the addition of lags arising from adjustment costs, is not robust in the face of empirical evidence. The particular structural equation, derived from that theory, which Jorgenson and his associates chose to fit to data, seems to perform well enough, but that equation treats output as an exogenous variable. The reduced-form expression implied by the same theory, which has prices, wages and the cost of capital (in which an interest rate variable is incorporated) as exogenous variables, but not output, fits badly, with wrongly-signed parameters being the rule rather than the exception. Brechling also shows that the equation which Jorgenson and his associates fit is not an appropriate reduced form for a cost-minimisation, as opposed to profit-maximisation, formulation of the neo-classical theory and that the appropriate reduced form fits the data badly.

In short, though interest rates might well systematically influence business investment by way of neo-classical mechanisms, Brechling's work shows that this proposition remains to be demonstrated as far as the United States' economy is concerned; and also, incidentally, casts doubts upon the account of the transmission mechanism implied by the FMP econometric model, since that model's treatment of investment draws heavily on Jorgenson's work. Brechling suggests that the supply side as well as the demand side of the capital goods market needs to be analysed explicitly and brought into the picture, before satisfactory tests concerning the interest sensitivity of investment demand can be carried out. In this, his work echoes the stress which Tobin (1969) and Brunner and Meltzer (e.g. 1976) lay on the role played by the supply price of newly-produced capital assets in the transmission mechanism.

One must be careful not to infer from the foregoing analysis that there is no evidence that business investment is affected by monetary factors. As Philip Lund (1971) and Fisher and Sheppard (1974) note, there is abundant evidence, from studies based on one form or another of the accelerator hypothesis, that output or sales variables seem to be important determinants of investment. Jorgenson's own empirical work, of course, leads to similar results. If monetary factors affect consumer expenditures, then sales or output variations, to the extent that these are the result of monetary changes, provide an important *indirect* channel whereby those same changes influence investment. This point, which is not a new one, having been explicitly set out as long ago as 1939 by A. J. Brown, is worth stressing, because, for the United States at least, there is a good deal of evidence to show that consumer expenditure is sensitive to monetary influences.

Michael Hamburger (1967) has found that interest rates played an important role in determining the demand for new durable goods over the period 1953–64. The demand for newly constructed housing is also well known to be sensitive to monetary factors. Credit availability effects, whose roots lie in imperfections in the mortgage market, play a significant role here according to the FMP model, although the work of Arcelus and Meltzer (1973) suggests that an orthodox interest rate mechanism, not supplemented by availability effects, can account for the influence of monetary policy on the housing market. The FMP model takes a 'life-cycle' approach to formulating the consumption function, and the effects of interest rate variations on the value of equities owned by households exert an influence on their levels of expenditure which constitutes an important component of the transmission mechanism which the model generates.

For Britain and Canada the evidence on all these issues is at least as mixed as it is for the United States. For both countries there do exist studies which find a significant role for interest rates in determining investment – Hines and Catephores (1970), or the investment equations of the London Business School (LBS) model for Britain, and the investment equations of both the RDX2 and CANDIDE 1.2 models of Canada, to give some examples. With the exceptions of RDX2 and Hines and Catephores, this work draws heavily and explicitly on that of Jorgenson, and none of it has been subjected to the same thorough scrutiny which Brechling brought to bear on studies of United States data. (It is worth noting that the builders of RDX2 were well aware of the existence of the problems subsequently raised by that work. C.f. Helliwell *et al.* 1971.) Accelerator type effects do seem to be important for investment in both countries, and, for Britain, Pravin Trivedi (1970) found a marginally significant role for interest rates to play in determining inventory investment, a result which seems to have eluded those working with Canadian data; though John Bryant (1978) has produced similar results for the United States.

The influence of monetary variables on consumption is less well established for Britain and Canada than for the US. In particular, the type of wealth effects that figure so prominently in the FMP model seem to be barely present in British data (c.f. Deaton 1972). The influence of interest rates as relative prices on the demand for consumer durables is recognised in the Canadian RDX2 model, while they are also allowed to influence overall savings behaviour. In this model also, credit availability influences the housing market, though in CANDIDE monetary influences are transmitted to this market solely by interest rates.

There is little debate about the importance of availability effects on the housing market as far as Britain is concerned, because there the typical response of building societies to a shortage of mortgage funds has been to indulge in explicit rationing, rather than to allow a sufficiently large interest rate increase to clear the market. Even when the 'Radcliffe view' about the relative unimportance of monetary policy was at the height of its popularity, the availability of mortgage funds was regarded as a key factor in the new housing market, and events of recent years have done nothing to alter anyone's views on this issue. The mechanism at work here involves the borrowing and lending rates of institutions involved in the mortgage market being sticky, so that a rise in market interest rates elsewhere attracts funds from these institutions, leading to a shortage of mortgages at going interest rates, and hence to credit rationing in the housing market. (The mechanism in question is described in the *Radcliffe Report* 1959, paragraphs 292–95.) It is hardly surprising, given the frequency with which legal restrictions on down payments and the periods of consumer loans were varied in the 1950s and 1960s, that credit availability effects seem to have been important in influencing the demand for consumer durables in

Britain during those years (c.f. Hilton and Crossfield 1970 and Garganas 1975).

Now, the evidence sketched out here would, taken at face value, suggest that 'money matters' to a greater extent in the United States' economy than in Britain, and perhaps than in Canada also. Crude correlations between money and money incomes are better determined in United States' data; to the extent that information on timing is relevant to the issue, there seems less ambiguity about the direction of causation between the variables in those same data; and the details of an IS–LM type of transmission mechanism are perhaps easier to trace in the case of the United States. An alternative, and simpler, interpretation of the evidence, however, is that such a framework, although reasonably well adapted to the study of the United States, particularly the United States of the 1950s and 1960s from which so many of the results we have cited above are derived, is, in other cases, an inadequate model for investigating the links between money and money income.

Three well-known shortcomings of the IS–LM approach to macroeconomic questions are particularly relevant to this point of view. Firstly, the model does not deal satisfactorily with the fact that variations in money income are made up of fluctuations in both real income and prices; secondly, it ignores linkages between the government's budget and the behaviour of the money supply; and thirdly, it is a model of a closed economy. It seemed until recently that these problems merely required that the model be extended, that equations be added to it. The large-scale econometric models mentioned above of course all do extend what is essentially an IS–LM framework in one way or another to cope with these factors. It was not apparent that such extensions would also require us to modify our views about the qualitative nature and likely stability of the linkages between money and aggregate demand which we have already discussed. However, as we shall now see, recent theoretical and empirical work has indeed forced us to do just that, and hence casts doubt upon the extent to which the evidence cited so far enables us to come to grips with all the questions we might like to ask about the transmission mechanism.

3. MONEY INCOME, REAL INCOME, AND PRICES

The IS–LM model set out earlier holds the price level constant and determines the level of real income. A common practice (though not one adopted by the builders of big models) in adapting it to the analysis of the determination of money income has been to replace real variables with nominal variables, to postulate that the way in which, and the extent to which, variations in the quantity of money affect money income is independent of the breakdown of changes in money income between real income and the price level. Such a procedure does of course underlie Friedman and Meiselman type studies, and it was defended by Friedman (1971) on grounds of theoretical convenience; it has also been implemented in empirical work using small-scale IS–LM models by Ernest Tanner (1969) and Moroney and Mason (1971).

If we consider the vertical segment of the 'reverse L' aggregate supply curve and set Y constant in equations (1) and (2), we may derive the following expression:

$$P = \frac{1}{Y[l_1 + (l_2/a)\{1 - k(1-t)\}] - (l_2/a)(A+G)} M_s \qquad (4)$$

A simple comparison of equations (3) and (4) makes it obvious that, in terms of this model, the quantitative nature of the relationship between money and money income will depend upon whether real income or the price level is varying. Only if either l_2 approaches zero or a approaches infinity, do equations (3) and (4) reduce to the same expression, namely:

$$PY = (1/l_1)M_s \qquad (5)$$

Here the money multiplier's size is independent of the breakdown of money income between real income and prices, but only because of the simplifying assumption, built into our model at the outset, that the relationship between the demand for money and real income is linear. In the special case of the model underlying equation (5), this assumption implies that the real income elasticity of demand for money is unity, and hence is equal to the price level elasticity of demand. If the demand for money is not unit elastic with respect to real income, then even if the potential effects of interest rate variations on velocity are assumed away by making the

LM curve vertical or the IS curve horizontal, the size of the money multiplier will vary with the division of money income fluctuations between real income and prices.

The evidence already cited on the role of interest rates in determining various components of expenditure makes it hard to believe in a horizontal IS curve, and the evidence against a vertical LM curve is overwhelming. Moreover, whatever might have been its value in earlier periods, the short-run real income elasticity of demand for money, particularly if money is defined narrowly, seems to have been significantly below unity in the United States, and in virtually every other developed economy as well, since World War II. The theoretically predicted value of unity for the price level elasticity of demand for money, on the other hand, is supported by a good deal of evidence. (For evidence on these matters, see Laidler 1977, Ch. 7.)

Thus, although the practice of treating the determination of variations in money income as a problem prior to, and separate from, that of breaking such variations down between real income and prices would, as Friedman (1971) argued, greatly simplify macroeconomics, and though it is easy enough to find premises in terms of which such a practice could theoretically be justified, those premises are factually wrong. How much money income will change in response to a given change in the quantity of money depends upon how much of that change comes in real income and how much in the price level; and this in turn implies that the mechanisms which determine the interaction of prices and real output must be treated as an integral part of the transmission mechanism which links the quantity of money to money income. These arguments make the evidence generated by reduced-form studies of the Friedman –Meiselman type cited earlier hard to interpret, as I have argued (Laidler 1971) (but note that there is an even more fundamental reason, which arises from analysis involving the Rational Expectations hypothesis, why we must regard price and output interaction as part of the transmission mechanism; this is taken up below, see pp. 135–138).

In recent years, the 'expectations augmented Phillips curve' has become the centrepiece of models which attempt to come to grips with price and output interaction. Two alternative accounts of the behaviour underlying this relationship are to be found in the literature. The first account interprets the relationship in equilibrium terms, and the second in disequilibrium terms. The distinction between these two approaches is critical as far as the subject matter of this essay is concerned: the very idea of a 'transmission mechanism', at least as it is usually thought of in disequilibrium terms, is hard to square with the equilibrium interpretation of the curve. This interpretation of the Phillips curve, which was anticipated by Irving Fisher (1911, Ch. 4, 1926), lies at the heart of the work of Lucas (1972, 1975), Sargent (1976) and Barro (1978) on what I have elsewhere referred to as the neo-Austrian approach to macroeconomics. It may be formulated in terms of labour market or output market behaviour, and it is convenient to adopt the latter formulation here for expositional purposes. (As the reader will see, to do this involves attributing less than perfect price information to firms, instead of to the labour force, but the end result of the analysis, as far as price output interaction is concerned, is the same as that obtained by the more elaborate analysis discussed in Essay 3 above. Hence nothing but expositional simplicity rests upon this choice.)

Consider an economy made up of perfectly competitive firms, with the output of each depending upon the relative price ruling for that output. Thus, where Y_{it} is the output of the ith firm in time t, P_{it} is the price of that output and P_{it}^e the general price level as perceived by that firm, we have

$$Y_{it} = f(P_i/P_i^e)_t \qquad f' > 0 \qquad (6)$$

Summing over all firms, ignoring distribution effects, and using conventional symbols for aggregate output and the general price level, we get

$$Y_t = F(P/P^e)_t \qquad F' > 0 \qquad (7)$$

Using lower case letters for logarithms, assuming a log linear form for F, and measuring units of output so that y takes the value zero when $p_t = p_t^e$, equation (7) may be written

$$y_t = h(p_t - p_t^e) \qquad h > 0 \qquad (8)$$

If we define the inflation rate as

$$\Delta p_t \equiv p_t - p_{t-1} \qquad (9)$$

and the expected inflation rate as

$$\Delta p_t^e \equiv p_t^e - p_{t-1} \qquad (10)$$

we may rewrite equation (8) as an expectations augmented Phillips curve:

$$\Delta p_t = (1/h)y_t + \Delta p_t^e \tag{11}$$

According to the foregoing analysis, therefore, the expectations augmented Phillips curve (11) is simply another way of writing an aggregate supply curve (8), which can be used instead of the textbook 'reverse L' relationship. It can be brought together with an aggregate demand curve derived from an IS–LM framework in order to determine simultaneously, *for given expectations about prices*, the level of real income and prices.

There is a difficulty here. We can think of a change in the quantity of money operating through the type of 'transmission mechanism' discussed in the preceding section of this paper to change the quantity of goods and services demanded at any given price level, and hence to shift the aggregate demand curve. In order to restore equilibrium, output expands along the aggregate supply curve in response to an increase in the price level. However, that increase in the price level simply happens, and is of just the right size to generate the output change that will clear the market. A full account of the transmission mechanism would explain where this market-clearing price level change, to which all buyers and sellers respond, comes from.

In Hicks' (1974) 'flexprice' markets, dominated as they are by specialist traders, neither producers nor consumers set the prices at which trade takes place. Dealers find it profitable to gather information which is then used to ensure that the prices which they set are in fact market-clearing prices. These prices in turn become data to which consumers and producers respond. If all markets operated in such a fashion, we would (as I have argued at length in Essay 3) have a factual basis for the foregoing 'Fisherian' account of the expectations augmented Phillips curve. However, if markets did so operate, it would be impossible for the portfolio disequilibria, and discrepancies between demand and supply prices which we have already described as underlying the aggregate demand side of the transmission mechanism, to arise. The existence of mechanisms to ensure that market-clearing prices are established sufficiently rapidly to make it worthwhile to model the economy 'as if' the price level and output were always determined by the intersection of aggregate demand and supply curves, would prevent such disequilibria from materialising. The transmission mechanism would be that of Walrasian general equilibrium economics, and not that of Keynesian macroeconomics.

As such commentators as Clower (1965), Leijonhufvud (1968) and Coddington (1976) have stressed, we require some degree of price stickiness to prevent markets clearing and to set a disequilibrium transmission mechanism to work. Hicks' notion of a 'fixprice' market provides a basis for such analysis. He notes that many markets (and in particular the labour market which I shall discuss below) are of a type in which price decisions are taken by, or negotiated between, the same agents who take quantity decisions. The term which he applies to such markets reflects his judgement that prices in them adjust only slowly towards market-clearing values. Thus, in an economy containing such markets, discrepancies between actual and market-clearing prices may arise and may play a role in the transmission mechanism. In short, although it is certainly an advantage of the Fisherian version of the expectations augmented Phillips curve that it is clearly grounded in orthodox equilibrium microeconomics, and although it cannot be claimed that the alternative interpretation which I shall now discuss has such well-established micro foundations, the latter does have the advantage of treating prices as being set by firms rather than being taken by them 'from markets' dominated by specialist price setters. Hence this alternative, which is largely due to Phelps (1969), provides a basis for the analysis of the role that 'fixprice' markets play in the transmission mechanism.

Think of each firm in the economy as forming an expectation of what price it must charge in time t in order to maintain its real level of sales constant. Suppose that each firm sets its actual price above or below that level depending upon whether it wishes to contract or increase its level of sales. For the economy as a whole, there will exist some level of output and sales at which the number of firms (suitably weighted by their shares in output) which want to expand sales just equals the number which wish to contract. At that output level, the value for the general price index which results from their individual price-setting behaviour will be equal to an index of the prices which they expected would keep their sales level constant. If output and sales for the economy as a whole exceed this 'natural' level, there will be a preponderance of firms wishing to contract, so that the actual price level will be set above the 'expected price level' and *vice versa*.

Putting the end product of the above argument into algebraic terms, picking a log linear form, with units chosen so that the log of the output level at which the actual and expected price level are equal is zero, and using the same symbols as before for the 'expected price level', even though it is conceptually a somewhat different variable, enables us to write

$$p_t - p_t^e = gy_t \qquad (8a)$$

which is obviously the inverse form of equation (8) from which we may derive

$$\Delta p_t = gy_t + \Delta p_t^e \qquad (11a)$$

The choice of which way round to write this equation is, in the present context, neither arbitrary nor irrelevant. The 'Phelpsian' account of its derivation reverses the direction of proximate causation between output and prices at the level of the firm's behaviour, and in doing so enables us to describe a further step in the transmission mechanism between money and money income in the same disequilibrium terms as we described the earlier steps. As before, think of an increase in the money supply leading to a higher level of demand for goods and services at any price level. As that higher level of demand, perhaps amplified by a Keynesian multiplier process, materialises in the form of a higher level of real sales and real output, the number of firms wishing to contract their sales, or prevent them from expanding, will increase. Thus the price level will rise relative to its expected level, as these firms revise upwards the prices they set for their individual products in response to quantity disequilibria. What happens then depends upon how expectations about prices, which we have so far held constant, respond to this sequence of events.

This process can be described in an alternative way, which brings out more clearly the desirability of treating price and output interaction as an integral part of the transmission mechanism between money and money income. A higher than equilibrium quantity of money in the economy causes attempts to substitute other assets, and current consumption, for money. Such behaviour on the part of households must lead to an increase in firms' sales, and, if output does not respond immediately to meet this increase, to a rise in their holdings of money (and perhaps of such liquid assets as trade credit) and a diminution of their inventories. The act of increasing prices is an integral part of firms' response to the asset disequilibrium just described, if the Phelpsian account of the Phillips curve is accepted. Jonson (1976a) gives such an account of the transmission mechanism, while Jonson *et al.* (1976) have explicitly based much of the dynamics of their small-scale econometric model of the Australian economy on it, with some success. As the reader will recognise, and as Jonson acknowledges, the underlying mechanics of this process are not unlike those that would follow from the operation over real time of the Patinkin (1956, 1965) – Archibald–Lipsey (1959) account of the Real Balance Effect, which I have discussed in Essays 2 and 3 above.

It would be wrong to claim that, in the present state of knowledge, the factors determining the extent to which such an asset disequilibrium would be met by price changes on the one hand, and output and inventory changes on the other, are understood. Barro's (1972) study of the pricing behaviour of a monopolist who faces a stochastic demand function, and lump-sum costs of price adjustment, provides a potentially useful starting point for anyone dealing with this problem. Mussa (1976) has extended Barro's work to incorporate an explicit analysis of the behaviour of goods inventories, though not of liquid asset holdings. Mussa also explicitly analyses the wage and employment decisions of his firm, and of course, assumptions about the behaviour of employment and money wages have been implicit throughout the preceding discussion.

As I have already noted, there exists an interpretation of the interaction of money wages and unemployment analogous to the Fisherian account of price and output interaction; an account in which the supply of labour, and hence employment, is made a positive function of the difference between the actual and expected level of money wages. The expected money wage level in turn depends on expectations about the price level and about labour productivity. This approach thus interprets all unemployment as being of the voluntary search variety, as I have elsewhere stressed. (See Essay 3.) Phelps' (1968) own original account of money-wage–unemployment interaction has firms forming expectations about the level of money wages which will maintain employment constant, and setting wages above, or below, that level depending upon whether they desire to expand or contract their labour force. There then emerges a 'natural' level of search unemployment at which there is equality between the expected and actual wage on both sides of the market. When firms wish, on average, to reduce their labour forces, there emerges downward pressure on money wages relative to expectations and unemployment goes above its 'natural' level, and *vice versa*. Therefore, in Phelps' early work also, unemployment varies as a result of voluntary quits, though in his later work with Taylor (1977) where money wages are tied down by long-term contracts, this is no longer the case.

Mussa's (1976) analysis, as does much earlier work of Brechling (1965), explicitly incorporates lump-sum costs of adjusting the stock of employees and permits the manhours worked per employee to be a variable. The number of employees, and the intensity with which they work, both become variables chosen by the firm along with wages, rather than being generated by supply side responses to wages set by the firm, as they are in Phelps' original model. I would conjecture that analysis of this type complements the so-called 'contracts' literature (see Essay 3, pp. 91–92) as a basis for generating sufficient money wage and price rigidity to permit deviations of unemployment from its 'natural' level to be interpreted as involving 'involuntary' unemployment of the type analysed by Patinkin (1956, Ch. 13), Barro and Grossman (1975, Ch. 2) and Malinvaud (1977). If this conjecture is right, such unemployment would arise from rational behaviour, not in the face of arbitrarily assumed wage rigidity, but in the face of a failure of wages to fall fast enough to keep the labour market cleared when the presence of adjustment costs, and other factors, make it rational for agents to set money wages by contract for extended periods.

However we interpret its nature, if, as unemployment varied about its 'natural' level, money wages as well as prices did not in fact fluctuate relative to their expected levels, as the expectations augmented Phillips curve predicts, then the British 'Keynesian' position (c.f. Kahn 1976, 1977), in which an exogenously given money wage rate is the principal determinant of prices, would be essentially correct. Only the mark-up between wages and prices would be susceptible to variation in response to market forces. The evidence on the interaction of prices, wages, output and employment has been surveyed elsewhere (see Laidler and Parkin 1975, Section 3, and Santomero and Seater 1978) and shows that the price level does vary (relative to expectations) with the level of real output, while the level of money wages varies (again relative to expectations) with unemployment. Also, although the point is not a vital one, most studies show that the ratio of prices to money wages does seem to vary with market pressures (though Godley and Nordhaus 1972, who work in terms of normal costs rather than simply current wages, provide an exception here). All this is true, not only of the United States, but of Britain, Canada and many other countries.

Unemployment and output changes seem to precede the price and wage changes associated with them. To the extent that one may make inferences about the direction of causation from data on timing, the evidence here supports the Phelpsian, rather than the Fisherian, interpretation of the expectations augmented Phillips curve. Hence it is compatible with a chain of causation such as I described earlier, which does not rely in any way on the assumption of sufficient price flexibility to ensure that markets are always cleared. Also, a pattern of wage–price–employment–output interactions such as I have just described is a feature of both the FMP model and of RDX2: theory and econometric modelling have thus complemented one another in developing this aspect of the analysis of the transmission mechanism.

Even so, one *caveat* is in order here, because data on the timing of changes in aggregate variables need to be treated with caution. Not only are price level data typically based upon posted prices, which tend to lag behind actual market prices, but it is also possible that the price index as a whole moves sluggishly even when particular individual prices, important as far as producing supply side quantity responses are concerned, are changing by a significant amount. Thus, the considerations which I have raised in the last paragraph, though they weigh against the Fisherian interpretation of the Phillips curve, need further analysis before they can be regarded as being definitely inconsistent with it.

To sum up the argument so far, there is a good deal of empirical evidence that the economy works 'as if' the processes I have been describing are in operation, but there still exist important gaps in our knowledge of this stage in the transmission mechanism. I have suggested that the Clower–Patinkin–Barro–Grossman treatment of involuntary unemployment and of the multiplier process might have a part to play in the analysis of the transmission mechanism, but this is yet to be demonstrated in any conclusive fashion.

Moreover, the labour market analysis I have described, even as it underlies the Phelpsian version of the Phillips curve, takes no account of the presence of powerful bargaining units on the supply side of the market, so that many find it hard to swallow as an account of the processes whereby unemployment affects wage bargaining in labour markets as they exist, despite the amount of support that it gets from the empirical evidence. The work to which I have already alluded on what Gordon (1976) has called the 'new-new microeconomics', dealing as it does with the factors determining the optimal terms and length of wage and employment contracts, and the reasons for wage rigidity within the contract period, does, however, promise to help us fill these gaps in our knowledge (see Hall 1980 for a recent survey of this area).

4. THE ROLE OF INFLATION EXPECTATIONS

The discussion of the preceding section held expectations about prices constant, and kept them in the background. We are now in a position to look more closely at the role which such expectations play in the transmission mechanism. Most recent work, because it has been done against a background of severe inflation, takes it for granted that future prices are expected to differ from current prices. Even the substitution of a constant expected *rate of inflation* for the constant expected *price level* implicit in IS–LM analysis somewhat complicates the analysis of the channels of causation that run between money and money income.

Equation (11a) tells us that, ignoring real growth, if output is held at its 'natural' level, prices, and hence money income, will increase at the same rate as that at which the price level is expected to increase. The existence of a stable aggregate demand for money function implies that this can happen only if the money supply also expands at the expected rate of inflation in order to validate the price increase in question. If inflation expectations remain constant over time, then so will the actual inflation rate, so long as the percentage rate of change of the money supply also remains constant at the appropriate value. Money income and the money supply thus grow at the same rate, but there is no sense in which one can be said to be 'causing' the behaviour of the other. As we shall now see, however, what really complicates matters is not the mere existence of inflation expectations nor, as is well known, that they influence nominal interest rates, and hence the demand for real balances, as well as price-setting behaviour; it is that they themselves change endogenously over time.

To begin with, the presence of endogenous inflationary expectations makes it inappropriate to follow IS–LM analysis in treating an increase in level of the nominal money supply as the typical expansionary policy and a decrease as the typical contractionary one. Once we permit inflationary expectations to enter as proximate determinants of the behaviour of prices, so that it is possible for any ongoing rate of inflation to be validated by the appropriate monetary expansion rate, it is in general more helpful to think of a *rate of monetary expansion* in excess of the expected inflation rate as expansionary, and a *rate of expansion* below the expected inflation rate as contractionary. Thus, in dealing with the 'transmission mechanism', we should, as Friedman argued as long ago as 1958 (though not on the grounds advanced here), be concerned with a series of events set in motion by a change in the rate of monetary expansion rather than in the level of money supply.

Let us now trace out the consequences of a particular expansionary policy, namely an increase in the monetary expansion rate occurring when the economy is initially in a full equilibrium situation. To do so, we must extend the transmission mechanism sketched out earlier to allow for the influence of endogenous inflation expectations on both price-setting behaviour and the time path of interest rates, but we must also say something about how such endogenous expectations are formed. Let us, for the moment, adopt a postulate, whose first-order adaptive expectations special case is widely found in the literature, particularly that of the early 1970s, but which is by no means uncontroversial because of that. Let us assume that agents form expectations of inflation by observing the time path of the actual inflation rate, and extrapolating from it in such a way as to ensure that, if a constant inflation rate persists over time, the expected inflation rate will eventually come into equality with it.

An increase in the rate of expansion of the money supply to a pace faster than that necessary to validate an ongoing anticipated inflation will first lead to a build-up of real money balances, whose implicit own rate of return will therefore begin to fall relative to that on other assets. As a consequence, a process of substitution into other assets and into current consumption will be set in motion, with interest rates, both observable and unobservable, falling. The ensuing increase in current production will set in motion a multiplier process. Instead of having described the whole transmission mechanism, as they would have done in the context of the IS–LM model, the last two sentences have sketched only the first step in a more complex pattern of events.

Along with the increase in output and employment just postulated goes a tendency for firms to increase their prices, and for money wages to rise to levels in excess of the values these variables were initially expected to take. Given that there initially exists a particular value for the expected rate of inflation, this involves an increase of the actual inflation rate *relative* to that expected rate. If, with the passage of time, the actual inflation rate influences the expected rate, the latter must also begin to rise. In its turn, an increase in the expected rate of inflation has two interrelated effects on variables involved in the transmission mechanism. It puts upward pressure on the rates of interest which assets denominated in nominal terms bear, and, in increasing the opportunity cost of holding money, accentuates the very portfolio disequilibrium which sets going the first stage of the transmission mechanism, and which accelerating inflation begins to offset. It also causes the inflation rate to accelerate further through its effect on price-setting behaviour. It is impossible to follow subsequent steps in this ongoing dynamic process with verbal argument. However, since the small-scale models of Laidler (1975, Ch. 7), Stein (1975) and Jonson (1976b) all contain elements of the process we are here describing, and since all three are dynamically stable, the proposition that this process is stable is defensible as a working assumption. I shall therefore adopt it and describe the new equilibrium to which the economy will eventually move, and show that we can derive some information about the path whereby that equilibrium is reached by considering its properties.

Because, as equation (11a) tells us, the expected and actual inflation rates will differ so long as output is not at its 'natural' level, the new equilibrium, like the initial one, will see the economy operating at such a level of real output. The expected rate of inflation will be higher in this new equilibrium, and so the quantity of real balances held by the public will be smaller. *If* money is 'super-neutral' so that the 'natural' output level is independent of the inflation rate, and of any past history of disequilibrium in the economy (both of these being dubious assumptions supported by no empirical evidence of which I am aware, and the former, as Laidler and Parkin 1975, Section 2 show, being contradicted by a good deal of theoretical argument), then we would also expect to find real rates of interest returned to their initial levels, with nominal rates having increased by the same amount as the inflation rate. If money is not 'super-neutral', then we might find real rates either higher or lower in the new equilibrium. In either event, though, a higher and more rapidly rising volume of nominal expenditure would be associated with higher nominal interest rates. If real balances are to be lower in the new equilibrium then, on average, during the transition towards it, the rate of inflation must exceed the rate of monetary expansion and might indeed follow a cyclical path. Moreover, if nominal interest rates at first fall, but end up at a level higher than that ruling initially, they must on average rise during the transition.

The above propositions about the economy's behaviour are supported by empirical evidence. The influence of the expected rate of inflation on the quantity of real balances demanded is well established empirically, and not just during rapid inflation of the Latin American type and hyperinflations such as those studied by Cagan (1956). Its influence is also present in data drawn from France (Melitz 1976) and the United States (Shapiro 1973, Goldfeld 1973), in the post-war period. Moreover, the influence of inflation on nominal interest rates is also clearly reflected in empirical evidence, and the inverse relationship between such rates and the demand for money is one of the best established results in applied macroeconomics (see Laidler 1977, Ch. 7). Evidence supporting the influence of inflation on nominal interest rates goes back to Irving Fisher (1896) but, more to the point here, the work of William Gibson (1970) has established, at least for United States' data, the tendency of nominal interest rates to fall, and then quickly to rise above their original level, in the wake of increases in the rate of monetary expansion and *vice versa* for decreases. Gibson attributes the subsequent rise in interest rates to induced increases in income, rather than to any increases in the expected inflation rate, but he bases his conclusion on what is now widely regarded as an implausibly long estimate of the delay with which interest rates respond to changes in the expected inflation rate; thus the argument here reinterprets his evidence, but not, I believe, along implausible lines.

5. RATIONAL EXPECTATIONS AND THE TRANSMISSION MECHANISM

The argument of the last few pages has been based on the assumption that the principal determinant of the expected inflation rate is the behaviour of the actual rate. The 'rational expectations' approach to modelling the formation of inflation expectations, which is based on the work of Muth (1961) but in the more recent literature has been pioneered by Walters (1971) and Lucas (1972), challenges this assumption, and does so in such a way as to make the transmission mechanism even more awkward to get to grips with than the above analysis would suggest. This approach is usually encountered along with a Fisherian approach to the Phillips curve, but is logically independent of that approach. As we have seen above (Essay 3, pp.83–86) it argues that, because rational economic agents will not make systematic errors, they will act 'as if' they form their expectations about the inflation rate by using the forecast that would be yielded by a correct model of the economy in which they are operating, and 'as if' they expected every other agent in the economy to form his or her expectations in the same way.

A thorough-going application of this approach raises a number of difficulties. It downplays the point, made by Frenkel (1975), that the gathering and processing of information is costly, so that many agents might not find it worthwhile to compute the (statistically speaking) optimal forecast of the inflation rate. As Benjamin Friedman (1975) has argued, it ignores the fact that agents are not automatically endowed with knowledge of the economy's structure, so that learning about it must be an ongoing process. And it ignores the fact noted by Laidler (1976), Poole (1976) and Modigliani (1977), and subjected to formal analysis by Stanley Fischer (1977) and Phelps and Taylor (1977), that, if they are bound by long-term contracts, agents will be unable to act upon new information, however it might affect their view of the future. It is one thing to *expect* the inflation rate to behave in a particular way, and quite another to act upon that expectation and hence *anticipate* the behaviour of the inflation rate.

Moreover, under rational *anticipations*, any change in the monetary expansion rate, not accompanied by an appropriate step change in the level of the money supply, will lead to an instantaneously explosive inflation or deflation, unless the money market is cleared by an instantaneous, *and unforeseen*, step change in the price level before those anticipations become effective. Otherwise, as soon as it is known that the rate of monetary expansion is about to change, agents must recognise, not only that the long-run equilibrium rate of inflation has increased, but also that, in the absence of a step fall in the money supply, the economy must move to the higher price level associated with an increased velocity of circulation. The latter change, if it is foreseen, involves a step jump in the price level and hence an infinite rate of inflation for an instant. In the face of this, completely rational agents would 'flee from money' and generate an explosion in the price level. This problem, which was recognised by Sargent and Wallace (1973), who got around it by introducing an infinitesimal time delay in the formation of rational expectations which permitted the step jump of the price level to take place without being anticipated, also turns up in the analysis of the inflation tax in a perfect foresight monetary growth model. (See, for example, Auerheimer 1974 and Marty 1976.)

Arguments such as the above cast doubt only on a particularly extreme form of the rational expectations idea. A looser version of the same hypothesis would recognise that agents' knowledge of the way in which the economy works is imperfect, that data on the behaviour of particular variables are expensive to generate and process, and that changed expectations do not immediately lead to changes in activities. It would nevertheless insist that, for some agents at least, it is possible to use extraneous information on the behaviour of such variables as the money supply, and others with which we shall deal in more detail below, in order to generate a more accurate forecast of the behaviour of the inflation rate than could be had simply by extrapolating from past data on that variable; to do so at a cost which makes the exercise worthwhile; and then to act upon that forecast. Poole (1976) and Clements and Jonson (1980) both advance arguments along these lines.

If, as Walters (1971), Jonson and Mahoney (1974), Rutledge (1974) and Barro (1977a, 1978) have suggested, some agents were to discover a stable relationship between the rate of monetary expansion and the inflation rate, were to use data on the time path of the money supply in forming expectations of inflation, and were then to act upon these expectations, their behaviour would to some degree 'short circuit' the disequilibrium transmission mechanism which I have described above. The effect would be to make the expected rate of inflation which underlies price-setting activities, and the determination of nominal interest rates, depend in some measure *directly* upon the behaviour of the money supply. Thus, if specialist dealers in security markets were to note that the rate of monetary expansion had increased, and to change the prices of securities to reflect changes in expectations of inflation, they could do so before any discrepancy between supply and demand in such markets in fact appeared. More important, if the rate of monetary expansion increased, and this very fact led some firms to expect that there could be an increase in the inflation rate, they would begin to increase the prices of their output at a more rapid rate, without any intervening chain of asset disequilibrium or output change being necessary to prompt such behaviour.

If *all* agents acted in this way, and expected all other agents to do the same, and if we accept the assumptions necessary to rule out instantaneous and explosive inflation, then the only effects of any change in the behaviour of the money supply would be on prices. The transmission mechanism, operating through portfolio disequilibrium and output changes, would never be called into play and monetary policy would have no short-run real effects. We have already seen that there are a number of reasons for not taking the extreme form of rational expectations, which underlies these propositions, too literally. That in no way detracts from the importance of the hypothesis for the analysis of the transmission mechanism; because, even if only some agents act upon 'rational' expectations, their activities imply the existence of yet another channel whereby monetary changes affect money income and expenditure, one which operates directly through expectations and their influence on price-setting behaviour.

Now, the arguments presented in this section have important, and, to a degree, destructive, implications for much of the evidence on the transmission mechanisms of monetary policy sketched out in Section 2. That is one of the important implications of the work of Sargent and Wallace (1975) and Lucas (1976). If the division of changes in money income between the price level and output must be regarded as an integral part of that transmission mechanism, rather than as a matter which can be analysed separately from it, then we must pay particular attention to the way in which endogenous, and variable, inflationary expectations impinge upon behaviour when we study that transmission mechanism. To begin with, this is of crucial importance in assessing how much attention we should pay to evidence on the influence of market interest rates on various categories of expenditure. As far as the demand for durable goods is concerned – both consumer and producer durables – it is real, rather than nominal, rates of interest that matter, or nominal rates taken in conjunction with expected inflation rates; and yet, all too often, it is nominal interest rates alone that have been used in empirical work, as Fisher and Sheppard (1974) have noted.

Of course, if the expected inflation rate is more or less constant, variations in nominal interest rates will reflect variations in real rates, and little if any harm is done by using the former. It is, perhaps, not without significance that work utilising United States' data drawn from periods starting after the end of the Korean War and terminating during the 1960s – such as, for example, Hamburger's study of the demand for consumer durables – has produced evidence showing an influence of nominal interest rates on expenditure; for this was a period of notable price stability. Moreover, the studies of Tanner (1969) and Moroney and Mason (1971), based on an IS–LM framework cast in nominal terms, seemed to produce satisfactory enough results, and used data from these years. This too is significant, because the foregoing discussion would imply that the IS–LM model adapted to determine money income is more likely to be viable at times and places where the expected rate of inflation is approximately zero, and fluctuates little, than at others.

Whenever or wherever there is any reason to suppose that variations in the actual inflation rate might have been reflected in variations in the expected inflation rate, the relevance of the simple IS–LM framework becomes suspect. The same circumstances render any correlation, or lack thereof, between nominal interest rates and expenditures of any type irrelevant to deciding upon the existence, or otherwise, of a well-determined linkage between monetary policy and nominal income. After all, it is real, and not nominal, interest rates which should influence expenditure decisions. Moreover, the rational expectations notion makes it possible to picture circumstances in which variations in the quantity of money can directly affect money income – specifically prices – without generating any evidence that expenditure decisions are sensitive to variations in interest rates, or to any other relative price fluctuations. Such linkages will come into play and be observable only when the consequences of monetary changes are not fully anticipated by the agents generating the data for us to study.

This means that the crude correlations between money and money income which we discussed earlier are more important than one might initially have supposed, or than many might think desirable, as pieces of evidence about the transmission mechanism. That such correlations vary in strength between time periods and across countries may no doubt be explained in part by the considerations that earlier led us to the conclusion that the division of money income fluctuations between output and price level changes is of vital importance. However, such an explanation still leaves questions about the direction of causation between the variables to be discussed further. Results on this matter are, as we have seen, somewhat more clear-cut for the United States than for other economies. In the following two sections of this essay, I shall consider how the potentially endogenous nature of the money supply impinges upon the transmission mechanism and hence upon the way in which we might interpret these results.

6. THE ENDOGENEITY OF THE MONEY SUPPLY

The standard IS–LM model usually treats the money supply as an exogenous variable, whose value is determined independently of fiscal policy, and it also deals with a closed economy. The structure of the model does not necessarily imply that the money supply must always be treated as an exogenous variable; but it does limit the cases in which it can become endogenous to those where the monetary authorities set a target for the nominal interest rate and are then forced to let the money supply adjust to any value necessary to achieve that target. It is certainly true that interest rates have frequently been held more or less constant by central banks, not least, for example, during the 1941–51 period in the United States, but the adoption of such a policy regime is of course far from being the only possible source of endogeneity in the money supply. The way in which the government decides to meet its own budget constraint, and the exchange rate regime it adopts, both have potentially important implications for the way in which the money supply will interact with other economic variables, and hence for the way in which we should interpret evidence about that interaction.

It was Carl Christ's (1969) paper which first drew widespread attention to the importance of the government's budget constraint. Government expenditure not financed by taxes or by borrowing from the public must be financed by borrowing from the banking system. This latter method of finance, the only one Christ analysed, necessarily involves money creation and will alter the structure of portfolios in the private sector. In a series of papers (e.g. 1976), Brunner and Meltzer have greatly extended Christ's analysis, analysing both money and bond financed fiscal policy in a model in which government debt, like money, is an imperfect substitute for private capital. Their work stresses the fact that policy-induced IS curve shifts must also lead to LM curve shifts, except in the special case in which changes in government expenditure are matched by equal changes in taxes. This is true even if we assume that government interest-bearing debt is not to any degree net wealth. Moreover, because anything but complete tax financing of government expenditure implies the creation of money and/or government debt, these shifts will persist for as long as any deficit arising from a fiscal policy change also persists (unless money and debt are created in just the right proportions to keep the LM curve stationary).

These considerations have important implications for macroeconomics in general and, for example, underlie the contributions of Blinder and Solow (1973) and Tobin and Buiter (1976) to the 'crowding out' debate. They argue that, provided government bonds are net wealth to a degree sufficient to ensure that a bond financed deficit sets in motion an expansion of output towards a stable equilibrium (or of the price level, if output is held constant at a capacity level), the equilibrium in question will occur at a higher value of output (or prices) than if the deficit were money financed. This at first sight counter-intuitive result stems from two properties of their models. First, equilibrium occurs when the budget is brought into balance by an expansion of income which increases tax revenues. Second, the government's cash outlays must necessarily be higher when its debt has been increased by the issue of interest-bearing bonds, than when it has been increased by the issue of non-interest-bearing money. The behaviour of the private sector is important only to the extent that it produces wealth effects strong enough to guarantee that the stable equilibrium about which inferences are drawn exists. Otherwise the characteristics of that equilibrium depend completely on the arithmetic properties of the government budget constraint. Thus, we need pass no judgement on its importance for macroeconomics in general to conclude that this aspect of the 'crowding out' debate is of only peripheral interest in the context of the problems under discussion here. Nevertheless, noteworthy implications for the way in which we discuss the transmission mechanism, and evidence about it, do flow from other aspects of the literature on the government's budget constraint.

First, we can hardly ignore the fact that if the monetary authorities of a country are expected to accommodate that country's treasury – as until the mid-1970s they were to a greater extent in Britain and Canada than in the United States – then expansionary fiscal policy will be accompanied by expansionary monetary policy. In such circumstances it is bound to be difficult for 'reduced-form' studies, that rely on correlations between money and autonomous expenditure on the one hand, and money income on the other, to distinguish between the direct influence of fiscal changes, and of the indirect influence which they have as a result of being financed by money creation. This is a point of which Kaldor (1970) made much. It will not in general be impossible so to distinguish, because it is the *rate of change* of the money supply, and *not its level*, which is related to the *level* of the budget deficit in these circumstances; any correlation over time between the level of the money supply and its rate of change will, though, lead to difficulties.

Further and related problems arise from government expenditures, as well as taxes, being variables which themselves depend in part upon real income and prices. The endogeneity of the deficit implicit in this fact, combined with the existence of the government budget constraint, entails the possibility of causation running from the level of money income to the rate of change of the nominal money supply, as well from the latter to the rate of change of nominal income. This would cause no problem if increases in money income could be relied upon to have a negative effect on the rate of money creation, because then the two-way causation would be easy to disentangle. There can be no *a priori* presumption that this will be the case, even though it is usual to think of an increase in money income leading to a fall in the budget deficit and hence in the rate of monetary expansion.

It is natural to think in the above terms, because one normally expects an increase in income to involve an increase in tax receipts and a fall in government expenditures. That is how 'built-in stabilisers' are expected to work. However, for some economies at least, it may be crucial to consider the division of changes in money income between real output and the price level before accepting such a conclusion. For example, in Britain, until 1977, government expenditure was planned in volume terms: nominal expenditures therefore automatically rose with the general price level. Moreover, government employees' salaries, and many transfer payments, have become increasingly sensitive to the price level in recent years, both in Britain and in Canada. To the extent that inflation influences nominal interest rates, debt servicing costs rise, not with the price level, but with the inflation rate. On the revenue side, Canadian income taxes are formally, albeit partially, indexed as they are in Britain, where marginal tax rates are also constant across a wide band of money income; the influence of inflation on effective real tax rates, which in the United States can be relied upon to contribute to a falling deficit in the face of inflation, is not so sharply present in these other countries. And none of this is to mention the often-noted tendency of political processes to introduce a positive dependence of government expenditures on tax receipts.

The point of all this is that, in countries such as Britain and Canada, in situations where the major source of an increase in money income is rising prices rather than rising real output, it is conceivable that the government's nominal deficit will increase rather than decrease. This is especially likely to be the case if we have a state of affairs in which rising money income is the net result of rising prices and falling output. If the nominal deficit is permitted by the authorities stably to influence the rate of monetary expansion (even though there is no logical reason why it should be), the latter in its turn will cause not just further increases in the level of money income, but an increase in its rate of change – in what could prove to be an explosive inflationary spiral. At the very least, there exists the possibility of the interaction between money and money income over time involving positive effects running in both directions. It would take detailed empirical work, of a type not yet carried out, to test the validity of this conjecture. However, if it is valid, then it might be difficult indeed to disentangle the complex causative patterns involved from the results generated by reduced-form equations of the type used in the studies mentioned earlier, or indeed from studies that employ Sims' methods. The extent to which problems of this sort have influenced the outcome of work of this type, for countries such as Britain and Canada, would be well worth looking into.

7. ENDOGENOUS MONEY AND EXPECTATIONS

A further and important implication of the existence of a government budget constraint for our knowledge of the transmission mechanism arises when we analyse it in conjunction with the rational expectations notion. Earlier I noted that, if there existed a stable relationship between the rates of monetary expansion and inflation, some agents might use direct observation of the rate of monetary expansion to form expectations about the behaviour of the inflation rate. However, if the money supply itself is an endogenous variable whose time path depends stably and predictably upon the size of the government's deficit, and the manner in which it is financed, rational agents could use information about the deficit, among other variables, to form expectations about the time path of the money supply in order to generate, in turn, expectations of inflation. We can thus conceive of the actual rate of monetary expansion as the sum of two components, one expected and the other unexpected. Expected variations in the monetary expansion rate upon which agents were free to act should lead directly, via a rational expectations mechanism, to variations in the inflation rate; but unanticipated variations should have effects on output and employment as well as on the inflation rate.

Empirical work by Barro (1977a, 1978) for the United States, and by Wogin (1976) and Saidi and Barro (1976) for Canada, has attempted to put this proposition to the test. They all attempt to divide the monetary expansion rate up between a forecast component and residuals from that forecast, and then to show that unemployment and output fluctuations correlate only with the residuals so derived. Moreover, Barro (1978) goes on to show that forecast changes in the monetary expansion rate are correlated with contemporaneous changes in the inflation rate.

Feige and Pearce (1976) might be thought to have produced results inconsistent with these applications of the rational expectations idea. They apply optimal time series forecasting techniques to United States data on inflation for the period 1953–71, and then show that information on the behaviour of the money supply does not permit any improvement to be made in inflation forecasts derived by these methods. However, under a stable policy regime, the feedback rules used by the monetary authorities to decide upon their policy actions would be implicit in the lag structure which Feige and Pearce's forecasting technique applies to the past behaviour of the inflation rate, and their technique would fail to isolate effects of money on prices even if they were present in the data. Thus their results are not in conflict with those of Barro, but they do show that his is not a strong test of the rational expectations hypothesis. Sargent (1976a) has stressed the need to test this hypothesis against data sets within which different policy regimes have been in force, in order to overcome the problem posed by considerations such as these.

It should also be noted that Barro's work is cast in terms of a model in which the Phillips curve is interpreted along Fisherian lines, and in which, therefore, there can be no question of a disequilibrium transmission mechanism, such as I am discussing in this essay, having any role to play. As I have argued in Essay 3 above, such a model is very hard to reconcile with a good deal of empirical evidence about the so-called 'short-run' demand for money function, so that I find many of Barro's results hard to accept at face value. Nevertheless, as I have also argued, there is no incompatibility between a traditional disequilibrium model of the transmission mechanism and the proposition that such a mechanism can be bypassed to the extent that agents monitor money supply behaviour when they form expectations about the future course of prices. Barro's results make it difficult to ignore this possibility, even if one does not accept all aspects of the model in terms of which they have been generated.

Application of the rational expectations idea to the analysis of the behaviour of open economies has been more extensive than the two studies of Canada already mentioned. In this context, it leads to a set of predictions which are supported by more, and perhaps stronger, empirical evidence than that which we have just considered. How the openness of an economy impinges upon the conduct of monetary policy and its transmission mechanism depends upon the exchange rate regime in force.

Consider first a fixed exchange rate regime. The maintenance of a fixed rate must involve a commitment by a country's monetary authorities to buy and sell their own currency at a fixed price in terms of others. Thus, unless sterilisation is feasible, they must surrender control over the quantity of money, exactly as they would were they to peg the price of bonds instead of the price of foreign exchange. The traditional view of the operation of a fixed exchange rate has always recognised the balance of payments as a source of monetary expansion or contraction unless reserve flows are sterilised; but the period of time over which sterilisation operations can be expected to be successful is widely agreed to have diminished markedly with the growth of international capital mobility in the 1960s. (On this matter see, e.g., Bell 1974.) Hence, I here neglect sterilisation operations as being a short-term complication which does not alter the essence of the analysis.

The traditional view of the balance of payments mechanism under fixed exchange rates would lead us to expect that, if the inflation rate in the world economy were to accelerate, and if the domestic authorities did not simultaneously undertake an expansionary policy, the home country's balance of payments would become increasingly favourable. Its rate of monetary expansion would increase in either case, and ultimately a readjustment of its domestic price level and inflation rate to values compatible with balance of payments equilibrium would take place. In this traditional view, the purely domestic aspects of the chain of causation would be no different from those through which a change in the monetary expansion rate would operate in a closed economy; although it is worth noting that the same characteristics of international capital markets which render sterilisation operations less viable, also put severe limits on the extent to which domestic interest rates can deviate from those ruling in the world economy, and hence on the role which they could play in that mechanism.

The rational expectations notion undermines this traditional view of the transmission mechanism in an open economy; which is perhaps just as well, since it has long been known to be incompatible with evidence generated under the gold standard. (See, e.g., Yeager 1966, Ch. 14.) If an increase in the world inflation rate is going to lead to an increase in the monetary expansion rate via the consequences of a balance of payments surplus, then rational agents would expect this to affect the time path of domestic prices. Hence domestic inflation expectations will be directly influenced by the time path of world prices. Domestic interest rates, even on assets not directly tradeable on world markets, would then rise when the world inflation rate increased. The effect of inflation expectations on price-setting behaviour would also result in there being a direct causative link running from world to domestic prices. If expectations are formed in this way, then monetary expansion, either coming through the balance of payments (or brought about by a change in the rate of domestic credit expansion), may be regarded as accommodating, rather than causing, any change in the time path of domestic money income which results from a change in the world inflation rate. Moreover, it is quite conceivable that variations in the path of money income, caused by changes in the world inflation rate, might lead, rather than lag behind, accompanying variations in the quantity of money.

The process I have just sketched out could give all the appearances of 'reverse causation' between money and money income in data generated by an open economy operating a fixed exchange rate, at least where the major sources of disturbance lay in the world economy, as I showed in the small model set out elsewhere (Laidler 1975, Ch. 9). The key element here is the role played by world prices, by way of their effect on inflation expectations, in determining domestic price-setting behaviour. In a pioneering study, Jonson, Mahar and Thompson (1974) showed that world prices had an important and systematic direct effect on inflation in Australia in the 1950s and 1960s. Parkin, Sumner and Ward (1976), in a study of wage–price behaviour in the United Kingdom, generated a similar finding for that country, as did Spinelli (1976) in a study of Italy for the period 1954–73. Cross and Laidler (1976) derived similar results from data on 19 countries for the years 1952–70 (the influence of world prices on expectations being at a minimum in the case of the United States). Furthermore, papers building on the work of Brunner (1974) and dealing with the United States (Dutton 1978), Germany (Neumann 1978), Sweden

(Myhrman 1979), France (Fourcans 1978), the Netherlands (Korteweg 1978), Italy (Fratianni 1978), and a number of open economies (Korteweg and Meltzer 1978) all test, among other things, for the direct influence of world inflation on domestic inflation and find a role for it to play. Note, though, that with the exception of the Korteweg, and Korteweg and Meltzer, studies, import prices, rather than world prices in general, are used in this work.

Exchange rate changes under a fixed rate regime also have, for given behaviour of the domestic credit expansion rate, predictable consequences for the balance of payments and hence the money supply. It is therefore noteworthy that Laidler (1975, Ch. 10) found that, over the period 1919–70, the qualitative nature of price and output interaction for Britain could be predicted with an expectations augmented Phillips curve that utilised error learning, except for the years following exchange rate changes. Moreover, Carlson and Parkin (1975) derived an estimate of the expected inflation rate for Britain directly from survey data, and found that it increased markedly, and otherwise inexplicably, after the November 1967 devaluation. Laidler and O'Shea (1980), in their small macro model of the United Kingdom, also found a significant 'catch up' effect of this devaluation on prices.

These results, dealing as they do with the behaviour of expectations in the wake of abrupt policy changes, provide evidence in favour of what I have termed the 'loose' version of the rational expectations hypothesis. Taken in conjunction with the more general arguments advanced earlier about the formation of inflation expectations in a fixed exchange rate open economy, they also go a long way towards explaining why British data, in particular, produce such ambiguous results about the direction of causation between money and money income in studies that rely on the timing of fluctuations in time series to generate evidence of causation. The reader should note here that although the authors of the above studies were explicitly aware that the openness of the economy made a difference to the manner in which expectations were formed, and that the nature of the exchange rate regime would also make a difference, they did not explicitly recognise that this could be regarded as a special case of the more general phenomenon which is now known as rational expectations. Thus there is an element of re-interpretation to the foregoing account of the work in question.

The expectations mechanism sketched above is not the only route whereby changes in world prices, or in the exchange rate, could impinge directly upon domestic prices, without the intervention of changes in the money stock. The 'mark-up' pricing hypothesis has long been an important component of models of the inflationary process, and plays a crucial role in determining prices in large macro models. In open economies, the role of import prices as a component of production costs has long attracted attention as a means whereby inflationary impulses could be directly imported from abroad. For example, Leslie Dicks-Mireaux (1961) and Lipsey and Parkin (1969) both found that such a variable could be given an important role in an aggregate price determination equation for Britain, while import prices contribute significantly to the prox-imate determination of the price level in both the LBS model of Britain, and the RDX2 model of Canada. I am aware of only one test, and a rudimentary one at that (contained in Laidler 1976b), which has attempted to discriminate between an expectations and an 'import cost-push' mechanism as the principal means by which world price level fluctuations are transmitted into open economies under fixed exchange rates. The results of that test favoured the expectations mechanism, but, given that there had been only one direct test of this question, any conclusion based on its outcome must be regarded as extremely tentative.

Either of the above mechanisms could in principle lead to an appearance of 'reverse causation' between money and money income in an open economy. However, it should be stressed that the appearance of rising prices accommodated by monetary expansion which might be generated by either mechanism would exist only at the level of the individual economy, so that the foregoing analysis helps us to interpret evidence only for individual open economies. Because it treats the behaviour of the price level in the rest of the world as exogenous, it cannot be looked upon as providing a complete account of the relationship between the behaviour of money and money income. A full treatment of the problems with which this essay is dealing, for a fixed exchange rate open economy, would have to include an account of what it is that determines the behaviour of money income at the level of the 'closed' world economy; and would treat the mechanisms described above as elements in the process whereby variations in economy-wide income impinge upon various regions of the economy. (See Parkin 1977a for a succinct account of what is involved in explaining the behaviour of the world price level in terms of that of a world money supply.)

The adoption of a flexible exchange rate gives the domestic monetary authorities the ability to do what they will with the money supply. This does not mean, though, that the transmission mechanism for monetary policy will be just as it would be in a closed economy, even if we ignore questions concerning expectations. For example, in the LBS model (as in RDX2) import costs play an important role in determining prices. Under flexible rates, the LBS model has expansionary monetary policy driving down the exchange rate. The subsequent rise in the domestic price of imports plays a key role in driving up domestic prices. (See Ball and Burns 1976.) Such a chain of causation, which also underlies Hicks' (1974, 1976) analysis of the role played by an economy's openness in the inflationary process, obviously could not be incorporated in a model of a closed economy. A completely flexible exchange rate is, in any event, an extreme case. When they abandon a fixed rate, monetary authorities frequently retain the notion that there is a desirable value, or range of values, for the exchange rate. If they do treat the exchange rate as a policy target, they must also stand ready to make the behaviour of the domestic money supply compatible with the maintenance of whatever range of values they decide to aim for.

Such a policy regime, often referred to as a 'dirty float', shares certain characteristics with a fixed exchange rate. Under it the domestic money supply is still open to influence from the rest of the world in a systematic way, so that events in the outside world are relevant to expectations about the time path of domestic prices. Thus, even with some degree of exchange rate flexibility, the traditional disequilibrium channels whereby monetary changes influence money income may be bypassed just as, it has been argued, they are bypassed under fixed rates. Arguments such as these might well explain why difficulties of interpreting money–money-income correlations, similar to those encountered with British data, also arise in studies of Canada, despite the economy having operated nominally flexible exchange rates for a good part of the post-war period. This conjecture receives support from the work of Caves and Feige (1980) who, using a Sims-type test, show that for Canada 'causation' ran primarily from the exchange rate to money, rather than *vice versa*, at least before 1975. This result, taken at face value, implies that, even under flexible exchange rates, monetary policy was geared to maintaining the exchange rate at a particular value, rather than to achieving domestic targets. However, things are not always so. For example, Howson's (1975) conclusions about post-1931 Britain, noted earlier, suggest that, in that episode, monetary policy was geared to achieving domestic targets and hence would be thought of as 'causing' the behaviour of the exchange rate.

The general implications of the matters discussed in this section for the transmission mechanism between money and money income are easy enough to draw, but are of profound importance for the way in which we view macroeconomics. We have seen that there is evidence consistent with the proposition that agents do use information on the behaviour of variables that influence the behaviour of the money supply to form expectations about inflation. However, if agents are free to act on their expectations, forecast changes in the money supply will impinge directly upon money income through the effect of those expectations on prices. Only changes in the rate of monetary expansion which are not anticipated will have their effects transmitted to money income through the traditional channels of portfolio disequilibrium, output changes and price reactions to output disequilibrium. Thus, the extent to which a particular change in the monetary expansion rate is divided up between an anticipated component and an unantici-pated one will influence the way its effects are transmitted. This division of course depends upon the way in which agents themselves form their expectations, and on the extent to which the nature of their individual contractual obligations leave them free to act upon those expectations. We have empirical evidence consistent with the view that this in turn depends upon such things as the way in which the authorities finance their budget deficits and the way in which they conduct themselves in the foreign exchange market. In short, the nature of the transmission mechanism for monetary policy itself depends in part upon the manner in which monetary policy is carried out and the way in which it interacts with fiscal and exchange rate policy.

Far from regarding the structure of the economy as something which may be taken as given for purposes of analysing alternative policies, we must recognise, as Lucas (1976) has argued, that it varies with the conduct of policy. If the structure of the economy through which policy effects are transmitted does vary with the goals of policy, and the means adopted to achieve them, then the notion of a unique 'transmission mechanism' for monetary policy is a chimera and it is small wonder that we have had so little success in tracking it down.

8. SUMMARY AND CONCLUSIONS

The principal theme of this essay is easily summarised. The IS–LM model provided a common theoretical framework in terms of which a spectrum of viewpoints about the nature of the transmission mechanism of the effects of monetary policy could be reduced to questions about the empirical magnitudes of the parameters of particular behaviour relationships. The model treated the money supply as an exogenous variable independent of fiscal policy, dealt with a closed economy, and offered no satisfactory way to analyse the division of changes in money income between real income and prices. Each of these shortcomings seemed open to a remedy that involved extending the structure without, at the same time, altering its basic properties; but, in the event, the attempt to solve these problems has led us to a fundamental reassessment of the nature of macroeconomic analysis.

At the heart of this reassessment lie the results of the search for the 'missing equation' which divides up changes in money income between real income and prices. To begin with, it has become apparent that the processes underlying this division must be treated as forming part of the transmission mechanism which links money and money income, rather than as involving a subsequent, and analytically separable, series of events. The expectations augmented Phillips curve, which is the most popular candidate to fill the role òf 'missing equation', rests on theoretical foundations which are as yet not fully developed, particularly in its disequilibrium version. There seems to be a good deal of empirical evidence in its favour; but the nature of the micro postulates, particularly as regards the labour market, which underpin the price stickiness upon which it is based, is still unclear and controversial. It is hardly surprising, therefore, that much debate about the transmission mechanism has in recent years centred on labour market behaviour.

Even so, it is not doubts about the way in which the forces of supply and demand operate in the labour market, which have undermined our conventional way of thinking about macroeconomic problems. Rather, it has been theoretical and empirical work on the role which price expectations play in determining all kinds of behaviour (including labour market behaviour), which has forced us to rethink so much of our analysis. If such expectations were related to the behaviour of particular economic variables in a stable and discoverable way, then even if such relationships differed between agents, the way in which they were determined could be treated as part of the structure of the economy. We could argue that, to the extent that we had not yet discovered such relationships, there existed a gap in our understanding of the structure of the economy, of the transmission mechanism through which policy, including monetary policy, operates to influence prices and output. That would be a problem, but not a basic one, because it could eventually be solved by empirical work.

However, the issue raised for macroeconomics by the emphasis we now lay upon expectations is more fundamental. If economic agents are capable of recognising that economic policy, and the institutional framework against whose background it is carried out, influence the environment in which they themselves operate, then it is plausible to postulate that information about the conduct of economic policy, and about that institutional background, will be used by at least some of them in forming their expectations. Hence, the way in which fiscal policy, or the exchange rate regime adopted by an open economy, interact with monetary policy will influence not just the values of those expectations, but the very manner in which they are formed. Moreover, we do have empirical evidence to suggest that this is more than just a theoretical possibility.

It follows from all this that there is no such thing as a unique transmission mechanism for monetary or any other kind of policy, knowledge of which will enable us first to discover how, in particular historical episodes, policies different from those actually implemented might have worked; and second, to choose in any current situation the best policy from a menu of alternatives. Rather, there is potentially a different transmission mechanism for every policy regime. If this is so, the contents of the famous 'black box' have no unique structure; which certainly would explain the difficulties we have encountered over the last two decades in trying to discover what that structure is. Whether it will prove possible, in building macro theories and designing macro policies, to generate empirically useful hypotheses about the way in which the nature of the transmission mechanism varies with the conduct of policy, so that it becomes feasible systematically to allow for the endogeneity of the transmission mechanism, even if only over a limited range of policy alternatives, must remain to be seen.

5

On the Case for Gradualism

1. INTRODUCTION

For more than a decade now, governments throughout the Western world have been struggling with the problem of combating inflation. With the passage of time, the view that inflation is essentially a monetary phenomenon, to be coped with by means of monetary policy, has gained wider and wider acceptance, not least among those responsible for the conduct of policy. In the public perception of these things there exists a body of doctrine, known as 'Monetarism', which seems to say that, if only the money supply is brought under control, so will be inflation. The proponents of this doctrine are often portrayed as suggesting that the cure for inflation is really rather a 'simple' matter, or 'simplistic' in the vocabulary of their critics. To put matters this way is misleading, and always has been.

The economic theory which underlies advocacy of a monetary cure for inflation is relatively straightforward. However, monetary policy affects variables other than the inflation rate and, if monetary policy is nevertheless devoted to achieving price level targets, it cannot be used for other ends. Also, and quite obviously, there exists a whole host of policy problems which are not monetary in nature, but which nevertheless might reasonably require the attention of governments while they simultaneously attempt to cope with inflation. All of these matters make the actual conduct of a monetarist anti-inflation policy anything but simple. This essay seeks to clarify the issues involved in the use of monetary policy, conceived of as control of the rate of growth of the money supply, to bring inflation under control, in the hope that proponents and opponents alike of such policy will come to have a better appreciation of the complexities that must inevitably arise if it is to be implemented successfully.

2. PRICE STABILITY AND A MONETARY RULE

The first step in designing policy to produce a non-inflationary economy is to set a reasonable and attainable goal. It is clearly impossible to achieve a state of affairs in which the cost of living for each and every member of the community remains constant on a day-by-day or even a year-by-year basis. Even if some overall measure of the general price level were to be held absolutely constant over time – and as we shall see in a moment, that is hardly an attainable goal – different members of the community would find their own personal cost of living varying, perhaps up and perhaps down, at any particular moment, as a result of relative price changes. For example, the relatively poor spend a larger proportion of their incomes on food than do the relatively rich. A bad harvest would cause the price of food to rise, and even if other prices fell so that the general price level were stable, that would still cause the cost of living to rise for the poor. There is no guaranteed way of avoiding bad harvests or the myriad other shocks which can cause relative price changes and it is therefore idle to pretend that everyone can be guaranteed a constant cost of living. The best that can be done as far as the price level is concerned is to follow policies which will ensure that, overall, taking one year with another, the rate of change of some reasonably representative price index will vary about a constant rate close enough to zero that the community finds any remaining tendency for prices to drift up (or down) tolerable. This is a modest goal, to be sure, but it has the great virtue of being attainable, and once attained, it ought to be sustainable as well.

In any country long-run stability in the inflation rate at a low level, once achieved, would be sustained if its Central Bank, or whatever other agency might be in control of such matters, maintained year in and year out a policy of making the supply of money grow at an appropriately chosen rate. The basis for this proposition is, in broad outline at least, the same now as it was when Milton Friedman set it out in 1960. Such a policy would work in any country where there existed some degree of price flexibility and an aggregate demand for money function which was, at least in the long run, stable. That seems to include just about every country which has ever been studied, and certainly advanced economies such as the United Kingdom, the United States and Canada.

Let us consider the demand for money first of all. The firms, households and other institutions which make up any economy use money – currency and bank deposits – to carry on their everyday business; and each one of them, on average, might be expected to keep by him an amount of cash that is related to the volume of market transactions he is involved in, and to the average price level at which those transactions take place. A wide variety of motives may be invoked to explain such behaviour (see Laidler 1977, Part 2), but the important matter from the point of view of policy is not why any particular agent might hold money, but whether the aggregate consequences of such individual behaviour can be described by a simple and stable function. Though any individual's desired money holding might, and perhaps does, fluctuate unpredictably over time, a great deal of empirical evidence tells us that such fluctuations tend to cancel out as we aggregate over individual agents; so that, in fact, for the economy as a whole there exists a reasonably stable relationship between the level of real national income and the general price level on the one hand, and the amount of money that the economy requires to carry on its business on the other.

Even so, I have referred to this relationship as *stable* and not *constant*. The relationship between money holding on the one hand and real income and prices on the other, is not one which can readily be observed on a day-by-day, or even on a quarter-by-quarter basis. It does begin to become apparent when we take our data year-by-year, though even here it is rather rough and ready. The relationship in question seems to involve the economy's demand for nominal money rising in proportion to the general price level (as basic economic theory would predict), and perhaps a little more slowly than real income. Even so, this relationship leaves ample room for year-by-year fluctuations in the economy's demand for money relative to real income and prices. Money typically bears interest at zero or at least low and rather inflexible rates; so when market interest rates are high, agents economise on money holding and devote more of their wealth to holding income-earning assets instead. Also, empirical evidence seems to show that short-term fluctuations in real income do not have so pronounced an effect on the quantity of money demanded as do longer term changes: that is, it is permanent, rather than current, income which affects the demand for money. And none of this is to mention the fact that sudden shocks to the money supply, or to variables on the demand side, can lead to the economy being temporarily pushed 'off' its long-run demand for money function altogether. (On all this see Laidler 1977, Ch. 7, 1980, and Essay 2 above.)

However, all of the factors I have just discussed are inherently temporary in nature and so, therefore, is their influence on the demand for money which, on average, taking one year with another, does grow steadily with real income and prices. It follows from this that, if the monetary authorities provide only enough money to accommodate the growth in the public's demand for cash which stems from real income growth (perhaps adjusted for any long-term changes in interest rates if there are any), there can be no room for prices to rise. A money supply which grows at a rate a little below the trend rate of growth of real income, the precise figure here being one which could only be settled after detailed quantitative work had been carried out on a specific economy, will serve automatically to stabilise prices at a roughly constant level. To see why, let us now consider what would happen if the price level did not remain constant, bearing in mind what has already been said about the importance of a degree of price flexibility.

Suppose in some economy or other, for some reason, perhaps the autonomous activities of trade unions or of a few large corporations in a particular sector of the economy, the price level began to rise; what would then happen? At first there would be very little in the way of an observable response. Agents would find themselves becoming short of cash as they tried to carry on the same volume of business at a higher and rising price level, but one would not expect them to take immediate action in response to this. A cash shortage is inconvenient, but not something which requires instant attention. However, if that shortage persisted, as it would in the case envisaged here, we might expect to see agents begin to take action to build their cash holdings up to a more comfortable level and the 'transmission mechanism' which I have described in some detail in Essay 4 above would come into play. Some agents would temporarily cut back expenditures on currently produced goods and services in order to let their cash build up; some would try to dispose of other assets which they were holding, such as bonds or equities; while others would attempt to extend their credit at banks and other financial institutions.

All this activity would, among its other effects, put upward pressure on interest rates, and therefore have two further effects. First, and less important, because the demand for money varies with interest rates, agents would become willing to live with less cash relative to their volume of business; this effect considered in isolation would tend to slow down the process of restoring the economy to a zero inflation rate. However, it is the second effect which is of crucial importance: higher interest rates would begin to impinge upon spending decisions, the investment decisions of firms no doubt, but also households' decisions to purchase durable goods such as housing and automobiles. These effects would supplement the direct effects on the demand for output of the activities of those seeking to restore their cash positions by immediately reducing their expenditure on goods and services. Overall, there would be created a downward pressure on demand, and hence on real income and employment, which would work against whatever forces were tending to push up prices in the first place. That downward pressure of demand would continue to grow so long as prices continued to rise, and would ultimately cancel out the pressure on prices.

Conversely, any tendency for prices, or real income for that matter, to fall would, if the supply of money were held on a constant growth path, be met by excess liquidity on the part of agents, a tendency for interest rates to fall and for the demand for goods to expand, thus putting upward pressure on output, employment and prices. In short, if the money supply grows at a constant rate, the real balance effect, broadly conceived (see Essay 2, pp. 45–51 above), for that is what we have been describing here, will act as a powerful built-in stabiliser for the economy, tending to maintain price stability without any direct action on the part of the authorities. Such a policy will not guarantee continuous 'full' employment or complete price level stability, as I have already remarked; but on average, taking one year with another, the inflation rate ought not to deviate too far from zero if such a policy is maintained, while unemployment should fluctuate around some constant rate, whose determinants will be discussed in due course.

The question must immediately arise as to whether we cannot do better than that. When prices begin to rise, why should not the authorities act to slow down the rate of growth of the money supply in order to speed up the economy's return to price stability? In principle there can be no doubt that this is possible, but problems arise in practice. If the authorities are to intervene in a helpful way, they must have a great deal of knowledge about what is happening in the economy, about what is going to happen, and about how the economy will react to their actions. They must ensure that their countervailing policy does not end up putting on too much pressure in the opposite direction or in putting on such pressure at the wrong time; because if it does either of these things, an active policy, however well intentioned, would make prices less stable over time than they would be were a simple rule adhered to. There is considerable doubt about whether we have enough knowledge of the structure of the economies we live in, or of the factors underlying the autonomous shocks to which they are subject, to be able actively to use the money supply as a stabilising device without thereby running a severe risk of doing more harm than good.

Moreover, we must also take account of what Thomas J. Courchene (1976) has called the 'Heisenberg effect'. When we say 'structure of the economy' here, we are not referring to something like the structure of a machine, but to a set of relationships which describe the actions of economic agents, of human beings. It is extremely unlikely, as Courchene has warned us – not to mention such advocates of the 'rational expectations' notion as Lucas (1976) and Sargent and Wallace (1975) – that such a structure will remain unchanged in the face of different types of policy actions on the part of the authorities, so that the problems to which I have referred will not easily be solved by the growth of quantitative knowledge. Human beings, in order better to plan their own lives, take account of what it is that policy makers are doing and are always therefore likely to surprise the policy makers with their reactions to the measures they take. The difficulties here are not, that is to say, merely the product of the current imperfect state of knowledge, but are inherent in the nature of human society and will always be with us. (On this, see also Essay 3, pp. 104–5 and Essay 4, pp. 142–52.)

All in all then, it is a matter of elementary prudence to suggest that policy makers should settle for the kind of simple rule which I am advocating here to govern the behaviour of the money supply and then stick with it. To implement such a rule will not ensure anything like perfection, but it is likely to lead to the perpetuation of a reasonable degree of price stability, if that is once achieved. However, to opt for a rule is not to opt for rendering monetary policy makers redundant ever afterwards, as we shall now see.

I have already noted above that the choice of a particular growth rate for the money supply would have to be based upon quantitative considerations. Assuming that one knew what the economy's underlying growth rate was, one would need to know the real permanent income elasticity of demand for money in order to choose a non-inflationary rate of monetary expansion. Further-more, it might also reasonably be added that one would have to know what was meant by the word 'money'. Currency in circulation plus deposits at banks is not a precise enough definition for practical application in a world in which the lines between deposits at banks, and their other liabilities, not to mention those between banks and other financial intermediaries, are, to say the least, unclear. In fact, these two issues are closely interrelated, not least because empirical evidence tells us that, on the whole, the more broadly is money defined, the greater is its real permanent income elasticity of demand. In a world in which the structure of financial institutions never changed, it might be sufficient to argue that it doesn't much matter which concept of money is to be controlled, so long as the relevant growth rate is consistently selected. After all, in a world without institutional change, if one monetary aggregate has its growth tied down on a non-inflationary path, then all the other aggregates might be expected to fall into line in due course.

The problem with all this is that institutional change does take place, and is notoriously difficult to predict before the event. In the financial system, one of its effects is to change the relationship between the abstract concept of 'money' and any particular collection of assets which, at any particular time, might be selected to stand for 'money' for the purposes of conducting policy. For example, a change which permits deposit accounts – time deposits in North American usage – to become subject to transfer by cheque clearly changes the meaning of any monetary aggregate which excludes such accounts, and indeed of one which includes them for that matter. Such a change would thus cause the demand for a particularly defined aggregate to shift, and perhaps its income elasticity of demand to change as well; and if the monetary growth rule was not changed to offset these shifts, all this would have implications for the behaviour of the price level.

Though one should not overstress the importance of such changes, they have nevertheless occurred in the past in many countries, and their effects on the demand for money have been observed to be significant (see Bordo and Jonung 1978, also Essay 1, pp. 7–8). Moreover, monetary institutions, and the people who operate them, are not immune to the general tendency of economic agents to react to the observed conduct of policy in ways which might surprise the policy maker. Thus, when it is said that it is important to tie down the growth rate of the money supply if a zero (or low and stable) inflation rate is to be sustained in any economy, this does not mean that the policy can be implemented simply by choosing a particular aggregate at a particular moment, calculating its income elasticity of demand *from past data*, and then legislating that, for ever more *in the future*, the precisely defined aggregate in question grow at a particular rate. The monetary system must be constantly monitored for institutional change to ensure that the chosen monetary aggregate and the growth rate targets set for it remain compatible with attaining the goal of price stability, and the relevant targets must, if necessary, be adapted to changed circumstances.

If all this seems suspiciously like a form of fine tuning to the reader, that is because this is exactly what it is. To adopt a monetary rule in the sense in which I am arguing for it here is not to abandon 'fine tuning', but to ensure that the money supply, rather than the levels of real income, employment and prices, becomes the proximate object of fine tuning. The case for adopting a monetary growth rule is that, by fine tuning the money supply along a target growth path, adapted as and when it becomes necessary to accommodate institutional change, one is more likely to achieve stability in income, employment, and particularly prices, than if one attempts to fine tune these variables directly. It should not be confused with arguments to the effect that the conduct of economic policy should in general be subjected to quasi-constitutional restrictions, for it exists quite independently of the ideological considerations which underpin these latter proposals. (The reader who is interested in these ideological matters will find Yeager 1962 well worth consulting.)

3. FISCAL POLICY AND GOVERNMENT BORROWING

Monetary policy is not carried on in a vacuum. It is but one of the macro-policy tools available to government, and cannot be implemented independently of the others. If a government undertakes a particular policy towards the growth rate of the money supply, then that puts constraints upon the conduct of fiscal policy. Any government, national or local, federal or provincial, must cover its current expenditures either from taxes or borrowing, or in the case of local and provincial governments in most countries, from grants from senior governments as well. In the present context, it is the central government which is of prime importance, because, in most countries, it is the central government, and the central government alone, which has the power automatically to borrow from the Central Bank if it deems it desirable. Indeed, in many countries, the Central Bank is to all intents and purposes a branch of the central government, and therefore completely subservient to its political decisions. Though that is perhaps how it should be in a democracy, one can understand the nostalgia of some economists for the days of truly independent Central Banks, because they did (and in the cases of Germany and Switzerland for example, still do) resist what they perceived to be political pressures towards inflationary policies more effectively than do those institutions which, like the Bank of England for example, are effectively just another branch of government.

The problem arises here because, when a government borrows from its Central Bank, it is, to all intents and purposes, printing money. As the Bank lends to the government, it adds a treasury liability to its own assets, and creates a new liability of its own, a deposit, which it hands over to the government. The government then spends this deposit, thus putting newly created money into circulation, and base money at that, because in most banking systems, Central Bank liabilities may be, and are, held by the commercial banks as reserves. Thus any increase in their quantity enables the banking system as a whole to expand its liabilities, and hence the money supply, by a multiple of that original increase. The implication here is quite straightforward. If a Central Bank is to ensure that the money supply grows along a particular path, year in and year out, then the volume of central government activity (and public sector activity where the central government is an important source of funds for the rest of the public sector) which can be financed by borrowing from the Central Bank must be consistent with the pursuit of that policy. Such borrowing must not fluctuate too much from year to year, and in the long run can grow only at about the same proportional rate at which it is intended that the money supply should grow.

Now, of course, the government of any country has many policy goals to pursue other than the control of the price level. National defence must be provided for, health and welfare programmes must be financed, relatively depressed regions of the country, or particular depressed industries, might be thought worthy of subsidies, and so on. One could argue at length about the merits of any particular government programme, or indeed, on a more fundamental level, one could engage in debate about the principles that should govern any form of government intervention in economic life. However, none of these matters is relevant as far as the current discussion is concerned. The implementation of a rule for money supply growth in order to ensure reasonable price stability is neutral as far as questions concerning the degree of government intervention in the economy are concerned. Its importance for fiscal policy arises because it puts constraints upon the way in which government expenditures are paid for, not because it constrains their overall level and structure.

The implementation of a monetary growth rule implies that the vast majority of government programmes must be tax financed or paid for out of the proceeds of bond sales to the non-bank public. Taxes depress private spending, as do bond sales to the extent that they put upward pressure on interest rates, but that is exactly what is required if government expenditure is to be expanded without putting undue inflationary pressure on the economy. If government spending is to be expanded in an economy operating in the region of capacity output, then private spending has to be reduced to make way for it. It is usually politically easier for governments to increase their expenditure than to raise taxes or drive up interest rates by bond sales. Thus, they always face a strong temptation to finance their spending by borrowing from the Central Bank, in what amounts to an attempt to hide from the population the true costs of their expenditure programmes. However, in such circumstances the private sector still has to release resources to the government. Inflation is simply the means by which this is accomplished when government spending is financed by borrowing from the Central Bank.

A commitment to a target for the rate of growth of some monetary aggregate forces the government to act in such a way that the costs of its expenditure plans are made readily apparent to the public which, in any event, must bear them. For a government to commit itself to a monetary growth target involves it in being self-disciplined about the way in which it finances its programmes. To say this is to recognise yet another aspect of the role of such a rule in the maintenance of price stability. However, to repeat a point already made, there is no reason to suppose that the implementation of a money supply growth rule puts any limits on the scope of government economic activity over any range which is politically relevant in contemporary Western economies. In this respect a monetary growth rate rule is politically neutral and is not an adjunct of a generally non-interventionist policy stance, except in the sense that the non-interventionist politician is likely to find the financial constraints implied by such a rule less onerous to meet than is his interventionist counterpart.

4. THE BALANCE OF PAYMENTS AND THE EXCHANGE RATE

So far the discussion has proceeded as if we were dealing with a closed economy, an economy which is not involved in trade with the rest of the world, or in the workings of world-wide financial markets. However, all Western economies are deeply involved with the world economy, and even the largest of them, the United States, is nowadays sufficiently 'small' in relation to that world economy to be potentially vulnerable to external shocks. If one asks what constraints the implementation of a monetary rule would place upon a country's choice of policies towards the foreign sector, it will soon be discovered that it is left with no choice but to allow exchange rate flexibility, if it is to be able to adhere to that rule in the presence of shocks coming from outside.

To see why, consider what would happen if a particular country was attempting to pursue a monetary rule calculated to generate domestic price stability at a time when there were strong inflationary pressures at work in the rest of the world. Suppose that under such circumstances that country tried to maintain a constant exchange rate between its currency and some representative 'rest of world' currency, or basket of currencies. Then, the prices of imported goods would begin to rise at home. At the same time, exporters would find it getting progressively easier to sell their products in world markets, and would therefore be tempted to raise their prices abroad and at home as well. As a direct result of these effects, there would develop simultaneously a balance of payments surplus and a tendency towards domestic inflation. A constant rate of monetary expansion, if it was maintained, would, of course, offset the tendency towards inflation, but the growth rate of the money supply could not in fact be maintained on target in the face of a fixed exchange rate and a balance of payments surplus.

A balance of payments surplus involves the inhabitants of the home economy receiving a net inflow of foreign currency. There is no reason to suppose that they will wish to accumulate and hold stocks of foreign exchange; instead they will present them to their commercial banks in exchange for domestic currency, and those banks in turn will present the foreign exchange to the Central Bank for redemption. The maintenance of a fixed exchange rate requires the Central Bank to be willing to buy foreign exchange presented to it in unlimited amounts and at fixed prices. Moreover, it must buy the foreign exchange with newly created liabilities of its own: that is to say, with newly created money. Thus, under a fixed exchange rate, a balance of payments surplus leads automatically to a step up in the rate of money creation in much the same way as does a step up in the rate at which the government borrows from the Bank.

It is sometimes argued that these consequences can be avoided by so-called 'sterilisation' operations, whereby, after purchasing foreign exchange, the Central Bank then sells government bonds on the open market in order to reduce the money supply again, leaving the overall quantity of money in circulation unaffected by the balance of payments surplus. The problem here is that such bond sales put upward pressure on domestic interest rates, and that such pressure leads to an inflow of capital. This in turn increases the balance of payments surplus and hence puts further upward pressure on the rate of monetary expansion. In the contemporary world, with its extremely efficient international capital markets, these effects would come through very quickly, in days or even hours, rather than months or weeks; so that sterilisation policies, which in the 1950s might at least have been capable of delaying the monetary consequences of balance of payments surpluses for a few months, are no longer likely to be effective even for a short period. The maintenance of a fixed exchange rate therefore makes it impossible for a Central Bank to guarantee the maintenance of any target growth rate for the money supply. The two are alternative rules for the conduct of policy, and in practice there is always the danger that they will prove incompatible with one another. Hence a flexible exchange rate is a necessary prerequisite for implementing a money supply growth rule.

It should be noted explicitly that the arguments just advanced do not claim very much on behalf of a flexible exchange rate as far as its ability to insulate the economy from foreign disturbances is concerned, nor should they, for strong claims in this regard cannot be defended. To begin with, it is now widely understood that there is a whole class of foreign disturbances, which will influence the real terms of trade which face any particular country, and will make their effects felt domestically regardless of the exchange rate regime. For example, when the world price of oil goes up relative to the prices of other goods, that makes the inhabitants of an oil importing country worse off, and those of an oil exporting country better off, regardless of the exchange rate regime. Furthermore, the effects of such a change on the profitability of oil using industries, or of industries which must compete domestically for inputs with oil production, will also be much the same under fixed or flexible rates.

If the rest of the world is subjected to monetary instability as a result of other countries' authorities permitting monetary growth rates to fluctuate, then, as Dornbusch (1976) has argued, that instability can, in the short run, be transmitted through the foreign exchange market to the economy of a flexible exchange rate country. These so-called exchange rate 'overshooting' effects occur because changes in the foreign monetary growth rate have an initial impact on foreign interest rates and a predictable, but delayed, impact on foreign prices. Thus assets denominated in the currency of a country where the monetary growth rate has decreased become doubly attractive to hold. The return they yield has increased and the expected future value of their currency of denomination has risen. The current value of that currency on foreign exchange markets has to rise immediately until these advantages no longer permit exceptional returns to be made by holders of these assets, and this, in general, involves the currency's value overshooting its new equilibrium value. This is just another way of saying that other currencies tend to over-depreciate on the foreign exchange market, and this in turn can generate short-term price level increases which are unrelated to any domestic cause. The way in which the abrupt tightening of monetary policy in the United States in 1980–81 put downward pressure on the exchange rates of all major currencies against the US dollar, and hence upward pressure on domestic prices and interest rates in the rest of the world, provides a vivid example of the practical importance of these overshooting effects.

Be all that as it may, the *only* advantage which is being claimed for a flexible exchange rate here is that, in permitting a country to adopt a money supply rule, it permits it to choose its own *long-run* average inflation rate. The case for a flexible exchange rate is identical to the case for permitting the authorities to choose the long-run average domestic inflation rate. That case does not involve a separate and distinct set of issues, and the only but all-important conclusion which arises from the foregoing discussion is that, if a monetary rule is to be adopted, then so must exchange rate flexibility.

5. UNEMPLOYMENT AS A POLICY PROBLEM

The previous two sections of this essay were concerned with the effect of the adoption of a rule for the monetary expansion rate on the means available for financing government expenditures and on policy towards the exchange rate. I have not yet said a word about policy towards unemployment, and yet in the quarter century after the Second World War 'full employment' was widely regarded as a more important policy goal than price level stability. I must now, therefore, say something about what the implementation of a monetary rule might do to a government's ability to pursue a 'full employment' policy. The first and most obvious thing to be said here is that, if monetary policy is to be geared towards the control of inflation, then it cannot also be actively deployed to pursue employment targets. However, the government of a modern economy has many tools other than monetary policy available to it. Therefore, to say that monetary policy cannot be used directly to influence the unemployment rate is not to say that a government should not have a policy towards that variable, or that it is lacking in means to carry out such a policy. Nor, as we shall see in a moment, is it to say that the pursuit of price stability by way of a monetary rule will not, in and of itself, have effects on that variable which are likely, in the long run, to be beneficial.

As with the pursuit of 'price level stability', so with that of 'full employment', it is important to have a goal which is in fact attainable. A state of affairs in which every member of the labour force has a job at all times is obviously not attainable (nor perhaps even desirable), so just what is a reasonable target to pursue on the employment front? A growing economy is inevitably in a state of flux. New products and processes are continually being introduced and the structure of output best suited to meet the desires of the population, and hence the structure of relative prices, is always changing. At any time, some sectors of the economy will be shrinking while others expand, and factors of production, not least labour, will have to move between them. One cannot expect such movement to take place instantaneously. Even when to change employment does not require him to gain new skills, it still takes time for a worker displaced in one industry to find a job elsewhere; and when the market for a particular type of skill shrinks with the industry in which the workers who possess it are employed, the process of moving between jobs is likely to take even longer. Moreover, it is not just the movement of existing members of the labour force between jobs which generates such frictional unemployment. When the young enter the labour force for the first time, they too take time to find suitable employment, and again, this is likely to take time – time during which they are unemployed.

When we talk, therefore, of trying to achieve 'full employment' in the economy, we must allow for the consequences of structural change and frictions in the economy in setting our goal. We must recognise that there is a 'natural', or 'minimum feasible', unemployment rate. Setting aside for the moment the difficult question of how one might go about estimating that unemployment rate, its very existence raises an important *caveat* for 'full employment' policies, namely that, no matter what arguments might be raised in their favour, the conventional tools of fiscal 'demand management' are not suitable devices for driving down that natural unemployment rate should it be judged to be unacceptably high. At best, such policies are appropriate to dealing with unemployment which arises from an overall shortfall in the level of aggregate demand below the economy's productive potential as constrained, among other things, by the friction present in the labour market. However, this does not mean that a modern government is powerless to affect the natural unemployment rate's level, if it does find it too high. The appropriate policies for dealing with such unemployment as arises from labour market frictions and structural change in the economy involve reducing those frictions, and hence making it easier for workers made redundant by technical change to acquire new skills, making it easier for people to move from labour surplus areas to labour shortage areas, or for firms to move in the opposite direction.

There is no space in this essay to set out and debate the merits of particular policies to deal with these problems. Which policy mix it is best to pursue in any time and place is likely to depend upon the particular characteristics of the problem as it manifests itself there. Sometimes extensive government subsidised job retraining schemes might be appropriate, and sometimes regional subsidies; but policies to reduce the natural unemployment rate need not always involve an increase in government intervention in the economy. In some cases, already existing policies contribute to keeping the unemployment rate up, and their removal would help matters. For example, in the United Kingdom, rent controls on private sector housing, and the heavy subsidies given to public housing tenants and owner/occupiers, taken together, greatly inhibit the geographical mobility of labour; so does the institution of mandatory redundancy payments. In the United States and Canada, minimum wage laws have a damaging effect on the employment prospects of the young and the unskilled. In all of these cases a reduction, rather than an increase, in government intervention in the markets would help the unemployment rate.

Now, quite obviously such policies for reducing the natural unemployment rate as I have mentioned above will not find universal support anywhere. The interventionist politician will be attracted by job-retraining schemes and regional subsidies and repelled by the abolition of housing subsidies, redundancy benefits and minimum wages. Anyone with an ideological attachment to market mechanisms will take just the opposite view. However, to argue for a monetary rule for the control of the price level does not imply that one should take one side or the other in such debates. If the growth rate of the money supply is to be kept on track, that does have implications for the way in which government expenditures are financed. However, as I have already stressed, it has no implications for the scale of such expenditures, or for the structure of government intervention in the economy. In particular, there is nothing about a commitment to a monetary rule which inhibits the pursuit of high employment by policies towards the labour market if that is deemed desirable.

One can, albeit tentatively, go a step beyond this, and suggest that the climate of price level stability which a monetary rule would create might itself have beneficial effects on the unemployment rate. To the extent that inflation itself is a source of confusion, uncertainty and friction in economic life, and to the extent that the protection against such uncertainty which can be afforded by indexation schemes of one sort or another is incomplete, then the absence of inflation will in and of itself promote the smooth workings of markets, not least the labour market, and to that extent reduce the natural unemployment rate. How important such a side effect of price level stability might be is, in the current state of knowledge, a debatable point; but qualitatively, at least, the effect is there, and ought not to be ignored.

The last few paragraphs have dealt with the 'natural' unemployment rate (which, it will by now be apparent is anything but a 'natural' phenomenon) or what a 'Keynesian' economist might call the 'irreducible' minimum unemployment rate, by which he would of course mean 'irreducible by demand management policies'. Now let us consider the effects of the adoption of a money supply growth rate rule on our ability to counter increases in the unemployment rate above this irreducible minimum. As I have already argued above in Essay 3, there is every reason to suppose that involuntary unemployment which results from a failure of the labour market to clear is, from time to time at least, a fact of life, rather than a figment of the Keynesian economist's imagination. In this context, again, the adoption of a money supply growth rate rule will have beneficial side effects, for reasons which have, in effect, already been discussed. If, for some reason, the levels of real income and employment were to begin to fall below their 'natural' levels, this would also tend to be associated with a reduction in the inflation rate and hence, in an economy in which a rule was being pursued, would automatically generate excess liquidity in the private sector. This, in turn, would stimulate spending and help to restore full employment. In short, a monetary rule acts as a built-in stabiliser for output and employment as well as for the inflation rate; and this is not to mention the possibility that its adoption would actually remove a source of instability from the economy, namely those destabilising shocks which actually originate in fluctuations, either intentionally induced or otherwise, in the rate of growth of the money supply.

Even so, there is no reason to suppose that the stabilising effects of a steadily growing money supply (suitably adjusted to take account of institutional change) would, by themselves, be sufficiently strong to ensure the maintenance of a comfortable level of employment at all times. They might be, but there can be no guarantee of this, and in any event, monetary weapons are not the only ones which might be deployed in an attempt at managing the level of aggregate demand. Fiscal policies involving variations in the scale of taxation and government expenditure are also available to be used to this end. Indeed, because they impinge directly upon the flows of income and expenditure in the economy, they are particularly well adapted to having a rapid impact upon the level of employment, an impact moreover which might be expected to die down over time as private expenditure is 'crowded out' by government spending, so that any mistakes made either in the scale or timing of fiscal policy are unlikely to have long-lived adverse macro effects (for a formal analysis of this in a dynamic IS–LM model, see Laidler 1975, Ch. 3). There is no reason to argue that the implementation of a rule for the rate of growth of the money supply should be accompanied by the abandonment of such policies. One can easily conceive of them having a role to play in ironing out those fluctuations in income and employment which would remain, even when a monetary rule was providing a background of long-term built-in stability to the economy.

However, there are a number of qualifications to the foregoing conclusion which merit explicit note. To begin with, and quite obviously, any government budget deficits which arise from the use of activist fiscal policy as a stabilisation device must be covered by borrowing from the public, and not by borrowing from the Central Bank, because only in this way can the conduct of fiscal policy be made consistent with the maintenance of a constant rate of monetary expansion. Second, fiscal policy's major roles in the economy are to influence the allocation of resources and the distribution of income. To the extent that its use for stabilisation purposes interferes with the pursuit of other policy targets, there might be important policy trade-offs to be taken into account in deciding how freely to use it for those purposes. Third, I have suggested that fiscal policies act quickly, and so they do once they are in place. However, the political process may be such that the process of implementation is slow and uncertain. This seems to be more of a problem, for example in the United States with its Congressional system of government, or in Italy with its multiplicity of political parties, than in Parliamentary systems dominated by two or three parties; but it remains a problem worth considering nevertheless.

Finally, I began this section of this essay by noting that there existed a 'natural' unemployment rate, and that it was only appropriate to use traditional demand management tools to increase employment if the economy was operating above this rate. We must, therefore, be able to measure the natural unemployment rate with some confidence if we are ever to be in a position to deploy fiscal weapons to influence employment and output in a useful fashion. The amount of disagreement that there has been in recent years about just what is the value of the natural unemployment rate in the United Kingdom or in the United States or Canada, or anywhere else for that matter, suggests that in the current state of knowledge we are in no position to estimate that rate with any degree of confidence at all.

The issues just raised should make one rather cautious about how much to expect from fiscal policy as an employment stabilisation device. However, note that only the first of them, the requirement that fluctuations in the deficit must be largely covered by borrowing from the public, has anything to do with the adoption of any sort of monetary rule. The others are quite independent of the case for a monetary rule and would have to be addressed by any advocate of fiscal policy, no matter what his views on the proper mode of behaviour for the Central Bank. Thus, to adopt monetary growth rate targets to control the price level does very little to constrain the use of fiscal policies to combat unemployment. Their adoption does not therefore require a down-grading of unemployment as a problem for policy. It leaves policy makers with ample scope to choose other means for achieving unemployment goals, should they wish to do so.

6. ANTI-INFLATION POLICY

The preceding sections of this essay have argued that the adoption of a constant rate of growth for the money supply, adjusted from time to time if institutional change in the financial sector seems to warrant it, will confer upon an economy, not perfect price stability or perpetual full employment, but at least a good prospect of achieving low and reasonably stable inflation and a level of employment which will fluctuate around its 'natural' rate. It has also been argued that such a monetary policy need not inhibit the authorities from attempting to reduce that natural unemployment rate by way of policies towards the labour market if they wish to do so, nor from attempting to iron out remaining fluctuations in employment about that natural rate with fiscal policy; although in the latter case I have expressed scepticism about how much could, in fact, be accomplished by such means. On the other hand, it has been noted that the adoption of such a package does place certain constraints upon some aspects of policy. In particular the implementation of a monetary rule implies acceptance that the great bulk of government expenditure be tax and bond financed, and that interest rates and the exchange rate be left to be determined by market forces at whatever level they might dictate.

The proposal, therefore, to use the money supply to provide a background of price level stability stops far short of guaranteeing perfection in economic life. At best it provides an environment in which the many other economic and social problems with which modern governments are expected to deal can be tackled. Which problems will be taken up, and the means used to cope with them, will undoubtedly vary from country to country, and from time to time as well, as power shifts among various political parties. The analysis underlying this essay tells us nothing about what ought to be done here, and certainly does not support the position often attributed to advocates of monetary policy by their opponents, though seldom with any justification, that the adoption of appropriate monetary policies will in and of itself do all that is needed to solve these other problems. Monetary stability merely creates an environment in which it is easier to tackle a whole array of social and economic problems. It does not constitute a solution to them.

The situation in which just about every economy in the Western world now finds itself is far from being one of monetary stability. Inflation, at rates that even fifteen years ago would have been regarded as unthinkable, is now endemic in the system, and it is not enough for the economist to point out that price level stability would be preferable to inflation, and that, once achieved, it can be maintained by keeping the money supply on an appropriately chosen growth path. He must say something about how it can be achieved, about how to get there from here. The answer which I would give to the question implicit here can be expressed in the single adverb 'gradually'. It is commonly agreed that the current world-wide inflation began in earnest in the mid-1960s, largely as a result of the key currency country of the Bretton Woods system, the United States, attempting to finance the Vietnam War by way of money creation; and that it was amplified by the attempts of individual countries to counteract the 1971–72 recession with fiscal and monetary policy. It took till the mid-1970s for the increase of the trend rate of inflation in most countries to come to an end and, since then, they have at best held the line against further increases in the long-run inflation rate. We have, that is to say, taken fifteen years to get into our current situation, and I can see no reason why we should not expect to have to take close to a decade to get back to where we were in the mid-1960s, as far as inflation is concerned.

It is my judgement that inflation is best tackled by way of a programme of slowly but surely reducing the rate of monetary expansion, by one or two percentage points a year, say, until a rate compatible with long-run price stability is reached; indeed that this is the only policy that is likely to be found tolerable. By this I do not mean that the policy is a pleasant one, but only that the alternatives are worse. The key factor underlying this judgement lies in the role played by expectations in economic life, and in particular the role which they play in the inflationary process. It is a commonplace, but an important one, that economic activity takes place over time. Decisions taken today are decisions taken for the future, and that future is an uncertain one. A firm deciding upon its production plans and its pricing policies must take a view about how much output it can sell, and at what prices, over the horizon for which it is planning. In negotiating a wage contract, both sides must base their bargaining positions, and the ultimate settlement, upon what they think are the prospects over the period of the contract for the particular industry they are involved in, and for the economy as a whole. Indeed the very planning period over which expectations must be formed is itself something which must be chosen, and not the least of the advantages of a climate of monetary stability is that it permits the horizon to be lengthened, and hence makes the planning problems of firms and households alike less onerous and time (not to mention resource) consuming to solve.

Wages and prices are set in terms of money, so that expectations about the time path of the purchasing power of money must become pervasive elements in economic decisions. Currently held expectations about the future inflation rate influence currently made decisions, not least those which are made about the future time path of particular wages and prices, so that there is a strong element of self-fulfilling prophesy about the behaviour of the price level. If all agents expect the price level to remain stable, each firm will set the money price of its own output on that expectation, and each wage bargain which is struck will also be based upon that expectation. The result of all these individual decisions will be that the general price will in fact tend to be stable. If, on the other hand, everyone expects the inflation rate to run at, shall we say, ten percent per annum into the relevant future, then that expectation will be built into the behaviour of wages and prices, and the inflation rate will indeed tend towards ten percent.

Now when we use the word 'expectation' here, we must be careful not to think of it as necessarily being a consciously constructed forecast of the time path of the inflation rate. For some economic agents, for example large firms or trade unions with specialised economic research departments, it will indeed be just that, but for many agents an 'expectation' about inflation amounts to little more than an uneasy feeling that prices are rising faster than they did. Moreover, it is not so much the state of anyone's psychology, or the quality of their explicit forecast (if they make one) which matters for the inflationary process, but the way in which expectations get translated into action. The large corporation or trade union might use its latest inflation forecast as an input into a carefully calculated pricing or wage bargaining strategy, but for less sophisticated agents the 'feeling' that prices are rising faster than they used to might translate into what amounts to a change in their habitual behaviour vis-à-vis price and wage setting. This is a point of some importance in the context of the current inflation, because it has now been going on for fifteen years or so. That in turn means that there now exists a whole generation of adults who, never having experienced anything different, take annual rates of price and money wage increases in double digits quite for granted. No doubt, as inflation is brought down, they will learn not to do so, and will develop new expectations and habits; but there is no reason to believe that they will do so quickly.

The arguments presented in the last few paragraphs imply that, once inflation is well under way, as it surely is in just about every Western economy by now, that complex of factors which we label with the deceptively simple word 'expectations' imparts a good deal of inertia to the behaviour of prices. Prices continue to rise in large measure because they have been rising. However, if the inflationary process is going to proceed smoothly, it needs to be validated by the behaviour of the money supply. If a ten percent per annum inflation rate is actually going to continue unchecked, the money supply must grow at a rate fast enough to accommodate whatever growth in the demand for money might emanate from real income growth and such, and then at a further ten percent to keep pace with rising prices. The policy strategy called 'gradualism' amounts to doing no more than slowly reducing the rate of monetary expansion over time until it will accommodate no inflation, and the reason for bringing about this reduction in the rate of monetary expansion slowly lies in the consequences for real income and employment of reducing the rate of monetary expansion.

As is implicit in the arguments presented in Essay 4, the main short-run – but not necessarily short-lived – effects of reducing the monetary expansion rate in an economy where inflation is well entrenched is not a reduction in inflation at all, but a down-turn in real activity and an increase in unemployment. When the monetary expansion rate is reduced, economic agents begin to run into the very type of cash shortage we discussed earlier, and their reaction to it will result in a fall-off in the level of aggregate demand for goods and services. However, when the individual firm experiences a decline in its sales, it has to decide whether that decline is a temporary aberration which can safely be ignored, or whether it portends a longer-term shift in market conditions. It takes time and resources to gather the kind of information needed to come to such a decision, so that the initial reaction to falling sales across the economy is a build-up of unwanted inventories of goods and not much else.

It is only when it becomes apparent to firms that the fall in demand is not a localised or transitory phenomenon that they will take action. Such action will involve cutting prices (which includes raising them by less than otherwise would have been the case) to boost sales, or cutting output, or a combination of such policies. The general presumption must be that their initial response will be more heavily weighted to the side of cutting output. In part, this is simply because cutting current output is complementary to increasing sales as a means of reducing unwanted inventories, and partly because it is sometimes cheaper for firms to adjust output than go to the expense of revamping their price-lists and informing their customers about this. More important, however, is the simple fact that wage contracts already entered into put a limit on the extent to which prices can be lowered without involving firms in losses. It is easier to cut output, put workers on short time, or indeed lay them off altogether, than to renegotiate an existing wage contract in a downward direction, not least because lay-offs only affect a part of the labour force, while wage cuts have to be negotiated with everyone.

Inflation expectations, the long-term contracts which embody those expectations, and the difficulty which firms, and indeed other agents too, must inevitably experience in distinguishing random fluctuations in demand from longer-term changes in its time path, all interact to cause a reduction in the monetary expansion rate to have its first major impact on output and employment. However, inflationary expectations are only one ingredient of wage and price setting behaviour. The appearance of excess capacity in the economy will lead firms to revise down their prices relative to their initial plans, and the associated unemployment will lead to a similar effect on the time path of wages as contracts come up for renegotiation. In time, therefore, the inflation rate will indeed begin to slow down. As it does so, expectations will begin to be revised downwards, habits will change, and the fall off in inflation will tend to become cumulative.

In due course, the falling inflation rate will catch up with the rate of monetary expansion, but it does not follow from this that the process we are describing would be then at an end. The inflation rate might not simply 'catch up' with the monetary expansion rate, but is likely instead to overtake it. If it does, agents will begin to find themselves with surplus cash, demand will begin to increase, and the process we have just described will reverse itself. Although monetary contraction will eventually lead to a permanently lower inflation rate, the approach to this long-run solution will be in a series of cyclical swings around the long-term trend, rather than along a smoothly converging path. There will be similar swings in income and employment about their natural rates and, in the current state of our quantitative knowledge, there is no reason to suppose that these swings might not be of several years' duration each. (A more formal analysis of these cyclical swings is given in Laidler and Parkin 1975, Section 4.)

The probability that, under a gradualist policy, the inflation rate is likely to follow a cyclical path is important for a number of reasons. First, it implies that there is no reason to expect any close correlation between the rate of monetary expansion and the price level during the, perhaps long drawn out, approach to a lower long-run average inflation rate, and that therefore the absence of any such correlation should not be read as evidence of the failure of such policy. Second, and closely related, the fact that, at some time after the implementation of policy, a satisfactory inflation rate has been achieved, does not mean that this inflation rate will be sustained. A temporary trough in the inflation rate is not the same thing as a lower long-run value for the variable, nor is an upswing in the inflation rate necessarily a sign that a gradualist policy is failing. However, these considerations undoubtedly make the problem of sustaining the political consensus necessary to maintain such a policy in place a difficult one, and must naturally lead to the question of whether or not one cannot do better than 'gradualism'.

Could one not, for example, so manipulate the money supply as to keep the inflation rate coming down smoothly, so that the success of the policy in question was obvious to the average observer? The answer here is straightforward, for the question implicitly asserts that a fine tuning policy towards the inflation rate would be preferable to a simple contraction of the rate of monetary growth. So it would, if such a policy could be designed, but it is vulnerable to all the objections already raised, in this and earlier essays, to fine tuning (see pp. 27, 104, 160 above). I would argue that, if those objections are taken seriously, as they should be, we are forced to conclude that, though desirable in principle, the policy here envisaged is unlikely to be feasible in practice.

As a matter of fact, a policy of fine tuning inflation out of the system is not often proposed, but it is frequently argued that gradualism is so likely to be slow and uncertain in its progress that a quick cure for inflation, involving a rapid – within a year, say – reduction in the monetary expansion rate, is preferable. Such a proposal is closely related to a belief in the 'Rational Expectations' hypothesis and is often defended by pointing out that, because so much of the inertia of the inflationary process comes from expectations, and because the expectations in question are held by self-interested maximising agents who are well capable of observing the stance of monetary policy, an announced and clear-cut change in policy might affect those expectations instantaneously. If it did, then it is argued that this announcement would have a marked effect on inflation directly, without the intervention of real income and employment fluctuations.

There is nothing the matter with the logic of the above argument, but it does take for granted the truth of certain empirical propositions over and above the proposition that economic agents are rational. First, it is one thing to change people's expectations with an announcement, and another to change their behaviour. Anyone tied into a long-term contract before the policy change is announced will have to live by it, or attempt to renegotiate it, and a change in his expectations will not have any immediate effect on his behaviour. Also, before it can change expectations, an announcement about a policy change must be believed, and there are two problems which suggest we cannot take it for granted that it will be. First, governments do change their minds, and because a policy is announced does not mean that it will be persevered with. Hence it is not rational to take government statements at face value, and agents do not in fact do so: consider for example the almost continuous speculation in the United Kingdom during the first two years of Mrs Thatcher's government about the possibility of a 'U-turn'. Furthermore, even if an agent believes that the government will stick to its policies, that belief will only affect his expectations if he believes that the policy will in fact work. Though monetarists believe that a slow-down in the rate of monetary expansion will reduce inflation, they must recognise that this belief is controversial. Indeed, it is a minority belief in some countries. If they do recognise this fact, they will also recognise the inconsistency of arguing that the main transmission mechanism for such a policy can be through changes in the expectations of people who do not believe in it, and the absurdity of concluding on such a basis that the policy will work relatively quickly and painlessly.

Not all advocates of a quick cure for inflation argue along the foregoing lines. Lipsey (1980), for example, agrees that a quick monetary contraction is likely to be more painful than a slow one while its effects last, but argues that the painful side effects will be over relatively quickly. Although one can be reasonably confident that the impact of such a policy would be to cause a rapid fall in inflation, and a sharp slow-down in real activity, it is not clear that the subsequent convergence of the economy to its natural unemployment rate would be any quicker than under a gradualist policy. Furthermore, although it may be that the cycles which a quick contraction might generate will be of a shorter duration than those brought on by a slow contraction, that does not necessarily follow either. In many economic models, the factors determining the period of any inherent cycle are not dependent on the size of the shock to which the model is subjected, and it would be a bold economist who speculated whether or not this was true of the dynamic processes underlying the interaction of monetary expansion, unemployment and inflation in the real world, particularly when these processes are themselves conditioned by the way in which expectations evolve over time. The fact is that we know next to nothing about these things. And this is not to mention that a 'short sharp shock' to unemployment might have unpleasant political consequences of its own.

7. SUPPLEMENTS TO MONETARY POLICY

I have argued above that the case for gradualism is not that it is painless, or politically easier to implement, than other policies, but that, in the present state of knowledge, its unpleasant effects are easier to foresee, and therefore assess, than those of alternatives. A quick cure for inflation might be less costly than a gradual one, but if it were, that would be the result of expectation effects, and of certain dynamic properties of market processes, on which, *ex ante*, we have no right to rely, for we have no evidence of their empirical relevance. Thus, a quick cure is also a risky one, and it is on what amounts to a declaration of ignorance that the case for the gradualist alternative rests. But the fact remains that the gradualist cure for inflation is likely to be painful, to involve unemployment and lost output over a number of years. Though few economists nowadays would advocate wage and price controls as an *alternative* to monetary contraction in the fight against inflation, there is still a substantial number of economists (e.g. Lipsey 1980, Tobin 1980, Bodkin 1981, Wirick 1981) who would advocate controls as a supplementary device likely to ease the real effects of monetary contraction.

Needless to say, the advocates of controls are in favour of 'effective' arrangements for reducing the rate of change of money wages and prices, but to stop at this point in making the case for controls is to stop too soon. Of course 'effective' controls would reduce inflation: that much is tautological, and the only opposition to 'effective' controls would be ideological. The place where there is room for serious economic debate is on the matter of whether or not any particular control scheme is likely to work in the first place, and this is an area where reasonable people can disagree. The advocates of controls seem to rest at least some of their case on the likely effects of the introduction of such measures on expectations about inflation. The arguments for and against this possibility are, in essence, the same as those I have already discussed in the context of the likely effects of the announcement of a tight monetary policy on expectations. If the announcement was believed, if a significant number of agents expected the announced policy to be effective, and if they were in a position to act upon that expectation, then the introduction of wage–price controls might indeed lower the actual inflation rate by this mechanism. It is one of the curiosities of recent debates about how to control inflation that those who seem to put the most faith in the benevolent effects of the announcement of monetary contraction on the inflation rate put the least faith in the announcement's effects of controls, and *vice versa*.

Lipsey (1980), who advocates both quick monetary contraction and controls as interlinked parts of an anti-inflation package, is one of the very few who have displayed consistency in their attitude towards announcement effects. He hopes that the joint effect of the announcement of controls and tight money would be beneficial, but he does not rely on this. My own views on this issue are more pessimistic than Lipsey's and start from an attitude of acute scepticism about announcement effects as a reliable basis for the design of economic policy. I have no more faith in the power of an announcement of controls to influence expectations in a significant way, and more important to influence behaviour, than I do in the power of an announced monetary contraction. However, at the same time, I cannot deny the logical *possibility* of such effects proving important in practice, although in the case of wage and price controls there is a theoretical basis to my scepticism. If announcement effects are to be of any more than passing importance, the change in expectations which they engender must, with the passage of time, be confirmed by experience. In the case of controls, this is unlikely to happen, because no set of controls can be comprehensive; in particular, in an open economy, prices originating in the foreign sector cannot be controlled, or at least not without the erection of an apparatus for direct quantitative controls on overseas transactions that most advocates of price controls would shy away from.

Under a fixed exchange rate regime, it is well established that the long-run trend of domestic prices is determined in the world economy. That is why, as I have already noted, the advocate of monetary gradualism for an individual country must also be an advocate of exchange rate flexibility. The issue to be faced here thus concerns the way in which wage and price controls would work against the background of a flexible exchange rate. Suppose, for the sake of argument, that controls were effective, either by way of influencing expectations or by some other means, in reducing the rate of wage inflation and the rate of change of the 'domestic component' of some relevant price index, below the values that they would otherwise take, given the stance of monetary policy. This would mean that there would be, at a given exchange rate and given world prices for those goods entering into the 'foreign' component of the price index, more real cash balances for the population to hold than would otherwise be the case. The advocate of controls hopes that the presence of such excess money balances in the economy would serve to keep up the level of real aggregate demand, and hence lead to a higher than otherwise level of real income and employment. The sceptic, such as myself, notes that their effect might well be felt mainly in the foreign exchange market, driving up the value of foreign currency, hence ensuring that the foreign component of the price index would be higher than otherwise.

If this latter effect was predominant, then the overall price inflation rate would be very much what it would have been in the absence of controls, although the structure of relative prices would be different. In particular, real wages would be lowered, and any expectations about price inflation engendered by the introduction of controls would be disappointed. Something very much like this seems to have happened during the 1973–74 experiment with wage and price controls in the United Kingdom (see Laidler 1976 for a fuller discussion), while Canada had a similar experience with controls, albeit in a much less dramatic and socially divisive way in 1975–77. (On the Canadian evidence, see Fortin and Newton 1981.) In both cases, controls seem to have amounted to policies to control real wages rather than inflation.

There is always the possibility that, next time around, it would be an increase in domestic output which would absorb excess cash balances. One cannot argue that an 'effective' wage and price control programme is *a priori* out of the question. Currently fashionable proposals of one form or another of tax-based incomes policies (see, for example, Weintraub 1981) do nothing to meet this issue though, for the innovative element in such proposals concerns the way in which controls will be made to affect wages and domestic prices in the first place. I am suggesting here that the main case against controls does not lie in the difficulty of enforcing them in those areas where it is conceivable that they might work, formidable though such difficulty might be, but in the impossibility of controlling the behaviour of the overall price index in an open economy with a flexible exchange rate. Only if output and employment react more rapidly to variations in the quantity of money balances in the economy than does the foreign exchange market, would there seem to be any hope of avoiding this problem. It is because I find such a possibility inconceivable that I remain sceptical about the desirability of using wage and price controls to bolster monetary contraction in the control of inflation.

Now, it should be clear that the main burden of my objection to using wage and price controls is not an ideological one, but rests instead on a judgement that they would not in fact achieve the end for which they might be used, namely reducing the unemployment that one would expect to accompany a gradualist approach to the control of inflation. However, there are other measures which might be used to ease the difficulties of the transition to a lower inflation rate. To begin with, if unemployment on a larger than usual scale is going to be the consequence of monetary contraction, then there is much to be said in favour of policies designed to ease the lot of the unemployed. If the authorities are going to undertake a policy which will have its adverse effects concentrated on a relatively small proportion of the population, and that is what undertaking a policy, one of whose predictable consequences is unemployment, amounts to, then it would seem only just to ensure that those who bear the brunt of the policy suffer as little as possible.

There is a strong case to be made along these lines, but there is a problem with it too that must be faced. The frictional and structural factors which underlie the economy's so-called natural unemployment rate arise, in part at least, from workers taking time to acquire new skills and to find new jobs when they become unemployed. The higher is their living standard while not working, the more careful would one expect them to be about selecting a new job, and hence the longer they will take about it. This is *not* to say that the unemployed are shiftless, nor is it to argue for making unemployment an unpleasant situation. However, it is to say that the higher the level of unemployment benefits, the higher is likely to be the level of unemployment. This is not just a matter of *a priori* speculation. We do in fact have a fair amount of empirical evidence about the effects of unemployment benefit variations on the unemployment rate. (See, for example, Grubel and Walker 1978.) However, this evidence is not cited here in order to make a case that unemployment benefits ought, after all, to be fixed at low levels when an anti-inflation programme is being designed. It would be foolhardy, in the current state of knowledge, to speculate as to whether we currently have too much or too little frictional unemployment. However, the effect of generous unemployment benefits on the natural unemployment rate is nevertheless a factor of which the policy maker must take account in deciding upon their appropriate level and structure. The reader should note, though, that policies designed to increase labour mobility, which I have discussed earlier, are available to offset these effects. The authorities do not have to await the arrival of price stability to implement such policies.

Of course, one way of stopping the unemployment rate ever getting too high during the transition to a lower inflation rate is to proceed slowly. That is what gradualism is about in the first place. However, inflation, as we know, also does social damage. This suggests that a useful accompaniment to a gradualist monetary policy might be measures designed to make it easier to live with inflation while the policy is working out. It is sometimes argued that such policies ought not to be introduced, lest this in some way reduce the political will to come to grips with inflation. That would be all well and good if all it would take to defeat inflation was political will, with no unpleasant side effects, and if there was a feasible way of solving the problem quickly, if only sufficient will-power was exerted. However, neither of these conditions hold, and it therefore seems to me that to eschew the use of policies for cutting down the adverse effects of inflation when they are available is quite pointless.

Some of the unpleasant effects of gradualism would be mitigated by the spread of indexation. Where one of the contracting parties to an agreement is the government, as in matters of taxation and pension obligations, there is much to be said for enacting indexation as a matter of law. When it comes to private contracts, this perhaps is not necessary. The very operation of capital markets ensures that expectations about inflation come to be reflected in nominal interest rates, and so there is no need for any active policy in this regard. As to wage contracts, that surely must be left to the parties involved to decide. To the extent that the inclusion of cost-of-living adjustment clauses in wage bargains makes money wage inflation less rigid in the face of subsequent reductions in price inflation, it is to be encouraged, since this effect would tend to increase the speed at which inflation would be brought down by a given gradualist policy, and decrease the amount of unemployment that might accompany it. This consideration suggests that the authorities might encourage the use of such clauses, but hardly amounts to a case for making them in any way mandatory.

However, it is important not to confuse indexation with a policy of guaranteeing that real wages never fall, and in practice there is a real danger of this happening, as the experience of the United Kingdom in 1975, or Australia over the period 1975–80, shows. Wage indexation is a device for ensuring that, once a wage bargain is struck, its real consequences will be what the parties to it intended. It is not a device to prevent the parties to a bargain agreeing to a cut in real wages should the conditions prevailing in whatever industry they are involved in seem to require such a change. What form of indexation is appropriate in any particular instance is not something that the outside observer can pronounce upon, and that is why the role of policy here should usually be the passive one of not preventing indexation, rather than the active one of attempting to enforce it.

8. THE PROBLEM OF MONETARY CONTROL

The process of reducing the rate of monetary expansion slowly over time in order to bring inflation under control is every bit as much a proposal to fine tune the money supply as is the proposal to keep money on a non-inflationary growth path once the inflation rate is at a satisfactory level. Thus, the advocate of gradualism must say something about the means whereby such fine tuning is to be implemented. Broadly speaking, two methods of monetary control are available. The first involves the Central Bank in manipulating interest rates, and the second the reserve base of the banking system.

The rationale for interest rate control can be put as follows. As a practical matter, it is possible to estimate a 'demand for money' function for the economy, using, shall we say, quarterly or even monthly data. Over such a short time period, the values of such arguments of that function as real income and the price level are in effect predetermined. The same may be said of the lagged values of any variables which might appear in the relationship. Some representative interest rate is also an argument in the demand for money function. Thus, so the argument goes, in order to hit a given target for the money supply within a quarter, the Central Bank needs only to calculate, given the values of the predetermined variables, the value of the interest rate which is compatible with its money supply target being demanded, set the rate at that level, and then leave it to the economy to move along its demand for money function. The econometric relationships underlying such an exercise are of course subject to error; but within reasonable limits, or so it is claimed, the rate of monetary expansion can be controlled by these means. There are a number of problems with the procedures I have just outlined. First of all, as I have argued in Essay 2 above, the short-run demand for money relationship upon which such a method of monetary control is based is not really a structural demand for money function at all, but a peculiar and ill-understood mixture of a long-run demand for money function and the reduced form of whatever model describes the portfolio behaviour of the private sector and banking system. Because it is so ill understood, such a relationship might prove less reliable in practice as a basis for gradualist policy than the results of empirical studies, carried out on data generated when the Central Bank was not implementing such a policy, might lead one to believe.

In any event, an absolutely crucial component of the case for using interest rate control methods is the existence of a well determined, and relatively elastic, demand relationship between the behaviour of the monetary aggregate chosen for control and the rate of interest. However, it is an elementary result of macroeconomics that, the more interest elastic is the demand for money, the less built-in stability does one get from adopting a monetary rule. The choice of interest rate control methods naturally then leads to the choice, as the centrepiece of policy, of a narrow money aggregate whose velocity varies relatively much with interest rates. Furthermore, the choice of such a narrow aggregate increases the chances of institutional change in the banking system undermining the effects of monetary policy. When a broad aggregate is to be controlled, there is more chance that such change will alter the composition of the 'money supply', leaving the significance of the aggregate unchanged. In the case of a narrow aggregate, such change is more likely to result in the evolution of monetary assets outside the scope of the chosen aggregate, assets which will, therefore, change the economic meaning of the aggregate. (On these issues see Courchene 1976, pp. 245–52, Howitt and Laidler 1979.)

A Central Bank which was determined to pursue a monetary target singlemindedly, and was in a position to resist any political pressure which might be brought upon it to do otherwise, might nevertheless be able to make interest rate control methods work. For example, after a shaky start in 1975–76, the Bank of Canada, while using these methods, has managed to keep within its money supply growth targets for over three years now. However, it is vulnerable to the criticism that the aggregate it has sought to manipulate has been sufficiently narrow as to be only a mildly efficient stabiliser of the inflation rate. Even so, the Bank of Canada has, from time to time, found itself under acute political pressure as a result of the behaviour of interest rates and the exchange rate. Other Central Banks which have attempted to use interest control methods have shown themselves less willing or, perhaps because of political pressures, less able to see those variables fluctuate enough to keep the money supply on track. (See Sumner 1980.) In practice they have not delivered a slow but steady contraction of the rate of growth of whatever monetary aggregate they have set targets for. The behaviour of the Federal Reserve system, at least until late 1979, illustrates this proposition well enough, as does that of the Bank of England over the 1979–80 period. The latter institution's problems were compounded by the fact that it tried to control the growth rate of a broad monetary aggregate, many of whose components bear interest at competitive market rates, by manipulating interest rates on assets that are highly substitutable for such 'money'. It is pointless here to speculate on how it managed to get itself involved in attempting this impossible task.

A key political problem with interest rate control is that, when it is used in this way, the interest rate itself tends to take on the attributes of a policy target in its own right. The authorities are seen by the public to be manipulating the interest rate, and come under political pressure to achieve a certain (typically 'low') range of values for that variable, in addition to, or instead of, any target for monetary expansion. That has happened in the United States and in Britain. When this happens, and if the rate of money creation nevertheless retains some importance for the authorities alongside the interest rate, they are left with little option but to try to control the rate of money creation by way of manipulating public sector borrowing. This happens because, given the value of the interest rate, there is a certain amount of public debt which the private sector will absorb over any time period. The difference between this amount and the overall borrowing requirement of the public sector determines how much the authorities must then borrow from the Central Bank, and therefore determines the size of public sector borrowing's contribution to monetary expansion. Hence if public sector borrowing can be controlled, then so can the money supply. This line of reasoning explains why, in Britain under the Thatcher government in particular, the authorities came to lay heavy emphasis on the control of the public sector borrowing requirement as a key component of monetary policy. A reluctance on the authorities' part to tolerate interest rate fluctuations has led to the government budget constraint imposing a much stronger linkage between fiscal and monetary policy than is strictly necessary. The fact that public sector borrowing is hard to predict, let alone control, when much government expenditure and revenue fluctuates according to statutory obligations which cannot quickly be changed, explains why, when such a linkage is imposed, it is inevitably the conduct of monetary policy that suffers.

For all the above reasons, then, interest rate control, whatever may be its merits in principle, is unlikely to be an effective means of carrying out a 'gradualist' monetary policy in practice. That is why the case for gradualism is so closely related to advocacy of 'base control' methods for the implementation of monetary policy. The phrase 'base control' is in some measure ambiguous. Some people use it to refer to a policy regime under which rules are set for the rate of growth of the monetary base *instead of* some broader monetary aggregate, and others use it to refer to a regime under which the monetary authorities manipulate the base, over which they can if they wish have direct control, *in order to bring about* a particular growth rate for some broader aggregate. Here I am using the phrase in the second sense.

There is nothing mysterious about the techniques of base control. They exploit the fact that there can exist a stable 'multiplier' relationship between the monetary base – the cash liabilities of the Central Bank – and a more broadly defined money supply concept. How stable such a multiplier will be does of course depend upon some factors beyond the monetary authorities' direct control, for example the preferences of the non-bank public vis-à-vis holding money in the form of currency as opposed to commercial bank deposits, as well as the banking system's demand for excess (that is, greater than required, or conventionally held) reserves. Also, the tightness of the Central Bank's degree of control over the base will depend upon the conventions it adopts to govern the granting of re-discount facilities to commercial banks which find themselves short of cash. However, it is within the discretion of the Central Bank to alter these conventions and it should be obvious that, the less automatic is the commercial banks' access to the discount window, the easier is it for the Central Bank to control the size of the monetary base.

Other factors which might influence the multiplier relationship are also susceptible to the control of the monetary authorities. Differential reserve requirements between different types of deposits, such as exist in Canada and the United States, or between different types of banks, such as exist in the United States, or a basic cash ratio that is so small that variations in the commercial banks' desired excess reserves come to dominate the multiplier, as is the case in Britain, can all lead to undue slippage between the monetary base and the money supply. However, these factors can be dealt with by way of administrative changes. There is no reason why there cannot be a uniform reserve requirement against all types of deposits which make up the monetary aggregate which the authorities wish to control. If the Central Bank were to pay interest to commercial banks on their reserve holdings, the main grounds on which the latter might object to such reserve requirements, namely that reserve requirements are a form of differential taxation on banks, would also be removed.

Of course, I am not suggesting that changes such as I am advocating here would be politically easy to implement in all times and places. Nor, if a Central Bank switched to a system of base control over a monetary aggregate after a history of stabilising interest rates, would agents in private markets find the transition a straightforward matter. When a Central Bank ceases to step in to iron out day-by-day interest rate fluctuations, it takes private agents a while to learn how to operate in the changed environment. Interest rates are volatile until private sector institutions learn how to take profitable advantage of such volatility and thereby compete it out of the system. The history of the United States in the wake of the Federal Reserve system's attempt to move to base control in the autumn of 1979 bears witness to the potential seriousness of such problems.

Now all this is to say that, if the authorities of a particular country opt for a gradualist policy, they should not take it for granted that they can implement such a policy without overhauling their monetary institutions to a greater or lesser extent. (See Poole and Lieberman 1972, and Duck and Sheppard 1978, for specific discussions of how US and British practices respectively could be modified to ease the use of base control methods.) Under the Bretton Woods system, and before that under the gold standard, interest rates were the key variables in the conduct of domestic monetary policy. It was by manipulating interest rates that Central Banks induced the kind of international capital market responses that enabled them to maintain their exchange rates fixed. Furthermore, under the Keynesian policy regime which was so predominant in the 1950s and 1960s, monetary policy was subordinated to fiscal policy, and the main job of the Central Bank was seen as ensuring that the interest rate effects of financing fiscal deficits did not offset whatever influence fiscal policy is intended to have. Here again it was the interest rate rather than some monetary aggregate which was the important policy variable.

The fact is that the monetarist proposal to put control of a monetary aggregate at the centre of policy is a radically new one as far as the behaviour of Central Banks is concerned. It should not therefore surprise anyone that the adoption of such a policy requires that monetary institutions be overhauled. The policy failures which have been experienced in so many countries over the last few years, not least in Britain and the United States where monetary targets have been more honoured in the breach than in the attainment, bear eloquent witness to the troubles that can be encountered if attempts are made to implement a monetarist policy using an institutional framework geared to carrying out Keynesian measures. Hence the overhaul is well worth carrying out.

9. CONCLUDING COMMENT

The basic theme of this essay is easily summed up: the use of monetary policy to establish and maintain control over the inflation rate is a complex matter, not because the economics that underlies such a policy regime is particularly difficult to grasp, but because of the way in which such a use of monetary policy impinges upon governments' ability to attain other policy goals, and to use other policy tools. A government which sets targets for the rate of growth of the money supply cannot also set targets for the exchange rate and interest rates, and it cannot also use monetary policy to manipulate the unemployment rate. Moreover, though it is still left with a good deal of freedom as far as fiscal policy is concerned, once money growth rate targets are set, its decisions about the financing of government expenditure are in large measure pre-empted. Also, in order to create a situation in which monetary growth targets are attainable in practice, institutional reforms in the financial sector of the economy may have to be undertaken. And none of this is to mention what is perhaps the most important of all problems in using monetary policy to cope with inflation, namely the fact that it undoubtedly creates unemployment as part of the transmission mechanism whereby it has its effects.

The above list of problems is formidable, and perhaps goes a long way towards explaining why the use of monetary policy to combat inflation has in practice been erratic and half-hearted in so many countries in recent years. Nevertheless, I find it inconceivable that inflation is going to be brought under control anywhere without monetary policy being systematically deployed to that end. Thus, the purpose of this essay has been, not to advance arguments against its use, but to state in a clear-cut fashion just what difficulties are likely to be encountered when it is used, in the hope that the old adage 'forewarned is forearmed' might be of some relevance to the design of successful anti-inflation policies.

References

Alchian, A. A. (1970) Information costs, pricing and resource unemployment; in Phelps, E. S. *et al.*, *The Microeconomic Foundations of Employment and Inflation Theory*, W. W. Norton.

Andersen, L. C. and Jordan, J. L. (1968) Monetary and fiscal actions: a test of their relative importance in economic stabilisation, *Federal Reserve Bank of St. Louis Monthly Review*, 50, (November), 11–24.

Ando, A. and Modigliani, F. (1965) The relative stability of monetary velocity and the investment multiplier, *American Economic Review*, 55, (September), 693–728.

Arcelus, F. and Meltzer, A. H. (1973) The markets for housing and housing services, *Journal of Money, Credit and Banking*, 5, (February), 78–99.

Archibald, G. C. and Lipsey, R. G. (1958) Monetary and value theory: a critique of Lange and Patinkin, *Review of Economic Studies*, 26 (69), (January), 1–22.

Artis, M. J. and Lewis, M. K. (1976) The demand for money in the United Kingdom 1963–1973, *Manchester School*, 44, (June), 147–81.

Artis, M. J. and Nobay, A. R. (1969) Two aspects of the monetary debate, *National Institute Economic Review* (August), 33–51.

Auernheimer, L. (1974) The honest government's guide to inflationary finance, *Journal of Political Economy*, 82, (June), 598–606.

Azariadis, C. (1975) Implicit contracts and underemployment equilibria, *Journal of Political Economy*, 83, (December), 1183–1202.

Baily, M. N. (1974) Wages and employment under uncertain demand, *Review of Economic Studies*, 41, (January), 37–50.

Ball, R. J. and Burns, T. (1976) The inflationary mechanism in the UK economy, *American Economic Review*, 66, (September), 478–84.

Ball, R. J. *et al.* (1975) The London Business School quarterly econometric model of the UK economy; in Renton, G. (ed.), *Modelling the Economy*, Heinemann Educational Books for the SSRC.

Bank of England (1970) The importance of money, *Bank of England Quarterly Bulletin*, 10, (June), 159–98.

Barrett, C. R. and Walters, A. A. (1966) The stability of Keynesian and monetary multipliers in the United Kingdom, *Review of Economics and Statistics*, 48, (November), 395–405.

Barro, R. J. (1972) A theory of monopolistic price adjustment, *Review of Economic Studies*, 39, (January), 17–26.

Barro, R. J. (1977a) Unanticipated money growth and unemployment in the United States, *American Economic Review*, 67, (March), 101–15.

Barro, R. J. (1977b) Long-term contracting, sticky prices, and monetary policy, *Journal of Monetary Economics*, 3, (July), 305–16.

Barro, R. J. (1978) Unanticipated money, output, and the price level in the United States, *Journal of Political Economy*, 86, (August), 549–81.

Barro, R. J. (1979) Second thoughts on Keynesian economics, *American Economic Review*, 69, (May), papers and proceedings, 54–59.

Barro, R. J. and Grossman, H. I. (1976) *Money, Employment and Inflation*, Cambridge University Press.

Barth, J. R. and Bennett, J. T. (1974) The role of money in the Canadian economy: an empirical test, *Canadian Journal of Economics*, 7, (May), 306–11.

Baumol, W. J. (1952) The transactions demand for cash – an inventory theoretic approach, *Quarterly Journal of Economics*, 66, (November), 545–56.

Bell, G. (1973) *The Eurodollar Market and the International Financial System*, Macmillan.

Bergstrom, R. and Wymer, C. R. (1974) A model of disequilibrium neo-classical growth and its application to the United Kingdom, London School of Economics International Monetary Research Programme (mimeo).

Blinder, A. S. and Solow, R. M. (1973) Does fiscal policy matter? *Journal of Public Economics*, 2, (November), 319–37.

Bodkin, R. (1981) The challenge of inflation and unemployment in Canada during the 1980s: would a tax-based incomes policy help? *Canadian Public Policy*, 7, (April), Supplement 204–14.

Bordo, M. and Jonung, L. (1978) The long-run behaviour of income velocity of circulation: a cross country comparison of five advanced countries 1870–1975, paper presented at the European Econometric Society Meetings (mimeo).

Bordo, M. and Schwartz, A. J. (1979) Clark Warburton: pioneer monetarist, *Journal of Monetary Economics*, 5, (January), 43–66.

Boughton, J. M. (1977) Does monetarism matter?; in Elmus Wicker (ed.), *Lilley Conference on Recent Developments in Economics, April 21–23*, Indiana University.

Brainard, W. C. and Cooper, R. N. (1975) Empirical monetary macroeconomics: what have we learned in the last 25 years?, *American Economic Review*, 65, (May), papers and proceedings, 167–75.

Brechling, F. R. (1965) The relationship between output and employment in British manufacturing industries, *Review of Economic Studies*, 32, (July), 187–216.

Brechling, F. R. (1974) Monetary policy and neoclassical investment analysis; in Johnson, H. G. and Nobay, A. R. (eds), *Issues in Monetary Economics*, Oxford University Press.

Brechling, F. R. (1975) *Investment and Employment Decisions*, Manchester University Press.
Brown, A. J. (1939) Interest prices and the demand for idle money, *Oxford Economic Papers*, 2, (May), 46–69.
Brown, A. J. (1955) *The Great Inflation, 1939–1951*, Oxford University Press.
Brunner, K. (1961) The Report of the Commission on Money and Credit, *Journal of Political Economy*, 69, (December), 605–20.
Brunner, K. (1970) The monetarist revolution in monetary theory, *Welwirtschaftliches Archiv.*, 105, 1–30.
Brunner, K. (1970) Issues of post-Keynesian monetary analysis; in Mayer, T. (ed.), *The Structure of Monetarism*, W. W. Norton.
Brunner, K. (1971) A survey of selected issues in monetary theory, *Schweizeriche Zeitschrift für Volkwirtschaft und Statistik*, (March), 1–146.
Brunner, K. (1974) Monetary management, domestic inflation, and imported inflation; in Aliber, R. Z. (ed.), *National Monetary Policies and the International Financial System*, University of Chicago Press.
Brunner, K., Cukierman, A. and Meltzer, A. H. (1980) Stagflation, persistent unemployment and the permanence of economic shocks, *Journal of Monetary Economics*, 6, (October), 467–492.
Brunner, K. and Meltzer, A. H. (1963) Predicting velocity: implications for theory and policy, *Journal of Finance*, 18, (May), 319–54.
Brunner, K. and Meltzer, A. H. (1971) The uses of money – money in the theory of an exchange economy, *American Economic Review*, 61, (December), 784–805.
Brunner, K. and Meltzer, A. H. (1976) An aggregative theory for a closed economy; in Stein, J. L. (ed.), *Monetarism*, North Holland.
Brunner, K. and Meltzer, A. H. (eds), (1978) *The Problem of Inflation*, Carnegie–Rochester Conference Series, Vol. 8, North Holland.
Bryant, J. (1978) Relative prices and inventory investment, *Journal of Monetary Economics*, 4 January, 85–102.
Buiter, W. H. (1980) The macroeconomics of Dr Pangloss: a critical survey of the new-classical macroeconomics, *Economic Journal*, 90, (March), 34–50.
Cagan, P. (1956) The monetary dynamics of hyperinflation; in Milton Friedman (ed.), *Studies in the Quantity Theory of Money*, University of Chicago Press.
Cagan, P. (1978) Monetarism in historical perspective; in T. Mayer (ed.), *The Structure of Monetarism*, W. W. Norton.
Cagan, P. (1979) *Persistent Inflation*, Columbia University Press.
Cagan, P. and Schwartz, A. J. (1975) Has the growth of money substitutes hindered monetary policy? *Journal of Money, Credit and Banking*, 7, (May), 137–60.
Carlson, J. A. and Parkin, J. M. (1975) Inflation expectations, *Economica NS*, 42, (May), 123–38.
Carr, J. and Darby, M. (1981) The role of money supply shocks in the short-run demand for money, *Journal of Monetary Economics*, 8, (September), 183–200.

Caves, D. W. and Feige, E. L. (1980) Efficient foreign exchange markets and the monetary approach to exchange rate determination, *American Economic Review*, 70, (March), 120–34.

Chick, V. (1973) *The Theory of Monetary Policy*, Basil Blackwell.

Chow, G. (1966) On the long-run and short-run demand for money, *Journal of Political Economy*, 74, (April), 111–31.

Christ, C. F. (1968) A simple macroeconomic model with a government budget constraint, *Journal of Political Economy*, 76, (February), 53–67.

Clements, K. W. and Jonson, P. D. (1979) Unanticipated money, disequilibrium modelling and rational expectations, *Economic Letters*, 2, 303–8.

Clower, R. (1965) The Keynesian counter-revolution: a theoretical appraisal; in Hahn, F. H. and Brechling, F. R. (eds), *The Theory of Interest Rates*, Macmillan.

Cobham, D. (1978) The politics of the economics of inflation, *Lloyds Bank Review* (April), 19–32.

Coddington, A. (1976) Keynesian economics: the search for first principles, *Journal of Economic Literature*, 14, (December), 1258–73.

Congden, T. (1978) *Monetarism – An Essay in Definition*, The Centre for Policy Studies, London.

Cooley, T. and Leroy, S. (1981) Identification and estimation of money demand, *American Economic Review*, 71, (December), 825–844.

Corry, B. A. (1961) *Money Saving and Investment in English Economics*, Macmillan.

Courchene, T. J. (1976) *Money and Inflation: An Evaluation of Recent Canadian Monetary Policy*, C. D. Howe Research Institute, Montreal.

Cross, R. J. and Laidler, D. (1976) Inflation, excess demand and expectations in fixed exchange rate open economies: some preliminary empirical results; in Parkin, J. M. and Zis, G. (eds), *Inflation in the World Economy*, Manchester University Press.

Deaton, A. (1972) Wealth effects on consumption in a modified life cycle model, *Review of Economic Studies*, 32, (October), 443–54.

DePrano, M. and Mayer, T. (1965) Tests of the relative importance of autonomous expenditure and money, *American Economic Review*, 55, (September), 729–52.

Dicks-Mireaux, L. A. (1961) The inter-relationship between cost and price changes, 1945–59: a study of inflation in post-war Britain, *Oxford Economic Papers* (NS), 13, (October), 267–92.

Dornbusch, R. (1976) Expectations and exchange rate dynamics, *Journal of Political Economy*, 84, (December), 1161–76.

Driscoll, M. J. and Ford, J. L. (1980) The stability of the demand for money function and the predictability of the effects of monetary policy, *Economic Journal*, 90, (December), 867–84.

Duck, N. W., Parkin, J. M., Rose, D. E. and Zis, G. (1976) The determination of the rate of change of wages and prices in the fixed exchange rate world economy 1956–71; in Parkin, J. M. and Zis, G.

(eds), *Inflation in the World Economy*, Manchester University Press.

Duck, N. W. and Sheppard, D. K. (1978) A proposal for the control of the UK money supply, *Economic Journal*, 88, (March), 1–17.

Dutton, D. S. (1978) The economics of inflation and output fluctuations in the United States 1952–74; in Brunner, K. and Meltzer, A. H. (eds), *The Problem of Inflation*, Carnegie–Rochester Conference Series, Vol. 8, North Holland.

Economic Council of Canada, (1975), *CANDIDE 1.2: A Description for Model Users*, Ottawa (mimeo).

Fausten, D. K. (1979) The Humean origin of the contemporary monetary approach to the balance of payments, *Quarterly Journal of Economics*, 93, (November), 655–74.

Feige, E. (1967) Expectations and adjustments in the monetary sector, *American Economic Review*, 57, (May), papers and proceedings, 462–73.

Feige, E. and Pearce, D. K. (1976) Economically rational expectations: are innovations in the rate of inflation independent of innovations in monetary and fiscal policy? *Journal of Political Economy*, 84, (June), 499–522.

Feige, E. and Pearce, D. K. (1979) The casual causal relationship between money and income: some caveats from the time series, *Review of Economics and Statistics*, 61, (November), 521–33.

Fischer, S. (1977) Long-term contracts, rational expectations and the optimal money supply rule, *Journal of Political Economy*, 85, (February), 191–206.

Fisher, G. R. and Sheppard, D. K. (1974) Interrelationships between real and monetary variables: some evidence from recent US empirical studies; in Johnson, H. G. and Nobay, A. R. (eds), *Issues in Monetary Economics*, Oxford University Press.

Fisher, G. R. and Sparks, G. (1975) A survey of empirical evidence on the structure of the Canadian monetary sector; in *Proceedings of Queen's University Conference on Monetary Issues*, Queen's University, Kingston (mimeo).

Fisher, I. (1896) Appreciation and interest, *Publications of the American Economic Association*, third series, II, (August), 331–442.

Fisher, I. (1911) *The Purchasing Power of Money*, Macmillan, New York.

Fisher, I. (1926) A statistical relation between unemployment and price changes, *International Labour Review* (reprinted as: I discovered the Phillips curve, *Journal of Political Economy*, 81 (2), pt. 1, (March/April, 1973), 496–502).

Fortin, P. and Newton, K. (1980) Labour market tightness and wage inflation in Canada, University of Laval (mimeo).

Fourcans, A. (1978) Inflation and output growth: the French experience; in Brunner, K. and Meltzer, A. H., *The Problem of Inflation*, Carnegie–Rochester Conference Series, Vol. 8, North Holland.

Frankel, S. H. (1977) *Two Philosophies of Money*, Basil Blackwell.

Fratianni, M. (1978) Inflation and unanticipated changes in output in Italy;

in Brunner, K. and Meltzer, A. H., *The Problem of Inflation*, Carnegie–Rochester Conference Series, Vol. 8, North Holland.

Frenkel, J. (1975) Inflation and the formation of expectations, *Journal of Monetary Economics*, 1, (October), 403–22.

Frenkel, J. (1980) Flexible exchange rates in the 1970s; in Laurence H. Meyer (ed.), *Stabilisation Policies: Lessons from the 70s and Implications for the 80s*, Washington University and Federal Reserve Bank of St Louis.

Frenkel, J. and Johnson, H. G. (1976) *The Monetary Approach to Balance of Payments Theory*, George Allen and Unwin.

Friedman, B. (1977) The inefficiency of short-run monetary targets for monetary policy, *Brookings Papers in Economic Activity*, 2, 293–335.

Friedman, M. (1956) The quantity theory of money: a restatement; in Friedman, M. (ed.), *Studies in the Quantity Theory of Money*, University of Chicago Press.

Friedman, M. (1958) The supply of money and changes in prices and output; in Joint Economic Committee of 85th Congress, 2nd Session, *The Relationship of Prices to Economic Stability and Growth*, US Government Printing Office, Washington, D.C.

Friedman, M. (1959) The demand for money – some theoretical and empirical results, *Journal of Political Economy*, 67, (June), 327–51.

Friedman, M. (1960) *A Programme for Monetary Stability*, Fordham University Press, New York.

Friedman, M. (1966) Interest rates and the demand for money, *Journal of Law and Economics*, 9, (October), 71–85.

Friedman, M. (1968) The role of monetary policy, *American Economic Review*, 58, (March), 1–17.

Friedman, M. (1969) The optimum quantity of money; in *The Optimum Quantity of Money*, Macmillan.

Friedman, M. (1970) A theoretical framework for monetary analysis, *Journal of Political Economy*, 78, (March/April), 193–238.

Friedman, M. (1971) A monetary theory of nominal income, *Journal of Political Economy*, 79, (March/April), 323–37.

Friedman, M. (1974) Inflation, taxation, indexation; in Lord Robbins *et al.*, *Inflation: Causes, Consequences, Cures*, Institute for Economic Affairs, London.

Friedman, M. (1975) *Unemployment Versus Inflation*, Institute for Economic Affairs, London.

Friedman, M. (1977) *Inflation and Unemployment: The New Dimension of Politics: 1976 Alfred Nobel Memorial Lecture*, Institute of Economic Affairs Occasional Paper 51, London.

Friedman, M. and Meiselman, D. (1963) The relative stability of monetary velocity and the investment multiplier in the United States, 1898–1958; in Commission on Money and Credit: *Stabilization Policies*, Prentice-Hall.

Friedman, M. and Schwartz, A. J. (1963a) *A Monetary History of the United States 1867–1960*, Princeton University Press (for the National Bureau of Economic Research).

Friedman, M. and Schwartz, A. J. (1963b) Money and business cycles, *Review of Economics and Statistics*, 45, (February), 32–64.

Friedman, M. and Schwartz, A. J. (1970) *Monetary Statistics of the United States*, National Bureau of Economic Research.

Frisch, H. (1977) Inflation theory 1963–75: a second generation survey, *Journal of Economic Literature*, 15, (December), 1289–1317.

Garganas, N. C. (1975) An analysis of consumer credit and its effect on purchases of consumer durables; in Renton, G. A. (ed.), *Modelling the Economy*, Heinemann Educational Books for the SSRC.

Gibson, W. E. (1970) Interest rates and monetary policy, *Journal of Political Economy*, 78, (May/June), 431–55.

Godley, W. (1981) Monetarism in three countries – the United Kingdom; in Crane, D. (ed.), *Beyond the Monetarists*, Canadian Institute for Economic Policy, Ottawa.

Godley, W. and Nordhaus, W. D. (1972) Pricing in the trade cycle, *Economic Journal*, 82 (327), 853–82.

Goldfeld, S. M. (1973) The demand for money revisited, *Brookings Papers on Economic Activity*, 3, 577–638.

Goodhart, C. A. E. (1975) *Money, Information and Uncertainty*, Macmillan.

Gordon, D. F. (1974) A neo-classical theory of Keynesian unemployment, *Economic Inquiry*, 12, (December), 431–59.

Gordon, D. F. and Hynes, A. (1970) On the theory of price dynamics; in Phelps, E. *et al.*, *The Microeconomic Foundations of Employment and Inflation Theory*, W. W. Norton.

Gordon, R. J. (ed.) (1974) *Milton Friedman's Monetary Framework*, University of Chicago Press.

Gordon, R. J. (1976) Recent developments in the theory of inflation and unemployment, *Journal of Monetary Economics*, 2, 185–219.

Granger, C. J. W. (1969) Investigating causal relations by econometric models and cross-spectral methods, *Econometrica*, 37, (July), 424–38.

Gray, M. R., Ward, R. and Zis, G. (1976) World demand for money; in Parkin, J. M. and Zis, G. (eds), *Inflation in the World Economy*, University of Manchester Press.

Grossman, H. I. (1981) Review of James Tobin: asset accumulation and economic activity, *Journal of Monetary Economics*, forthcoming.

Grubel, H. G. and Walker, M. (eds) (1978) *Unemployment Insurance*, The Fraser Institute, Vancouver, B.C.

Hahn, F. H. (1980) Monetarism and economic theory, *Economica* NS, 47, (February), 1–18.

Hall, R. (1980) Employment fluctuations and wage rigidity, *Brookings Papers on Economic Activity*, 1, 91–123.

Hamburger, M. J. (1967) Interest rates and the demand for consumer durable goods, *American Economic Review*, 57, (December), 1133–53.

Harberger, A. C. (ed.) (1960) *The Demand for Durable Goods*, University of Chicago Press.

Harrod, R. F. (1971) Discussion Paper; in Clayton, G., Gilbert, J. C. and Sedgwick, R. (eds), *Monetary Theory and Monetary Policy in the 1970s*, Oxford University Press.

Helliwell, J. F. *et al.* (1971) *The Structure of RDX2*, Bank of Canada Staff Research Papers, No. 7 (2 parts).

Hicks, J. R. (1974) *The Crisis in Keynesian Economics*, Basil Blackwell.

Hicks, J. R. (1976) Must stimulating demand stimulate inflation? *Economic Record*, 52, (December), 409–22.

Hilton, K. and Crossfield, D. H. (1970) Short-term consumption functions for the UK, 1955–66; in Hilton, K. and Heathfield, D. F. (eds), *The Econometric Study of the United Kingdom*, Macmillan.

Hines, A. G. and Catephores, G. (1970) Investment in UK manufacturing industry 1956–67; in Hilton, K. and Heathfield, D. F. (eds), *The Econometric Study of the United Kingdom*, Macmillan.

Howitt, P. W. (1974) Stability and the quantity theory, *Journal of Political Economy*, 82, (January/February), 133–51.

Howitt, P. W. (1979) Evaluating the non-market-clearing approach, *American Economic Review*, 69, (May), papers and proceedings, 60–64.

Howitt, P. W. (1981) Activist monetary policy under rational expectations, *Journal of Political Economy*, 89, (April), 249–69.

Howitt, P. W. and Laidler, D. (1979) Recent Canadian monetary policy, a critique; in Purvis, D. and Wirick, R. (eds), *Proceedings of Queen's University Conference on Economic Policy*, Queen's University, Kingston (mimeo).

Howson, S. (1975) *Domestic Monetary Management in Britain 1919–38*, University of Cambridge Department of Applied Economics Occasional Paper 48, Cambridge University Press.

Johnson, H. G. (1962) Monetary theory and policy, *American Economic Review*, 52, (June), 335–84.

Johnson, H. G. (1972) *Inflation and the Monetarist Controversy* (De Vries Lectures, 1971), North Holland.

Johnson, H. G. (1972) The monetary approach to balance of payments theory; in *Further Essays in Monetary Economics*, Allen and Unwin.

Jones, R. A. (1976) The origin and development of media of exchange, *Journal of Political Economy*, 84, (August), Part 1, 756–75.

Jonson, P. D. (1976a) Money, prices and output: an integrative essay, *Kredit und Kapital*, 4, 499–518.

Jonson, P. D. (1976b) Money and economic activity in the open economy: the United Kingdom, 1880–1970, *Journal of Political Economy*, 84, (September/October), 979–1012.

Jonson, P. D., Mahar, K. L. and Thompson, G. J. (1974) Earnings and award wages in Australia, *Australian Economic Papers*, 13, (June), 80–98.

Jonson, P. D. and Mahoney, D. M. (1973) Price expectations in Australia, *Economic Record*, 48, (March), 50–61.

Jonson, P. D., Moses, E. R. and Wymer, C. R. (1976) A minimal model of the Australian economy, Reserve Bank of Australia Discussion Paper 7601, Sydney (mimeo).

Jonson, P. D. and Trevor, R. G. (1980) Monetary rules: a preliminary analysis, Reserve Bank of Australia Research Discussion Paper 7903 (Revised September, 1980), Sydney (mimeo).

Jorgenson, D. W. (1967) The theory of investment behaviour; in Ferber (ed.), *The Determinants of Business Behaviour*, National Bureau of Economic Research.

Jorgenson, D. W., Hunter, J. and Nadiri, M. I. (1970) A comparison of alternative models of quarterly investment behaviour, *Econometrica*, 38, (March), 187–212.

Jorgenson, D. W. and Stevenson, J. A. (1967) Investment behaviour in US manufacturing 1947–60, *Econometrica*, 35, (April), 169–220.

Kahn, R. F. (1976) Inflation: a Keynesian view, *Scottish Journal of Political Economy*, 23, (February), 11–15.

Kahn, R. F. (1977), Mr Eltis and the Keynesians, *Lloyds Bank Review*, (April), 1–13.

Kaldor, N. (1970) The new monetarism, *Lloyds Bank Review*, (July), 1–18.

Kantor, B. (1979) Rational expectations and economic thought, *Journal of Economic Literature*, 17, (December), 1422–75.

Karni, E. (1980) A note on Lucas's equilibrium model of the business cycle, *Journal of Political Economy*, 88, (December), 1231–41.

Keynes, J. M. (1936) *The General Theory of Employment, Interest and Money*, Macmillan.

Korteweg, P. (1978) The economics of inflation and output fluctuations in the Netherlands 1954–75; in Brunner, K. and Meltzer, A. H. (eds), *The Problem of Inflation*, Carnegie–Rochester Conference Series, Vol. 8, North Holland.

Korteweg, P. and Meltzer, A. H. (1978) Inflation and price changes: some estimates and tests of alternative theories; in Brunner, K. and Meltzer, A. H. (eds), *The Problem of Inflation*, Carnegie–Rochester Conference Series, Vol. 8, North Holland.

Laidler, D. (1966) The rate of interest and the demand for money – some empirical evidence, *Journal of Political Economy*, 74, (December), 545–55.

Laidler, D. (1968) The permanent income concept in a macroeconomic model, *Oxford Economic Papers*, 20, (March), 11–23.

Laidler, D. (1971) The influence of money on economic activity: a survey of some current problems; in Clayton, G., Gilbert, J. C. and Sedgwick, R. (eds), *Monetary Theory and Policy in the 1970s*, Oxford University Press.

Laidler, D. (1975) *Essays on Money and Inflation*, Manchester University Press.

Laidler, D. (1976a) Inflation in Britain: a monetarist perspective, *American Economic Review*, 66, (September), 485–500.

Laidler, D. (1976b) Inflation – alternative explanations and policies: tests on data drawn from six countries; in Brunner, K. and Meltzer, A. H.

(eds), *Institutions, Policies and Economic Performance*, Carnegie–Rochester Conference Series on Public Policy, Vol. 4, North Holland.

Laidler, D. (1977) *The Demand for Money – Theories and Evidence* (2nd edn), Harper and Row.

Laidler, D. (1980) The demand for money in the United States: yet again; in Brunner, K. and Meltzer, A. H. (eds), *The State of Macroeconomics*, Carnegie–Rochester Conference Series on Public Policy, Vol. 12, North Holland.

Laidler, D. and Parkin, J. M. (1970) The demand for money in the United Kingdom 1956–67: preliminary estimates, *Manchester School*, 38, (September).

Laidler, D. and Parkin, J. M. (1975) Inflation – a survey, *Economic Journal*, 85, (December), 741–809.

Laidler, D. *et al.* (1976) *Study on the Possible Part Played by Certain Primary Non-Employment Incomes in the Inflationary Process in the United Kingdom*, Commission of the European Communities, Brussels.

Laidler, D. and O'Shea, P. (1980) An empirical macro-model of an open economy under fixed exchange rates: the United Kingdom, 1954–1970, *Economica*, May, 47 (186), 141–58.

Lange, O. (1942) Say's Law: a restatement and criticism; in Lange, O. (ed.), *Studies in Mathematical Economics and Econometrics*, University of Chicago Press.

Leijonhufvud, A. (1968) *On Keynesian Economics and the Economics of Keynes*, Oxford University Press.

Leijonhufvud, A. (1981) The Wicksell connection: variations on a theme, in *Information and Coordination*, Oxford University Press.

Lewis, M. (1978) Interest rates and monetary velocity in Australia and the United States, *Economic Record*, 54, (April), 111–26.

Lieberman, C. (1980) The long-run and short-run demand for money revisited, *Journal of Money, Credit and Banking*, 12, (February), 43–57.

Lipsey, R. G. (1960) The relationship between unemployment and the rate of change of money wage rates in the United Kingdom, 1862–1957, *Economica* NS, 27, 1–31.

Lipsey, R. G. (1979) World inflation, *Economic Record*, 55, (December), 283–96.

Lipsey, R. G. and Parkin, J. M. (1970) Incomes policy: a reappraisal, *Economica* NS, 36, (May), 115–38.

Lucas, R. E. Jr (1972) Expectations and the neutrality of money, *Journal of Economic Theory*, 4 (2), 103–24.

Lucas, R. E. Jr (1975) An equilibrium model of the business cycle, *Journal of Political Economy*, 83, (November/December), 1113–44.

Lucas, R. E. Jr (1976) Econometric policy evaluation; in Brunner, K. and Meltzer, A. H. (eds), *The Phillips Curve and the Labour Market*, Carnegie–Rochester Conference Series, Vol. 1, North Holland.

Lucas, R. E. Jr (1977) Understanding business cycles; in Brunner, K. and Meltzer, A. H. (eds), *Stabilization of the Domestic and International*

Economy, Carnegie–Rochester Conference Series, Vol. 5, North Holland.

Lucas, R. E. Jr (1980) Methods and problems in business cycle theory, *Journal of Money, Credit and Banking*, 12, (November), Part 2, 696–715.

Lucas, R. E. Jr and Rapping, L. A. (1970) Real wages, employment and inflation; in Phelps, E. S. *et al.*, *The Microeconomic Foundations of Employment and Inflation Theory*, W. W. Norton.

Lund, P. J. (1971) *Investment: The Study of an Economic Aggregate*, Oliver and Boyd, Edinburgh.

Macesitch, G. (1964) The quantity theory and the income–expenditure theory in an open economy: Canada 1926–58, *Canadian Journal of Economics and Political Science*, 30, (August), 368–90.

Macesitch, G. (1969) The quantity theory and income–expenditure theory in an open economy revisited, *Canadian Journal of Economics*, 2, (August), 448–52.

MacKinnon, J. G. and Milbourne, R. D. (1981) Monetary anticipations and the demand for money, Queen's University, Kingston (mimeo).

Malinvaud, E. (1977) *The Theory of Unemployment Reconsidered*, Basil Blackwell.

Marty, A. L. (1976) Comment on Frenkel and Sjaastad, in Parkin, J. M. and Zis, G. (eds.), *Inflation in the World Economy*, University of Manchester Press.

Mayer, T. (1978) *The Structure of Monetarism*, W. W. Norton.

McCallum, B. (1976) Rational expectations and the natural rate hypothesis: some consistent estimates, *Econometrica*, 44, (January), 43–52.

McCallum, B. (1978) Inflation and output fluctuations – a comment in the Dalton and Neumann papers; in Brunner, K. and Meltzer, A. H. (eds), *The Problem of Inflation*, Carnegie–Rochester Conference Series on Public Policy, Vol. 8, North Holland.

McCracken, P. *et al.* (1977) *Towards Full Employment and Price Stability* (The McCracken Report), OECD, Paris.

Melitz, J. (1976) Inflationary expectations and the French demand for money 1959–70, *Manchester School*, 44, (March), 17–41.

Meltzer, A. H. (1963) The demand for money: the evidence from the time series, *Journal of Political Economy*, 71, (June), 219–46.

Meltzer, A. H. (1965) Monetary theory and monetary history, *Schweizerische Zeitschrift Volkswirtschaft und Statistik*, (Spring), 409–22.

Meltzer, A. H. (1969) Money intermediation and growth, *Journal of Economic Literature*, 7, (March), 27–56.

Meltzer, A. H. (1977) Anticipated inflation and unanticipated price change: a test of the price specie flow theory and the Phillips curve, *Journal of Money, Credit and Banking*, 9, (February), Pt. 2, 182–205.

Mill, J. S. (1844) On the influence of consumption upon production; in *Essays on Some Unsettled Questions in Political Economy*, London.

Minford, P. (1980) A rational expectations model of the UK under fixed and floating exchange rates; in Brunner, K. and Meltzer, A. H. (eds), *The State of Macroeconomics*, Carnegie–Rochester Conference Series on Public Policy, Vol. 12, North Holland.

Mishan, E. J. (1958) A fallacy in the interpretation of the cash balance effect, *Economica* NS, 25, (May), 106–18.

Modigliani, F. (1977) The monetarist controversy or, should we forsake stabilization policies? *American Economic Review*, 67, (March), 1–19.

Modigliani, F. and Ando, A. (1976) Impacts of fiscal action on aggregate income and the monetarist controversy: theory and evidence, in Stein, J. L. (ed.), *Monetarism*, North Holland.

Moroney, J. R. and Mason, J. M. (1971) The dynamic impacts of autonomous expenditure and the monetary base on aggregate income, *Journal of Money, Credit and Banking*, 3, (November), 793–814.

Mortensen, D. T. (1970) A theory of wage and employment dynamics; in Phelps, E. *et al.*, *The Microeconomic Foundations of Employment and Inflation Theory*, W. W. Norton.

Mussa, M. (1976) Output and employment in a dynamic model of aggregate supply, London School of Economics (mimeo).

Muth, J. F. (1961) Rational expectations and the theory of price movements, *Econometrica*, 29, (May), 315–35.

Myhrman, J. (1979) The determinants of inflation and economic activity in Sweden; in Lindbeck, A. (ed.), *Inflation and Employment in Open Economies*, North Holland.

Neumann, M. (1978) The impulse–theoretic explanation of changing inflation and output growth: evidence from Germany; in Brunner, K. and Meltzer, A. H. (eds), *The Problem of Inflation*, Carnegie–Rochester Conference Series, Vol. 8, North Holland.

Niehans, J. (1978) *The Theory of Money*, Johns Hopkins University Press.

Ostroy, J. and Starr, R. (1974) Money and the decentralisation of exchange, *Econometrica*, 42, (November), 1093–114.

Parkin, J. M. (1977a) A monetarist analysis of the generation and transmission of world inflation 1958–71, *American Economic Review*, 67, (February), papers and proceedings, 164–71.

Parkin, J. M., Sumner, M. T. and Jones, R. A. (1972) A survey of the econometric evidence on the effects of incomes policy on the rate of inflation; in Parkin, J. M. and Sumner, M. T. (eds), *Incomes Policy and Inflation*, University of Manchester Press.

Parkin, J. M., Sumner, M. T. and Ward, R. (1976) The effects of excess demand, generalised expectations and wage–price controls on wage inflation in the UK; in Brunner, K. and Meltzer, A. H. (eds), *The Economics of Wage and Price Controls*, Carnegie–Rochester Conference Series on Public Policy, Vol. 2, North Holland.

Patinkin, D. (1956) *Money Interest and Prices* (1st edn), Row-Peterson, New York.

Patinkin, D. (1965) *Money Interest and Prices* (2nd edn), Harper and Row.

Patinkin, D. (1967) *On the Nature of the Monetary Mechanism: The 1967 Wicksell Lectures*, Almqvist and Wicksell, Stockholm.

Patinkin, D. (1969) The Chicago tradition, the quantity theory and Friedman, *Journal of Money, Credit and Banking*, 1, (February), 46–70.

Phelps, E. S. (1967) Phillips curves, expectations of inflation and optimal unemployment over time, *Economica* NS, 34, (August), 254–81.

Phelps, E. S. (1968) Money wage dynamics and labour market equilibrium, *Journal of Political Economy*, 76 (4), pt. II, 678–711 (amended reprint in Phelps, E. S. *et al.*, 1970).

Phelps, E. S. *et al.* (1970) *Microeconomic Foundations of Employment and Inflation Theory*, W. W. Norton.

Phelps, E. S. and Taylor, J. B. (1977) Stabilizing powers of monetary policy under rational expectations, *Journal of Political Economy*, 85, (February), 163–90.

Phillips, A. W. (1958) The relation between unemployment and the rate of change of money wage rates in the United Kingdom, *Economica NS*, 25, (November), 283–99.

Poole, W. (1976) Rational expectations in the macro-model, *Brookings Papers on Economic Activity*, 2, 463–505.

Poole, W. and Lieberman, C. (1972) Improving monetary control, *Brookings Papers on Economic Activity*, 2, 293–335.

Purvis, D. D. (1980) Monetarism – a review, *Canadian Journal of Economics*, 1, (February), 96–121.

Radcliffe Committee (1959) (Committee on the Working of the Monetary System), *Report*, HMSO, London.

Reid, M. (1962) *Housing and Income*, University of Chicago Press.

Robinson, J. (1970) Quantity theories old and new, *Journal of Money, Credit and Banking*, 2, (November), 504–12.

Rutledge, J. (1974) *A Monetarist Model of Inflationary Expectations*, Lexington Books, Lexington, Mass.

Saidi, N. H. and Barro, R. J. (1976) Unanticipated money, output and unemployment in Canada, University of Rochester (mimeo).

Santomero, A. M. and Seater, J. J. (1978) The inflation–unemployment trade-off – a critique of the literature, *Journal of Economic Literature*, 16, (June), 499–544.

Sargent, T. J. (1976a) Testing for neutrality and rationality; in Sargent, T. J. and Wallace, N. (eds), *Rational Expectations and the Theory of Economic Policy Part II, Arguments and Evidence*, Research Department, Federal Reserve Bank of Minneapolis, *Studies in Monetary Economics*, 3.

Sargent, T. J. (1976) A classical macroeconomic model for the United States, *Journal of Political Economy*, 84, (April), 207–38.

Sargent, T. J. and Wallace, N. (1973) The stability of models of money and growth with perfect foresight, *Econometrica*, 41, (November), 1043–48.

Sargent, T. J. and Wallace, N. (1975a) Rational expectations and the theory of economic policy, Research Department, Federal Reserve Bank of Minneapolis, *Studies in Monetary Economics*, 2.

Sargent, T. J. and Wallace, N. (1975b) Rational expectations, the optimal monetary instrument and the optimal money supply rule, *Journal of Political Economy*, 83, (April), 241–54.

Shapiro, A. A. (1973) Inflation, lags, and the demand for money, *International Economic Review*, 14, (February), 81–96.

Simmel, G. (1907) *The Philosophy of Money* (translated 1978 by T. Bottomore and D. Frisby), Routledge and Kegan Paul.

Sims, C. A. (1972) Money, finance and causality, *American Economic Review*, 62, (September), 540–52.

Slutsky, E. (1937) The summation of random causes as the source of cyclic processes, *Econometrica*, 5, (April), 105–46.

Solow, R. M. (1968) Recent controversies on the theory of inflation: an eclectic view; in Rousseas, S. (ed.), *Symposium on Inflation: Its Causes, Consequences and Control*, The Calvin K. Kazanjian Economics Foundation Inc., Wilton, Conn.

Solow, R. M. (1979) Alternative approaches to macroeconomic theory: a partial view, *Canadian Journal of Economics*, 12, (August), 339–54.

Solow, R. M. (1980) On theories of unemployment, *American Economic Review*, 70, (March), 1–11.

Spinelli, F. (1976) The determinants of price and wage inflation: the case of Italy; in Parkin, J. M. and Zis, G. (eds), *Inflation in Open Economies*, Manchester University Press.

Stein, J. L. (1976) Inside the monetarist black box; in Stein, J. L. (ed.), *Monetarism*, North Holland.

Stein, J. L. (1976) *Monetarism*, North Holland.

Sumner, M. (1980) The operation of monetary targets; in Brunner, K. and Meltzer, A. H. (eds), *Monetary Institutions and the Policy Process*, Carnegie–Rochester Conference Series, Vol. 13, North Holland.

Tanner, J. E. (1969) Lags in the effects of monetary policy: a statistical investigation, *American Economic Review*, 59, (December), 794–805.

Tobin, J. (1947) Liquidity preference and monetary policy, *Review of Economics and Statistics*, 29, (May), 124–31.

Tobin, J. (1956) The interest elasticity of transactions demand for cash, *Review of Economics and Statistics*, 38, (August), 241–47.

Tobin, J. (1958) Liquidity preference as behaviour towards risk, *Review of Economic Studies*, 25, (February), 65–86.

Tobin, J. (1965) The monetary interpretation of history, *American Economic Review*, 55, (June), 464–85.

Tobin, J. (1969) A general equilibrium approach to monetary theory, *Journal of Money, Credit and Banking*, 1, (February), 15–29.

Tobin, J. (1972) Inflation and unemployment, *American Economic Review*, 62, (March), 1–18.

Tobin, J. (1980) Stabilization policy ten years after, *Brookings Papers on Economic Activity*, 1, 19–71.

Tobin, J. and Buiter, W. (1976) Long-run effects of fiscal and monetary policy on aggregate demand; in Stein, J. (ed.), *Monetarism*, North Holland.

Trivedi, P. K. (1970) Inventory behaviour in UK manufacturing, *Review of Economic Studies*, 37, (October), 517–36.

Tucker, D. (1966) Dynamic income adjustment to money supply changes, *American Economic Review*, 56, (June), 433–49.

Walker, M. (ed.) (1976) *The Illusion of Wage and Price Control*, The Fraser Institute, Vancouver, B.C.

Walters, A. (1965) Professor Friedman on the demand for money, *Journal of Political Economy*, 73, (October), 545–51.

Walters, A. (1971) Consistent expectations, distributed lags and the quantity theory, *Economic Journal*, 81 (322), 273–81.

Weintraub, S. (1981) A prices and incomes policy; in Crane, D. (ed.), *Beyond the Monetarists*, Canadian Institute for Economic Policy, Ottawa.

White, W. H. (1978) Improving the demand for money function in moderate inflation, IMF *Staff Papers*, (September), 564–607.

White, W. H. (1981) The case for and against disequilibrium money, IMF (mimeo).

Wiles, P. (1973) Cost inflation and the state of economic theory, *Economic Journal*, 83, (June), 377–98.

Williams, D., Goodhart, C. A. E. and Gowland, D. H. (1976) Money, income and causality: the UK experience, *American Economic Review*, 66, (June), 417–23.

Wilson, T. (1976) The natural rate of unemployment, *Scottish Journal of Political Economy*, 23, (February), 99–107.

Wirick, R. (1981) The battle against inflation – the Bank of Canada and its critics, *Canadian Public Policy*, 7, (April), Supplement, 249–59.

Wogin, G. (1980) Unemployment and monetary policy under rational expectations: some Canadian evidence, *Journal of Monetary Economics*, 6, (January), 59–68.

Yeager, L. (ed.) (1962) *In Search of a Monetary Constitution*, Harvard University Press.

Yeager, L. (1966) *International Monetary Relations*, Harper and Row.

Author Index

Subject Index